TEACHING THE LITERATURE OF TODAY'S MIDDLE EAST

Providing a gateway into the real literature emerging from the Middle East, this book shows teachers how to make the topic authentic, powerful, and relevant.

Teaching the Literature of Today's Middle East:

- Introduces teachers to this literature and how to teach it
- Brings to the reader a tremendous diversity of teachable texts and materials by Middle Eastern writers ranging from Nobel-prize winners to authors waiting to be discovered
- Focuses on authentic literature in translation that is appropriate and engaging for secondary and university students, including autobiography, young adult, and graphic novels
- Takes a thematic approach that allows students to understand and engage with the region, address key issues, consider American involvement, reflect on the representation of the Middle East in European literature, and come to know Americans with Islamic backgrounds
- Includes stories from the author's own dynamic and engaging classroom, and shares student insight and reactions
- Includes a chapter on how to effectively work with and teach Muslim students
- Utilizes contemporary teaching methods, including cultural studies, lit circles, blogs, YouTube, class speakers, and film analysis
- Directly and powerfully models how to address controversial issues in the region, including American involvement, Palestinian rights, "terrorism", feminism, economic inequality, and Orientalism

Written in an open, personal and engaging style, theoretically informed and academically smart and highly relevant across the field of literacy education, this text offers teachers and teacher-educators a much needed resource for helping students to think deeply and critically about the politics and culture of the Middle East through literary engagements.

Allen Webb is Professor of English Education and Postcolonial Studies at Western Michigan University.

TEACHING THE LITERATURE OF TODAY'S MIDDLE EAST

Allen Webb

With David Alvarez, Blain H. Auer, Monica Mona Eraqi, Jeffrey A. Patterson, and Vivan Steemers

Routledge
Taylor & Francis Group
NEW YORK AND LONDON

First published 2012
by Routledge
711 Third Avenue, New York, NY 10017

Simultaneously published in the UK
by Routledge
2 Park Square, Milton Park, Abingdon, Oxon OX14 4RN

Routledge is an imprint of the Taylor & Francis Group, an informa business

Library of Congress Cataloging in Publication Data
Teaching the literature of today's Middle East / Allen Webb, with David Alvarez . . . [et al.].
p. cm.
Includes bibliographical references.
1. Middle Eastern literature – Study and teaching. 2. Middle East – In literature-Study and teaching. 3. Muslims in literature-Study and teaching. I. Webb, Allen. II. Alvarez, David Edward, 1965–
PJ809.T43 2012
809'.8956071–dc23 2011017264

ISBN13: 978-0-415-87437-3 (hbk)
ISBN13: 978-0-415-87438-0 (pbk)
ISBN13: 978-0-203-83255-4 (ebk)

Typeset in Bembo and Stone Sans
by Florence Production Ltd, Stoodleigh, Devon

They shall beat their swords into plowshares, and their spears into pruning hooks;

nation shall not lift up sword against nation, neither shall they learn war any more.

Isaiah 2:4

I think that's what I liked most about this class, that everything we read had a direct correlation to what is going on in the world in today's day and age, versus learning about allegory and symbolism from ancient pieces of literature.

John Ebbing, Student in Allen Webb's course addressing the literature of today's Middle East

CONTENTS

PREFACE

My daughter Jessica was in junior high school at the time of the 9/11 attacks. During the days afterwards, her teacher sought to create greater sympathy and understanding of the Arab world by showing the students in her class, including Jessica, Walt Disney's film *Aladdin*. Obviously, however, the story of Aladdin had nothing whatsoever to do with either the 9/11 event or the real lives of people in the Middle East today. In fact, the film *Aladdin* has been extensively criticized as a racist portrayal of Arabs. But *Aladdin* was the only thing my daughter's well-meaning teacher could think of as a resource to help her students begin to understand the Middle East and, perhaps, sympathize with or at least get a different idea about Middle Eastern peoples than what was currently filling the news.

My daughter's teacher was not alone in not knowing where to start with teaching about the Middle East. Of course, we live in a time where the Middle East is at the very center of the world economy, global politics, and foreign policy. The events of 9/11, the Iraq and Afghan wars, and the continuing Global War on Terror are defining issues of our times. The on-going Israeli-Palestinian conflict (perhaps the greatest threat to world peace), the Arab democracy movement in Tunisia, Egypt, Libya, Syria, nuclear tensions, oil crises – we hear about these and related events from the region every day. Along with international conflicts, significant immigration from the Middle East to the West has led to disturbing stereotypes and controversy, including over Islam. Yet, teachers and professors have had almost no idea of what kinds of texts, materials, or approaches they might use to teach authentically about the Middle East, and, especially, to explore the lives, perspectives, and evolving experiences of the people who live there. This book intends to fill that gap.

Most readers of *Teaching the Literature of Today's Middle East* will vividly remember the 9/11 attacks and the debates in the United States and around the world about the wars in Iraq and Afghanistan. Yet by the time you read this book, from the viewpoint of our students, the 9/11 attacks and the wars they occasioned may be "ancient history" – meaning they took place before they can remember or even before they were born. Nonetheless the need for American and English-speaking young people around the world to know more about the Middle East will not have abated. And the complex factors that led to and have followed the 9/11 attacks are still in play. The Middle East, especially the contemporary Middle East, is an area that our curriculums have too long ignored, to the loss, mis-education and even peril of our students, and the world.

From Afghanistan to Palestine, from Morocco to Iraq, there is a vibrant and exciting literature by living authors that can bring to us the diverse personal experiences and perspectives of this vital region of the world. For my students, and for others about whom this volume reports, contemporary Middle Eastern literature has broken stereotypes, transformed worldviews, developed personal connections, humanized Islam and Muslim people, and helped them learn about Arabs, Turks, Jews, Kurds, Persians, and Pushtans. Their thinking about the Middle East has become substantially richer and more complex.

Years ago I began focusing the literature classes I was teaching on the Middle East because I was concerned about the willingness of my government to intervene in the area and the lack of information of many in the U.S. about the region. I still have this concern. Estimates of the number of Iraqis who have died as a result of the American invasion range between a hundred thousand and more than a million, and, at the time of this writing, no satisfying resolution to the conflict appears in sight. Today, in 2011, my students no longer remember when America was not at war in Iraq and Afghanistan, the longest wars in American history. Many of my students, their family members, and friends have served, currently serve, or will serve in American military interventions in the region. Joe Kincheloe believes that "A new critical education based on an appreciation of difference can help the United States redress some of its past and present policies toward the diverse Islamic world. While these policies have been invisible to many Americans, they are visible to the rest of the world – the Islamic world in particular." (5)

I have always wanted to make my teaching relevant; today it seems imperative that my students better understand the Middle East.

Although I significantly address the wars in Iraq and Afghanistan, the book has a much broader focus. I bring to the reader a tremendous diversity of teachable texts by wonderful Middle Eastern writers, from Nobel-Prize winners to authors waiting to be discovered by teachers and students. I refer to a wide range of countries and themes and to a diversity of materials, much of it in translation, that teachers can include in their classes including novels, autobiography and memoir, film, short stories, graphic texts, essays, anthropological writing, and so on. I tell stories from my own classroom, share student insight and reactions, utilize contemporary teaching methods, including literature circles, blogs, You Tube, class speakers, field trips, film analysis, and online resources. All of these potential curriculum and research materials need to be thought about carefully and critically, and in this book I offer resources, ideas, and strategies that you can use to thoughtfully integrate Middle Eastern literature into classes at the college, high school and middle school levels – just the kind of background knowledge and resources that will help you become with time, study, and experience, a more informed and better prepared teacher of literature from the Middle East.

The book utilizes a thematic, cultural studies approach relevant to English, language arts, and social studies classes from middle school through to college. This approach allows students to understand and engage with the region, consider complicated issues from multiple perspectives. As I foreground the representation of Middle Eastern people by Middle Eastern authors, we will examine themes from their writing including the failure of democracy in many Middle Eastern countries, the changing role of Islam, the experiences of women, wars and conflicts in the region, American intervention and the experience of people with Middle Eastern and Islamic backgrounds currently living in the West. We will also consider Orientalist representations of the Middle East in European and American literature and film. Throughout, I provide background information and teaching approaches that will help teachers to directly address controversial social, cultural, historical, political and religious questions, the very questions that enliven our curriculum and bring it up-to-date.

This book also includes writing by outstanding college and high school teachers I know and work with who have also been teaching Middle Eastern literature and culture in ways that support and complement this project. Blain Auer, a recent PhD in religion from Harvard's Islamic Studies program, helps us think about teaching the Quran to American students in Chapter 1. Monica Eraqi, a high school social studies teacher now working on a doctorate in curriculum and instruction focused on the Middle East, has taught at two different high schools in Southeastern Michigan, including Hamtramck High School, where 70 percent of the students are Muslim. In Chapter 4 she reports on a year-long high school social studies course she created focused on the Middle East. Jeff Patterson, an outstanding high school teacher working with alternative education students in rural Michigan and presenter at National Council of Teachers of English (NCTE) state and national conferences, reports on a semester-long senior English class he developed focused on literature, film, and research on the Iraq War. David Alvarez, professor of English, PhD in Comparative Literature and expert in postcolonial studies especially the literary relationship between North Africa and Spain, writes about his experience teaching recent literature about the migration of North Africans to Europe. Vivan Steemers, professor of translation studies and author of a recent book on the publication history of North African literature, writes a chapter for teachers about issues created by the translation and publication of

Middle Eastern writing. Throughout the book there is also evidence of reading and research undertaken by very able graduate and undergraduate research assistants – all of them my students at Western Michigan University: Peter Larr, a secondary history teacher; Sarah Davis, a secondary English teacher; and Jen Barns, student of Arabic and aspiring secondary teacher in English and social studies. Western Michigan University, and Michigan as a whole, have relatively large populations of Muslim and of Middle Eastern students, so I guess it is not surprising that all of these professors and teachers work or were trained in this state.

Clearly, this book is "multi-vocal." In addition to the outstanding teachers and scholars who have directly helped in the writing, this volume draws, as the acknowledgments make clear, on the contributions of many scholars, teachers, writers, and friends – and it includes comments from dozens of college and high school students. Sometimes you may notice colloquial expressions or grammatical inaccuracies in quotations from high school or college students. While I have sometimes condensed student remarks or corrected grammar, the enthusiasm and authenticity of student writing, their reactions, perspectives, and developing insights, provide direct and valuable evidence of the learning process in the study of literature of the Middle East. I thought putting "[sic]" inside of their direct quotations would seem heavy handed, so I have avoided that as well. In recent years when I have taught Middle Eastern literature, several times a week my students and I write blogs responding to our reading and extending our in-class discussion. These linked, academic blogs emerge as an interactive form of public writing – and because student blog posts, as well as papers and essay tests, provide rich insight for teachers, I have liberally drawn on them. You can visit the original blogs we wrote from my website, AllenWebb.net. (For more information on the Internet, blogging, and teaching literature see my book *Literature and the Web: Reading and Responding with New Technologies*, written with Robert Rozema.)

It makes sense to read this book from beginning to end. The early chapters provide important introductory material and information that later chapters build on. At the same time, teachers with specific concerns can jump to specific sections. There is a chapter focused on approaches to take when teaching Muslim students (Chapter 10). I imagine a teacher especially in need of that information going directly to that section. Or, teachers of British or American literature courses may want to look at the chapter about integrating Middle Eastern literature with the canon (Chapter 12) before reading one of the other chapters. So keep an eye on the table of contents and go to those sections that interest you, bearing in mind that reading through the whole book is important to developing a comprehensive understanding of issues involved in teaching about today's Middle East.

My emphasis in this volume is on the *content* of literary texts and cultural works. Many of these works are excellent texts for studying literary terms, genres, narrative point of view, narratology, allegory, symbolism, irony, and so on. At times I will refer to this kind of possibility, and the book welcomes teachers with interest in questions of form, language, and narration to many works that will make fine additions to their curriculum. Nonetheless my primary focus is not on literariness but on teachers and students coming to understand today's Middle East, a goal I consider just as appropriate to English, language arts, and humanities classes as to social studies and history. Focusing on content, the best curriculum brings together a variety of genres and texts including literary works, film, historical and cultural texts, speakers, and so on.

Don't be put off by the fact that I sometimes reference Wikipedia and have even quoted from readers' comments on Amazon.com. It is not that I believe either of those sources fully reliable. Wikipedia is an amazing, evolving resource and provides information and ideas that are in the public sphere, likely commonly believed or, as they frequently are in Wikipedia entries regarding the Middle East, openly disputed. Sometimes it is important to know ideas or disputes that are out there, even if they are not documented by scholars in traditional, refereed paper publications. Sometimes these easily accessible online references open up possibilities for further and deeper research. In writing this book I have also undertaken extensive reading of those "old-fashioned" sources: hard-bound and paper books, literary works and literary scholarship, historical and cultural monographs, and library research. I try to clearly indicate my sources and references, whether online or paper. For every literary work I recommend, I have read or examined many more. I try to recommend only the best and most appropriate texts, and my final determination has always been based on my willingness to use the text with my own students.

Attentive readers will recognize that I have an agenda. I want teachers to develop curriculums that will lead students to deeper, more complex, and more meaningful understandings of the Middle East than circulate in popular culture, the mass media, news reports, and political speechifying. This means that the materials I recommend often challenge dominant thinking and go against the grain of simplification and stereotype. The perspectives I present are likely to challenge established us-versus-them politics and foreign policy often found in America, the English-speaking world, or the so-called "West" where we and our students live. In this sense, I want students to be informed and active citizens, careful and critical thinkers who can see the complexities and ask questions about what they are told. Teachers and students should both be asking questions about the curriculum itself, about how to make it more inclusive, balanced, and meaningful.

For my own classes, and for the curricular materials I recommend to teachers in this book, I have tried to use texts that are authentic, that would be recognized by people from the Middle East as literature they know or that would speak to their own self-understanding. Sometimes Middle Eastern works most marketed to English-speaking readers represent the experience of a small, elite class or set of cosmopolitan individuals who have been able to find their way to be translated, or who have become expatriates from their home country and now live in America or Europe and write in English (or French). Sometimes, despite their elite background, their writing may still speak more broadly. Sometimes because these works have been popular in the West, it makes sense to teach them, though we must be aware, as my graduate student Katie Burbo points out,

> Literature is more than an art, it's an industry, meaning that someone must decide what will be published, translated, and distributed . . . Middle Eastern texts that make it through translation and into the U.S. sometimes serve the purpose of preserving pre-existing stereotypes.

These important issues of translation and publication are thoughtfully addressed by Vivan Steemers in Chapter 11. Throughout *Teaching the Literature of Today's Middle East* I will frequently point to ways in which individual texts are not fully "representative" of any region, nation, ethnic group, language, gender, or community.

While I do recommend some poetry and short stories, the bulk of my recommendations are for shorter novels, novellas, graphic novels, autobiographies and films that I believe are especially appealing to English-speaking secondary and college students. Portraying dynamic characters in rich social contexts, the novel in particular is an effective form for cross-cultural study, useful not only in literature classes but also in history, social studies, and humanities. As Bakhtin argued long ago, the novel brings together multiple perspectives, languages, cultures, social classes, and literary forms. Writers frequently use novels to address social conflict, problems, and tensions. Novels offer rich and engaging reading experiences. Novels frequently draw on memoir, narratives of growing up, family, schooling, and community life. An encompassing and flexible genre, the novel has been taken up by Middle Eastern writers and modified to address their own language, literary traditions, and point of view. In recent decades the outpouring of novels from the region and by authors with Middle Eastern backgrounds make this genre increasingly available. And novels can serve as anchor texts in thematic curricular units that draw on a wide range of materials.

While the novel and novel-like works are excellent vehicles for the kind of study proposed in this book, depending on your situation it may be challenging to integrate novels or longer works into existing curriculums. A novel read by a whole class of students requires more time and more commitment than a poem, short story, or film. For that reason, I have tried to be extremely careful about the novels I recommend. I focus on literature that will both expand the knowledge and understanding of our students, and that will appeal to and engage them. Often these works will be more meaningful in the context of additional information, other materials, and a more fleshed out curriculum – and this book is rich with suggestions and ideas. The longer novels I do recommend, such as Yashar Kemal's *Memed, My Hawk* (395 pages) or *Rooftops of Tehran* (345 pages) by Mahbod Seraji, are page-turners, feature younger protagonists, engaging plots and strong emotions that will capture and hold the attention of teenage and young adult readers.

In preparing to teach Middle Eastern literature and write this book I read many of the most celebrated authors from the Middle East, including Nobel laureates such as Naguib Mahfouz and Orhan Pamuk, as well as many lesser known, but justly recognized writers such as Gamal al-Ghitani and A.B. Yehoshua. Many of these writers write for adults in the Middle East and much of their writing demands a level of reader sophistication that makes their works too difficult for the vast majority of high school and even college students, at least non-majors in literature or Middle Eastern studies. Sometimes their writing is primarily historical, requiring complex background knowledge or set in a period remote from "today's Middle East." There are outstanding novels that I do not address in this book simply because of length, for instance Abdelrahman Munif's *Cities of Salt* (640 pages). I have taught and do recommend carefully selected shorter works by Mahfouz and Pamuk. Many of the longer, difficult works are still great reads for teachers, can inform our thinking and teaching, and may be suitable to recommend to highly motivated students on an individual basis, especially after they get a start with more approachable texts. When I introduce a text for teaching I provide the year of publication, number of pages, and my recommendation for age level. I make these grade level recommendations based on my assessment of reading difficulty (not only readability level but also on difficulty and maturity of content) – interpret my recommendations depending on your students, community, and approach to teaching. This book is not comprehensive. I don't think any book on teaching literature from such a huge region and diversity of languages and cultures could be comprehensive. There are so many authors I have yet to discover, so many works I haven't read, and so many not yet in translation. Yet, I do set forward a rich diversity of materials and approaches to teaching about the Middle East.

As a former high school teacher now teaching college but working on a daily basis with secondary teachers and future secondary teachers, I am well aware that particularly at the middle school and high school level it is a challenge to change curriculums and purchase new texts. Let me make several suggestions to my secondary colleagues. Of course, one can start with short stories, You Tube clips, and films. A surprising number of texts are available online, including full versions of novels. It wasn't until our bookstore ran out of copies of *Aunt Safiyya and the Monastery* that a student discovered, and shared with me, that the University of California Press has put the whole novel online, available for free. After getting started with one text, students can do independent or group reading using library or other resources. An outstanding approach is to use literature circles (see Daniels) where students read a text in small groups and the expense of a class set of books can be distributed among five or six titles that can even be read by all students on a rotating basis. As I suggest in Chapter 12, literature from the Middle East can be paired with works that are already being taught in courses in British, American, or World literature, creating dialogic opportunities. As one of four authors of the Michigan State Board of Education High School Content Standards and Expectations (2006), I am well aware of the impact of the curricular standards movement, common assessments, and standardized testing in secondary education. Units focused on Middle Eastern literature can and should be included in many different courses in ways that meet and exceed national, state, district, and department standards. In fact, sometimes these standards allow teachers to argue for the inclusion of new materials. From a traditional perspective, Middle Eastern texts can also be included when studying literary genres, styles or techniques, or when including "informational texts" alongside literary works, or having students do research and argumentative writing (all emphasized in the national Common Core Standards, as of this writing adopted by 44 states). Middle Eastern texts make for fascinating comparison works when examining specific themes, including but not limited to growing up, family life, friendship, death, facing challenges, political oppression, civil rights, and so on. Contemporary Middle Eastern literature is an important component for social studies, history, humanities, and women's studies courses, as each chapter in this book demonstrates. Teaching about the contemporary Middle East in a high school social studies class is the focus of Chapter 4 by Monica Eraqi, a chapter that college teachers and literature teachers will also find relevant.

Few teachers will be able to teach a full semester class addressing Middle Eastern studies or literature – though such a class would certainly be timely and of educational value. Instead, incorporating a few works read in common, moving to literature circles, and extending to independent reading allows students to develop knowledge about the texts they are reading that they can share with the rest of the class. In this way a wide variety of texts and perspectives can be included, and we can begin to address the serious paucity of knowledge of the Middle East. While this volume offers excellent primary and secondary materials, the range of Middle Eastern literature available in translation is ever increasing. Teachers willing to explore bookstores, libraries, and the Internet will identify other writers from the Middle East that they will want to include in their curriculums. Incorporating literature from the Middle East can go beyond individual classes to school or district-wide initiatives. For example, in Parchment, Michigan, at the time I visited them, the school districts' English teachers were considering including at least one significant Middle Eastern literary work at each grade level, 7–12.

Another powerful way to examine stereotypes at the college or secondary level is to bring in outside speakers – as you will see many have been delighted to talk to my students. There are people from the Middle East or with significant experience in the region living in all parts of the U.S. and the English-speaking world, and they are often open to visiting classrooms. The website Islamic Finder.com is a terrific way to find Islamic resources in your area in the U.S. and Canada – just enter your postal zip code. A woman from Egypt who had only been in the U.S. for a few weeks came to my class. My students were surprised that she wore jeans and spoke contemporary idiomatic English – she broke stereotypes and inspired discussion and reading about Islamic women. A Turkish man showed slides of modern Istanbul and a film clip about Turkish rock music.

A Zionist defended Israel's treatment of Palestinians. An Iranian discussed his perspective on his country being described by American leaders as part of the "Axis of Evil." A Jordanian described two different schools he had attended in Jordan, one in the city where the women students wore jeans and short skirts and one in the countryside where women predominately wore burqas. An organizer of Iraq War protests in our community lectured my students on how the American invasion violated international law. A team of three American soldiers with extensive on-duty experience in Iraq and Kuwait talked about the psychological impact of these wars on American troops.

There is currently a kind of renaissance (to use a Eurocentric word) of Middle Eastern writing, and this book will draw on many of the best and most popular authors both in translation and works written in exile or by ex-patriots in English. Every day it seems I hear about another great read from or about the Middle East. I am sure that even in the time it takes this book to go to press, there will be more than one new, interesting, and appropriate title for teaching. At the same time, I don't believe *Teaching the Literature from Today's Middle East* will be quickly out-dated. The texts I recommend and the topics and issues they address are selected to be relevant and meaningful for years to come. As new works emerge, the texts and authors I recommend here will remain touchstones.

We are all aware of how fast the world is changing, how the expanding market place, the increasing interdependence of nations, rapidly developing technology and communication, and exchange of cultural information from advertising to film to the Internet is transforming daily life, making possible and disseminating new forms of behavior and value systems, and challenging traditional practices and beliefs. These changes are taking place in the Middle East just as dramatically, or even more so, than in the rest of the world. Different patterns of life emerge not only between generations but even between siblings. Readers of Middle Eastern literature need to be highly conscious that a book published in 2000 may depict a reality very different from one published in 1980, and one published in 2010 may be quite different from one from 2005. Today's Middle East is neither yesterday's nor tomorrow's, but understanding with some sympathy and depth any location or recent period will help make sense of the rest.

Nancie Atwell has said, "Teachers of adolescents must read, must write, and must teach from our literate experiences and literary passions." (Atwell 313.) This book is going to introduce far more texts that you likely can read or teach, but you can learn from each chapter, develop knowledge and passion, choose those works and develop curriculum appropriate to your class and your students, and begin further exploration. Passionate and informed teachers will need to take the lead to help their colleagues, departments, schools, districts, universities, and states recognize the value and wisdom of teaching literature from today's Middle East.

ACKNOWLEDGMENTS

The author expresses his sincere appreciation to the many people who helped with this book. First and foremost contributing authors including Vivan Steemers, Jeff Patterson, Monica Eraqi, David Alvarez, and Blain Auer – you have made this book so much richer. My graduate research assistants Sarah Davis and Peter Larr, former high school English and social studies teachers, have done a great deal of reading that has extended the range of this volume. Certain undergraduate students, many of them themselves going into teaching, have also made important contributions, Jennifer Barns, Lauren Griffith, and Ali Moossavi, in particular. So many students who have advanced my thinking and allowed me to quote them here – your voices and insight are greatly welcomed!

My dear friends Mustafa Mughazy, Mustafa Mirzeler, and Jahan Aghdai have made enormous contributions to this book and to the project, recommending texts, helping me understand social, historical and cultural contexts, reading and commenting on portions of the manuscript, and supporting me every step of the way. Elizabeth Hearne read the manuscript and provided many suggestions that enhanced the balance and complexity. Mike Jayne also provided editorial help. My graduate students Zaydun Al-Shara and Hanan Hashem Aly read and provided feedback on sections of the book.

Several outstanding writers of Middle Eastern origin have spoken with me and shared insights for this project, including Mahbod Seraji, Firoozeh Dumas, Naomi Shihab Nye, and Hedy Habra. I have worked with teachers teaching Middle Eastern works and appreciate their help; they include Lindsey Steenbergen, Katrina Davidson, and Becky Gordon. The Kalamazoo Islamic Center and many of its members have been wonderful resources, especially the imam H.N. Akbar.

My friends and fellow graduate students Kavous Seyed-Emami and Tugrul Ilter deeply informed my thinking. My late, dear friend Blair Harcourt's father,

Hugh Harcourt, professor of philosophy at the American University of Beirut and Birzeit, gave me my first list of Middle Eastern texts to read and teach in 1983. Other scholars have been an important help including Maysam Behravesh, Ilana Nash, Alan Hart, Amy Damaschek, Todd Kuchta, Phyllis Bennis, Elsa Marston, Sarah Brouillette, Kristen Bergen, Khachig Tölölyan, Howard Hastings, Bengisu Rona, Gwen Tarbox, Adam Chamy, Scott Slawinsky, and Phil Egan. Like so many others, I owe a debt of appreciation to the late Edward Said and many who have followed in his wake. Rick Beach told me Naomi Silverman is the best editor in the industry; now I know he is right. Emilie Littlehales at Routledge also made a careful reading of the manuscript. Despite all this help, I am sure this book still has gaps, shortcomings, and distortions – those are my fault entirely. A special thanks to my wife, Cindy Pietras, who has ever matched my rants, raves, frustrations, and excitements with calm thoughtfulness.

SPECIAL ACKNOWLEDGMENTS

The extensive involvement and thinking of my students has enriched this book. I quote from the writing of thirty-eight different students, many more than once – you will enjoy getting to know them. These students have graciously given their permission to use their words. Many students not quoted also contributed by their participation in discussion, writing, and research.

List of students quoted (in order of appearance)

John Ebbing
Katie Burpo
Dan Brim
Molly Grube
Virginia Shedd
Marie Teitgen
Lauren Axt
Rachael Denham
Kristen Felts
Chelsea Leatherman
John Spreitzer
Janelle Mirch
Ashley Hillyard
Mary Hitt
Sara Soenen
Jen Wiley
Saralynn Bush
Ashley Auberman
John Novak
Lisa Anderson
Carly Fricano
Amanda France
Sara Pollard
Anne Morgan
Craig Downer
Kendra Matko
Heather Winowiki
Linda Cross
Maria Benson
Megan Carlson
Katie
Molly White
Sara Keeler
Diane Hall
Brian Lane
Frankie Velazquez
Owen Horton
Victor Jimenez

PERMISSIONS ACKNOWLEDGMENTS

"Literature from the Modern Middle East: Making A Living Connection," *English Journal*, 1/09. This article was a starting point for the book. A large section features in Chapter 7 and it is referenced in several other chapters.

Figure 7.1 Data for the table acquired from ProCon.org, a 501(c)(3) nonprofit public charity online at www.procon.org

The following acknowledgments are to the photographers of the listed figures:

Figure 1.4 Muhammad Mahdi karim, www.micro2macro.net
Figure 2.1 Daniel Mayer
Figure 2.2 Seçkin Resimler
Figure 2.3 Dan Lundberg
Figure 3.1 Zharif Hussein
Figure 3.2 Jari-Pekka Kaitainen
Figure 4.1 Bjørn Christian Tørrissen
Figure 5.1 David Bohrer
Figure 5.3 Charles W. Gill
Figure 6.1 Leslie A. Shively
Figure 6.2 Grace Beahm/*The Post and Courier*
Figure 7.2 Justin McIntosh
Figure 9.1 Dane Hillyard
Figure 10.1 Shane McCoy
Figure 12.2 *The Rubaiyat*, Arthur Szyk
Figure 12.3 Alhambra James Cavanah Murphy

1

CULTURAL AND RELIGIOUS CONTEXTS

The "Middle East" is an enormous and diverse region of the world linked together by historical, cultural, linguistic, and religious connections, including legacies of the empires of Greece, Rome, the Arabs, the Ottoman Turks, and European and American imperialism. The region can be defined in a number of ways. For the purpose of this book I will use the definition that includes North Africa (Morocco, Algeria, Tunisia, Libya, Egypt, Sudan, Eretria, Somalia), the traditional "Middle East" (Saudi Arabia, Yemen, Oman, Israel, Palestine, Lebanon, Syria, Turkey, Jordan, Iraq, Iran, Kuwait, Arab Emirates, Qatar, Bahrain) and, especially because of the contemporary conflict there, Afghanistan. Even though this definition is certainly broad enough for this project, it could be even broader as many other countries might also be considered part of the "Middle East" (including Western Sahara, Mauritania, Ethiopia, Armenia, Azerbaijan, Turkmenistan, Kazakhstan, and Uzbekistan, even Pakistan). The region we will consider the "Middle East" has a current population of about 540 million people (the United States has 307 million) and an area of nearly 8 million square miles (the United States comprises 3.8 million square miles). The Arabian Peninsula by itself is about the same size as the United States east of the Mississippi plus Texas and California. The enormous region of the Middle East represents a great diversity of land forms at the intersection of three continents, including mountain ranges, seas, oceans, rivers fed by winter snowfall, fertile soils as well as deserts, Mediterranean and temperate climates.

We should recognize also that the term "Middle East" is not one that originates in the region or reflects how people who live there name or define themselves. Instead it is a Eurocentric expression that likely first emerged in the 1850s in the British offices administering their India colonies.

> The very appellation ["Middle East"] is a creation of colonialism, for this region is "Middle" simply because the point of reference, in more than one way, is Europe. People who live in these countries understand themselves to be "Middle Easterners" only in relation to the West, and use the term primarily within the context of discussion of geopolitical considerations and configurations of world powers. Their own self-designated parameters of identity would not include this category. No one would say: As a Middle Easterner, I . . . , while people do say, "as an Arab," "as an Egyptian," "as a Muslim," in addition to "as a woman," "a physician," "a Marxist," etc. If people of the region want to use a more encompassing designation that transcends national, linguistic, or religious classifications, they tend to use the term, "peoples of the third world."
>
> *(Al-Nowaihi, 283)*

The term "Middle East" is surprisingly recent. It gained recognition when it was used by an American naval strategist in an article published in 1902 to designate the area between Arabia and India (Koppes, 95). Parts of this region had also been known as the "Near East," as opposed to the "Far East" of China, Korea, and Japan. It wasn't until the 1950s that the term began to be used by U.S. government officials.

Portions of what we now call the "Middle East" were politically connected by Greek, Roman, Persian, and Byzantine Empires, but the most important empire for shaping modern linguistic and cultural identity of the region was the Arab empire that arose in the first generations after Muhammad's death (632 CE) and lasted nearly 800 years. By 750 CE the Arab empire included Arabia, Syria, Egypt, North Africa, Spain, Persia, Armenia, Afghanistan, and portions of Pakistan and India – a significantly larger area than we now call the "Middle East." Variations of the Arabic language are spoken across North Africa and the Arabian Peninsula as the map indicates.

BOX 1.1 APPROXIMATE NUMBER OF SPEAKERS OF MIDDLE EASTERN LANGUAGES

- Arabic 280 million native speakers, 250 million non-native
- Persian 60–70 million
- Turkish 70 million
- Kurdish 26 million
- Hebrew 7 million
- Armenian 7 million
- Berber 10 million

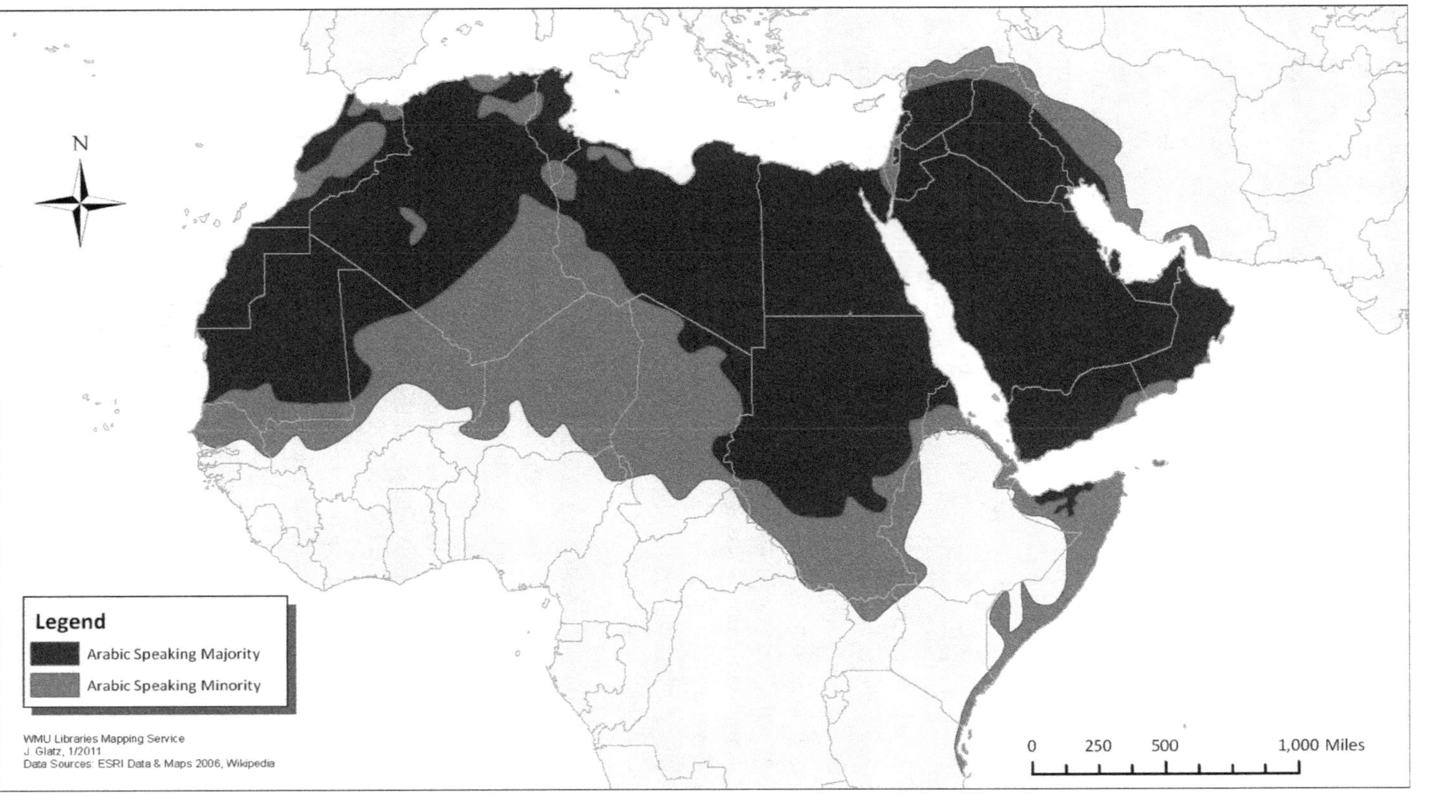

FIGURE 1.1 Approximate Number of Speakers of Middle Eastern Languages

At the time of Muhammad, the Arabs were frequently described as sharing virtues necessary for nomadic life in the desert, "bravery in battle, patience in misfortune, persistence in revenge" (Ochsenwald, 19). There was an emphasis on protection of the weak, defiance of the strong, hospitality to the visitor, and generosity to the poor. Loyalty to the tribe and fidelity to promises were highly valued. Codes of desert revenge existed to enforce justice under a system without formal government and penal codes. There were also ideals that might be seen as loosely democratic, with clans independent from each other, decisions made by assemblies of chiefs, and unity created by negotiation.

Islam spread quickly not simply from conquest, but because the Muslims were found to be more liberal than previous empires and local authorities. Muslim rule generally meant religious freedom and lower taxes. Non-Muslims could not bear arms, but were allowed to maintain their own laws and culture. Muslims were actively involved in commerce, facilitated by reading, writing and a common language. Indeed, the European "dark ages" was a time of Arab cultural flowering. Muslim culture assimilated Greek, Roman, Persian, and Hindu learning and Arabic provided a *lingua franca* for theology, philosophy, science, and the humanities, including poetry. While there was certainly oppression of women in the Arab empire (and in Europe at the same time, of course) during Muhammad's day some women had significant freedom and public roles. Interestingly, the veiling and seclusion of women was not originally a Muslim practice – it was adopted from Byzantium.

As the Arabic language became increasingly used throughout the enormous region of the Middle East, the definition of who was "Arab" also evolved. An "Arabic" person became someone who identified as Arab on ethnic, linguistic, or cultural grounds. "Arab" was never a religious category – there were Christian and Jewish Arabs long before Islam, and significant numbers of Arabs today are Christian and Jewish. "Arab" was not a racial category: there are white, black, and brown Arabs.

In the fifteenth century the Arab Empire was replaced by the Ottoman Turks. The Ottomans had accepted Islam, and the sultanate and caliphate (political and religious governance) were eventually centered in Constantinople, modern day Istanbul. The Ottoman Empire was one of the largest, richest, and longest lasting in world history. It included an enormous territory in areas we now consider Middle East, North Africa, and Europe. The Ottoman Empire was a multi-ethnic state where Turkish was the language of governance, Arabic the language of religion, and many citizens also spoke one or more local or regional languages. The Ottoman Empire was multi-religious; for most of its history the majority of its citizens were Christian (in Southern and Eastern Europe as well as throughout the Middle East) and there were many flourishing Jewish communities accepted after they fled from persecution or were expelled from countries in Europe, especially Spain and Portugal. (At one time or another Jews were also expelled from England, France, Germany, Poland, Russia, and many other countries.) The diverse

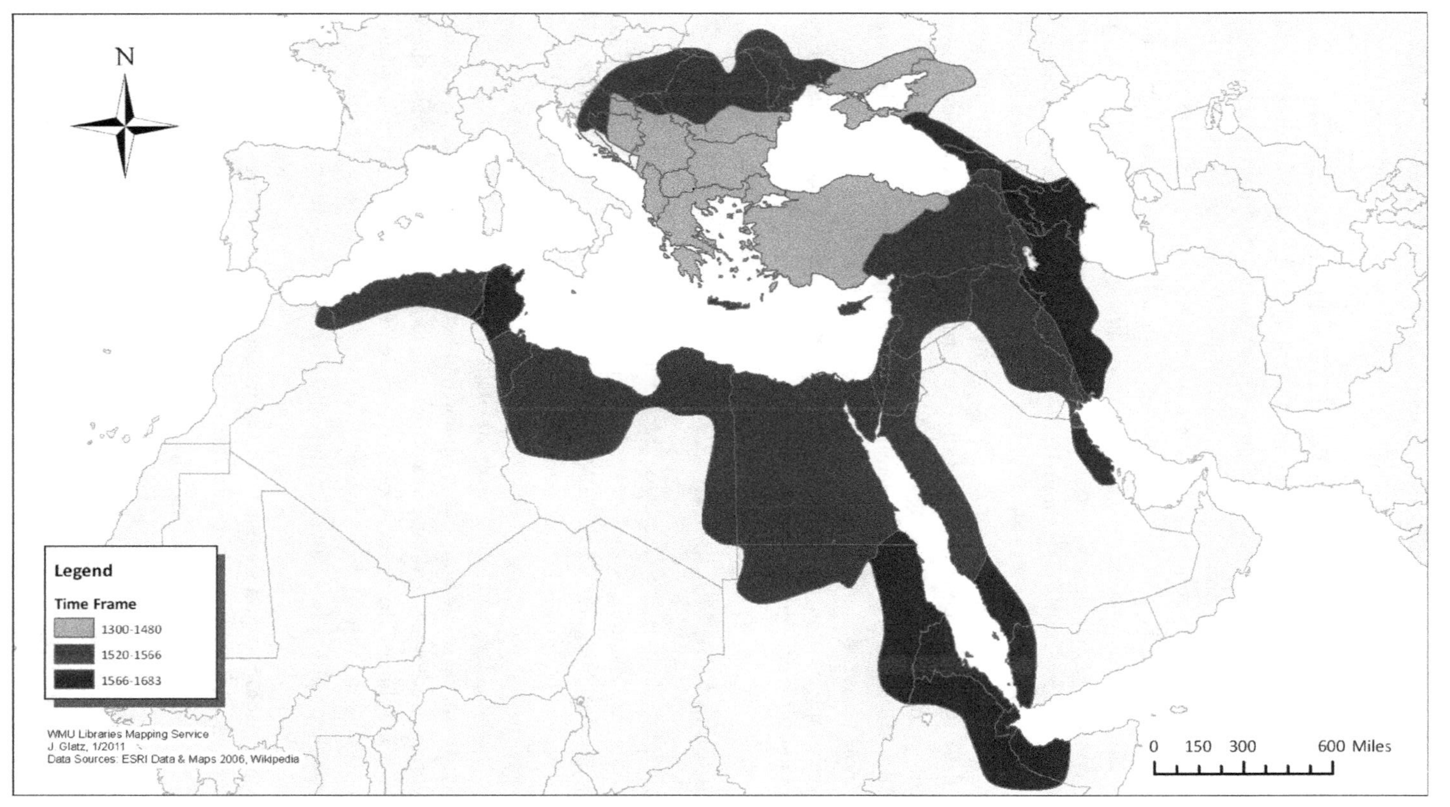

FIGURE 1.2 Ottoman Empire

and sometimes conflictive ethnicities and religions (including Sunni vs. Shiite Islam) were more or less held together under the aegis of empire. There was extensive trade and the Sultan accumulated enormous wealth. Like the rest of the world at that time, most people were employed in agriculture. Again like the rest of the world, outside the capital cities and the military, formal education beyond religious teaching was poorly developed. Given the extent of the empire, rural areas were sometimes loosely governed, local elites had significant authority, and at times banditry was common. Throughout the Ottoman period various efforts were initiated to reform land ownership, standardize military training and, especially near the end of the empire, to establish technical education on the Western model, including the education of women. The extensive and lengthy Ottoman Empire further developed political, social, and cultural connections between the Middle East and North Africa. The region of Iran remained separate, though Islamic and subject to the Caliphate in Istanbul. Corruption, intrigue, and the cost of conquests weakened the Ottoman Empire and the rising power of Europe increasingly threatened its rule.

After World War I and the defeat of the Ottoman Empire, the victorious European powers dominated the region. Since the end of World War II increasing American intervention in the region has profoundly shaped today's Middle East. I narrate this crucial history in Chapter 5.

Religions of the Middle East

The Middle East is the home to many religions, including the three great monotheistic "religions of the book," Judaism, Christianity, and Islam. Teaching contemporary literature from the Middle East the theme of religion will come up. Religion permeates life. Consider, for instance, the importance of religion to the British literature we teach in schools, from *Beowulf* and *The Canterbury Tales* to John Donne and John Milton, to Graham Greene and T.S. Eliot. Religion will also come up in the study of the Middle East because English-speaking students have many stereotypes and misconceptions, above all about Islam, but also about Judaism and about Christianity. Conflicts between Islam, Christianity, and Judaism have had much more to do with control over land and economic resources than differing religious belief (a topic I return to at several points), though the conflicts have provoked religious misunderstanding and animosity. Some measure of religious education, and some effort to address and dispel religious stereotypes is an appropriate part of teaching literature of the Middle East.

Judaism

At 4,000 years old, Judaism is the oldest monotheistic religion in the world. World Jewish population is estimated to be about thirteen million, with about five million in the U.S. and a like number in Israel. In the Jewish faith no one person or organization has authority on theological or legal matters, which have been interpreted for centuries by rabbis and scholars from the Hebrew Bible, the Torah, and from commentaries such as the Talmud and Midrash. There are many different beliefs in Judaism; the faith tends to be organized as Orthodox, Conservative, or Reformed, depending on how liberally texts are interpreted. The study of the Torah is considered a means of understanding God, and there is a long and deep scholarly tradition in Judaism. Because of its complex history, Judaism does not fit simply into categories as a religion, an ethnicity, or a culture, but draws on all of these. Indeed, the very definition of who is "Jewish" is debated. Some Jews view themselves as "secular" meaning that Judaism may be an important aspect of their lives, but they typically don't attend synagogue, hold traditional beliefs, nor engage in religious practice. The Ashkenazi ("Western") Jews, who comprise 80 percent of the world's Jewish population, trace their ancestry to medieval Jewish communities along the Rhine River in Germany that spread through Eastern Europe and spoke Yiddish, a Germanic language much influenced by Hebrew. Sephardic Jews, up to 20 percent of Jews, are descended from those who were expelled from Spain and Portugal in 1492 and 1497, though the term is also used more broadly to include Jews of North Africa and Asia (these Jews are also referred to as Mizrahim). The Jews who were expelled from Spain settled in Morocco, Turkey, throughout the Ottoman Empire, and elsewhere.

Traditionally Jews pray three times a day, with a fourth prayer on holidays. The Shabbat or Sabbath is a day of rest from sundown on Friday to just after sundown on Saturday. Jewish holidays include Yom Kippur (a day of fasting and forgiveness of sins), Rosh Hashanah (new year), Passover (commemorating the exodus from Egypt), and Hanukkah (re-dedication of the temple). Of course, there is so much more to learn about Judaism, and many helpful books and resources. I have found many Jewish people, including rabbis, to welcome the opportunity to speak with students about the Jewish faith.

Teaching about the Middle East, especially Israel and the Israel–Palestine conflict, may bring up for students, parents, or community members the issue or topic of anti-Semitism. Given the long history of anti-Semitism in our culture and in literature in English, including in our most canonized authors, it is important for teachers to address it. My 2001 book *Literature and Lives* opens with the story of my experience teaching Elie Wiesel's *Night*, and bringing an Auschwitz survivor, Diana Golden, to my high school classroom. In that book I set forward materials and approaches for teachers to address the Holocaust in an historically grounded way, and I offer ideas for helping students examine anti-Semitism in literature including in works by Chaucer, Shakespeare, Dickens, George Elliot, Ezra Pound, and T.S. Eliot. Over my thirty years of teaching I have continued to bring Holocaust literature and survivors to speak to my students, now future teachers themselves, and to take future teachers to synagogues and invite rabbis to my class to help students learn about the Jewish faith and the history of the Jewish people. I also continue to publish on the topic of teaching about anti-Semitism ("A Multimodal Approach to Addressing Anti-Semitism," 2006). In *Literature and Lives*, I describe how "teaching a Holocaust unit touched something in me that began to enlarge my vision of English teaching" (Carey-Webb, 3). In important ways, the values, commitments, and approaches I have learned as a teacher addressing anti-Semitism have brought me to this current project, addressing literature of today's Middle East.

All in all, our students need to learn to recognize and resist the long history of racism, discrimination, pogroms, expulsions, and genocide against Jewish people. And, they need to know that anti-Semitism is alive today in global conspiracy theories, right-wing militias, and outright violence and racism against Jews. Indeed, and perhaps for good reason, many Jewish people around the world think of Israel as the sanctuary of last resort, should anti-Semitism again represent a danger.

Because Israel plays this role, and because Jewish people have suffered so much, especially in the Holocaust, it is difficult for many people, including many Jewish people, to criticize Israel. Yet, teachers who read, teach, and address the contemporary Middle East are going to come across literary, cultural, historical, and political works that openly and powerfully criticize Israel, particularly its treatment of Palestinians and its Arab neighbors. This book includes such works, and it is also important that we and our students read and understand them. *Teaching the Literature of Today's Middle East* also presents literature and film from Israel appropriate for teaching to young adults. Arabs are ethnically Semitic people, and, as I have discussed and we will see further, there are similarities in racist depictions of Arabs and of Jews.

Let me be clear on one point. It is possible to teach about the Middle East and/or criticize the politics of the state of Israel, without being anti-Semitic. Teachers who address the Middle East should know that some of the strongest criticism of Israel, and specifically Israel's treatment of Palestinians, is made by Israelis themselves, and by prominent American Jews from Noam Chomsky to Jon Stewart. While there are different versions of Zionism, one of the fundamental ideas of political Zionism is that Jewish people have a special right to the land of Israel, a right that supersedes the claims of the Palestinians who formed the vast majority population there preceding World War II and who, in the present day, still constitute about half the population of Israel and the Palestinian territories controlled by Israel. Yet, there are orthodox Jews who believe that Zionism is "totally contrary to traditional Jewish law and beliefs and the teachings of the Holy Torah" ("What is Zionism?"). Alan Hart's readable three-volume history of the Israel–Palestine conflict makes the case, as his title indicates, that *Zionism*: [is] *The Real Enemy of the Jews*. Hart argues that many of Israel's actions are both inconsistent with the moral and ethical values of Judaism and dangerous to the state of Israel and to Jewish people since these actions, unless reversed, may foster a worldwide anti-Semitic backlash. While there is an effective American pro-Israel lobby (The American Israeli Public Affairs Committee, AIPAC) there is also a lobby of American Jews (J Street), which criticizes many Israeli policies and calls for a peaceful two-state solution with a safe and viable homeland for the Palestinians. Helping students gain awareness of the debates over Israel and Zionism, and more diverse and balanced perspectives than those commonly available in the American and English language mainstream media, is a crucial task for teachers addressing Middle Eastern literature. This topic is the focus of Chapter 7 of this book.

Christianity

Christians are another important and diverse group in the Middle East. I am not going to provide here an overview of Christianity and its differing beliefs and denominations. I do want to make clear, however, that not only did Christianity start in the Middle East, but Christian groups have existed since antiquity in the Middle East, and have often had peaceful relations with their Muslim neighbors. In Egypt there are over nine million Coptic Christians speaking a language descended from ancient times. The generally positive interaction between Christians and Muslims in Egypt is explored in the novel *Aunt Safiyya and the Monastery*, a great work for the classroom (as mentioned in the *Preface* this text is available as a free text online; teaching it is discussed in Chapter 3). In Lebanon, Christians constitute nearly half of the population and include both Maronites and Greek Orthodox believers. Chaldean and Assyrian Christians have been in Iraq since the second century, and the traditional language in these churches is Syriac, a descendent of Aramaic, the language thought spoken by Jesus and his disciples. The largest Christian church in Iran is the Armenian Apostalic Church (dating to 300 AD). The Iranian constitution recognizes the rights of Christians and they are allotted representation in the Iranian parliament. Syria has a substantial Christian community, perhaps 10 percent of the population, both Greek Orthodox and Catholic. There are Arab Christians in Israel and the occupied territories, though their numbers are in decline. While Christians in Iraq were not persecuted under Saddam Hussein, they have suffered greatly and many have fled since the American-led invasion. There are also Kurdish Christians, Ethiopian Christians, and small numbers of Christians across North Africa – they have been especially persecuted in the Sudan. There are also expatriate Christians throughout the Middle East, including the Gulf States and Saudi Arabia.

Islam

Certainly the religion most students think of first when they think of the Middle East is Islam and Muslims constitute the vast majority populations throughout the region, except in Israel and Lebanon. Islam is also the religion our students are likely to know the least about, and is thus the most important to address.

There is no such thing as an essential or unified "Islamic world" or "Muslim viewpoint." There are over 1.5 billion Muslims in the world and practitioners

BOX 1.2 TEACHING ABOUT RELIGION IN THE PUBLIC SCHOOLS

Religion in the Public Schools: A Joint Statement of Current Law, widely available on the Internet and distributed to all public schools in America during the Clinton administration, is a collaborative document signed by over thirty religious and civil rights groups that span the religious and political spectrum, from the American Civil Liberties Union to the evangelicals, and including Jews, Muslims, Christians, Sikhs and Humanists. This statement outlines the religious rights of students in the public schools and the law regarding the teaching of religion in America. It makes clear that while teachers may not conduct religious services in the classroom or expect or require students to adopt specific religious beliefs, teaching about religion, the history of religion, comparative religion, and religious sacred texts "are all permissible public school subjects." Moreover, the document makes the point that "it would be difficult to teach art, music, literature and most social studies without considering religious influences." In other words, teaching students about any religion, including Islam, assigning reading from the Bible, the Torah, or the Quran, inviting informational speakers to the classroom to talk about religion, examining stereotypes about Christians, Muslims, and Jews – important topics on their own or in conjunction with literary or historical studies – is perfectly legal and appropriate in American public schools.

are not only in the Middle East and North Africa, but also throughout Asia – southern, central, and southeastern. There are Muslims in China, Russia, and India – Indonesia is the world's most populous Muslim country. There are Muslims in Europe, in South America and the Caribbean. There are approximately 7 million Muslims in the United States (compared to 6.5 million Jewish people, and 3 million Native Americans). There are Muslims of every political point of view, every racial group, speaking an enormous diversity of languages. Only about 15 percent of Muslims worldwide are Arabs. As with Judaism and Christianity, there are a diversity of denominations, sects, practices, groups, schools, brotherhoods, movements, and beliefs within Islam, inclusive of Suni and Shiite but also Wahabi, Sufi, Ahmadiyya, Twelver, Usalism, Akhbarism, Ismaili, Hanafi, Shafi'i, Maliki, Ash'ari, Maturidi, Murji'ah, Salafism, Baralwi, Al-Ikhwan Al-Muslimun, Nizari, Bohra, Kharijite, Qadiri, Naqshbandi, Mouride – and many more. There are also groups closely connected to Islam that some practitioners may or may not always consider Islamic, the Druse, Zikri, Ahmadiyya, and the American group, the Nation of Islam. There are faiths much influenced by Islam but clearly not Muslim, including Baha'i, Sikhism, and Nuwaubu.

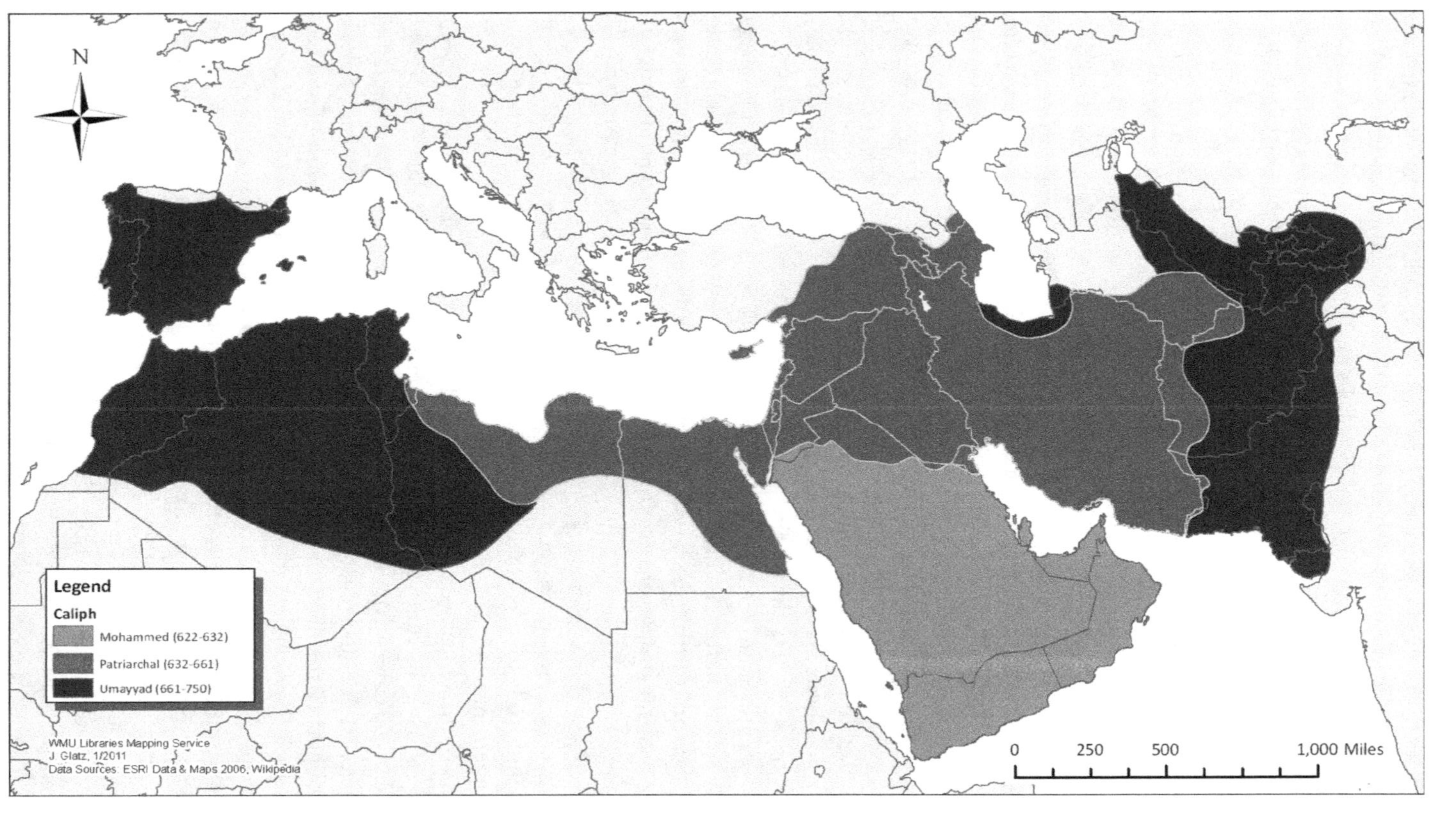

FIGURE 1.3 Islamic Caliphate

Saying something definitive about Islam is difficult. The famous literature professor Edward Said (his important book *Orientalism* is discussed below) has argued that Islam takes many forms. Said links this diversity to the history of Islam,

> As the religion grew enormously in the century after Muhammad's preaching and career, the faith spread into hundreds of different regions and cultures, from China and India in the east to Morocco in the west, to Europe in the north, and to Africa in the south. Each region and people who came under its sway developed its own kind of Islam. Thus, Islam is a world of many histories, many peoples, many languages, traditions, schools of interpretation, proliferating developments, disputations, cultures, and countries. A vast world of more than 1.2 billion people stretched out over every continent, north and south, including now the Americas, it can't adequately be apprehended or understood simply as "Islam" . . . One should therefore begin by speaking about Islams rather than Islam . . . far from there being a simple one-to-one correspondence between Islam (whatever construction one may put on it) and every believing or faithful Muslim, there is on the contrary a whole set of profound conflicts at the very heart of one and the other, conflicts between absolutism and tolerance, between the doctrinaire and the liberal, between commitment and skepticism, to mention only a few; and, once we add matters of language, culture, history, politics, community, and school of interpretation in all the various parts of the world, the question of Islam and Muslims becomes virtually unapproachable from any simple or summary point of view.
>
> *("Impossible," 71)*

In this contentious variety and complexity Islam is like Christianity and Judaism. All three religions encompass many points of view, understandings, and interpretations.

Given the difficulty of addressing Islam, there are basic points about the religion that are likely to come up when reading texts set in the Middle East or with Muslim characters. Muslims believe in one god, and that Muhammad is his prophet. Muhammad is not comparable to Christ in the Christian tradition because Muhammad is not divine, instead he is the last prophet in a long line of prophets. "Allah" is the Arabic word for God, and means the same God worshiped by the Jews and Christians – "Allah" is the word used to mean "God" in Christian churches in Arabic speaking countries. The Quran is the inspired word of God revealed to Muhammad in Arabic. Muslims believe that Islam fulfills the monotheistic religions of Judaism and Christianity. In the Quran, Abraham, Moses, and Jesus are recognized as prophets.

When teachers address Islam they often talk about the Five Pillars of Sunni Islam, the belief in one God with Muhammad as his messenger, daily prayer, fasting during Ramadan, giving of alms, and, when possible, pilgrimage to Mecca

(Hajj). Though there is value in students knowing "the Five Pillars," teachers should also aim to develop in students a deeper understanding of the religion, and help them recognize the fundamental similarity of ethical principles between faiths. (Additional ideas for teaching about Islam and also about support and respecting Muslim students are found in Chapter 10.) There are many fine sources to introduce the study of Islam, and I list several at the end of the chapter. A popular resource is the writing of British author Karen Armstrong whose books on religion and Islam are readable (age 16–college) and generally respected. Armstrong argues that,

> The Muslim interpretation of the monotheistic faith has its own special genius and has important things to teach us. In all the great religions, seers and prophets have conceived strikingly similar visions of a transcendent and ultimate reality . . . I believe that Muhammad had such an experience and made a distinctive and valuable contribution to the spiritual experience of humanity. If we are to do justice to our Muslim neighbours, we must appreciate this essential fact.
>
> (Islam, *13–14)*

The Judeo–Christian tradition does not have the monopoly on either monotheism or concern for justice, decency, compassion and respect for humanity – these are certainly important to Islam, as our examination of Middle Eastern literature will demonstrate.

Some people think of the Wahabism of Saudi Arabia as "pure" or "traditional" Islam, but this is a mistake. Armstrong says,

> Wahhabism is only an Islamic sect. It developed in the eighteenth century and was similar to the Christian Puritan sect that flourished during the seventeenth century in England, the Netherlands and Massachusetts. The Puritans and the Wahhabis both claimed to be returning to the original faith, but both were really an entirely new development and a response to the unique conditions of the time.
>
> *(Armstrong, 1993, 13)*

The 1976 film *The Message* staring Anthony Quinn tells the story of the beginnings of Islam and the prophet Muhammad, though, in the film, Muhammad is never directly depicted. The film is available online, and scenes could help students understand the historical story central to the Muslim faith. On the Amazon website for the film, M. Higgins writes,

> I am a middle school teacher and I use this movie to teach my students about Islam. It is very popular with them. I find it interesting that the kids are cheering for Muhammad and his followers by the end of the film.

> Thinking of Moslems, as "the good guys" is something our media and culture has not traditionally done, so I really appreciate the ways this film challenges societal prejudices.

Especially given current tensions and controversies, teaching about Islam is relevant to students of all ages.

Dr. Blain H. Auer helps us think about an engaging approach to beginning to teach about Islam.

FIGURE 1.4 Kaaba in Mecca

BOX 1.3 TEACHING ABRAHAM – BLAIN H. AUER

Reading Abraham across religious traditions is an effective tool for bridging gaps of cultural difference. Abraham is perhaps *the* figure who symbolizes the core values of monotheism shared by Jews, Christians, and Muslims. What is little understood by students unfamiliar with Islam is the central role Abraham plays within the Islamic tradition. He is the builder of the Kaaba in Mecca, thus founding the first place of worship to God. He has the role of progenitor of both Jewish and Arab genealogies, one through

continued . . .

his wife Sarah and their son Isaac and the other through Hagar (Hajar in Arabic) and their son Ishmael. Just as in Judaism, he is viewed as the patriarch of the Arabs and Muslims.

Abraham is central to the religious beliefs and practices of Muslims around the world. Events from his legendary life are reenacted by Muslims during the annual pilgrimage to Mecca, the Hajj. Muslims visit Mecca to circumambulate the Kaaba, a building of worship to God that it believed to have been constructed by Abraham. Next to the Kaaba is a reliquary (a vessel of some sort that houses objects connected to important religious figures) known as the station of Abraham, the place where Abraham stood while building the structure. It contains a slab of rock that bears the imprint of Abraham's footprints. Adjacent to the Kaaba but within the confines of the Great Mosque of Mecca is a place where Hagar ran in the desert looking for water to give to her infant son Ishmael. In God's mercy he produced a spring of fresh water known as Zam-Zam. Muslims visit this spring to collect the precious water to drink and share with family and friends.

The pilgrimage to Mecca also reenacts the most famous story from the life of Abraham, the sacrifice of his son. In the Quran it is told that God tested Abraham's obedience, commanding him to sacrifice his son. When Abraham proved himself to God by raising the knife against his son he was spared this horrific act and God produced a ram as a substitute. Muslims across the globe commemorate Abraham's trial by sacrificing an animal, an event that takes place near the end of the Hajj. This is known as the Great Festival (*id al-kabir*) or the Festival of the Sacrifice (*id al-adha*). Another reenactment associated with Abraham's sacrifice is the stoning of Satan. In Muslim lore Abraham was tempted by Satan to disobey God's command and not sacrifice his son. Abraham was not deceived into committing this sin and he threw stones at Satan driving him away. During Hajj pilgrims hurl small pebbles at three pillars that symbolize the places where Satan attempted to corrupt Abraham.

One effective tool for communicating this rich religious history is through a comparative reading of the sacrifice of Abraham in the Quran and the Bible. The version of Abraham's sacrifice is one of the most lengthy narratives in the Quran and is found in Surah 37: 99–113. This is significant because the Quran is not a collection of stories in the manner of the Bible. Overall, it is commandments, instructions, and guidance given to humanity directly in the voice of God. This makes the Quran very difficult to read from cover to cover if it is approached like a conventional book and Muslims generally do not read it in this way. The fact that Abraham's sacrifice is one of the most complete stories in the Quran only confirms its centrality. Actually, the Quranic passage is a little shorter than the Biblical version, which is nineteen "verses" in length and is found in Genesis 22: 1–19.

continued . . .

The word "verse" does not get across the full meaning of how the Quran is organized. *Aya* is the Arabic word used here, which means "sign." While *surah*, generally translated as "chapter," literally means a fence or row.

There is an overall affinity between the versions found in the Bible and the Quran. Abraham is called upon by God to sacrifice his son. Both versions explicitly state that God was testing Abraham. However, Abraham behaves differently in each version. In the Quran, Abraham invites his son to decide on how they should proceed with God's command. In Genesis, Abraham keeps his son in the dark about the truth of the impending sacrifice. Genesis contains many more details than the Quran, such as reference to the carrying of the wood and the knife by the son, as well as the appearance of the ram. These are absent from the Quranic version. Finally, the Quranic version is told in the first person, giving it a more direct feeling. While doing this cross-reading one student remarked that "it feels like it is talking to me." Genesis, on the other hand, is told in the third person positioning the reader as a passive observer to monumental events. One important element, though not explicit in the Quran, is the fact that Muslims today believe that it was Ishmael who was chosen to be sacrificed. Jews and Christians believe it was Isaac. This difference is the basis for the understanding of each religious community's claim to a special chosen status before God. Each argues that only the most cherished son would have been selected for the sacrifice. There are many other elements that students will pull out of their encounter with these two texts. It can provide important points for discussion on what it means to be a prophet, the qualities of sacred texts, and the understanding of the historical origins of Judaism, Christianity and Islam.

BOX 1.4 CONNECTING THE QURAN AND THE BIBLE

To help students understand the connection between Islam and Christianity, I have had them read Surah 3 and 19 of the Quran, the Surahs that address the story of Mary (called Maryam in Arabic). Of course, my students read the text in translation – we also look at several different translations of a few verses so they can see that by not reading the text in the original Arabic they are missing some of the meaning. (The Center for Muslim–Jewish Engagement at the University of Southern California has an online version of the Quran showing multiple translations.)

continued . . .

My student Dan Brim responded to reading the Quran:

> I knew absolutely nothing about Islam or the Quran prior [to] today's reading. I was a taken a bit off-guard. All of the names that I grew up with, Adam, Noah, Moses, Father Abraham, Mary, Jesus, they were all there. Of course, there was different interpretation as to how their significance (especially the importance and value of Christ). I had no idea they were a part of the Islamic religion, not even a little bit.

Molly Grube states:

> Many people are of the belief that Christians and Muslims share nothing in common, when quite the opposite is actually true. Christianity, Islam, and Judaism all stem from the same core beliefs. I always knew that, but I still found myself slightly surprised when I was reading "Maryam." Another light bulb went on to signal to me the connection between Christianity and Islam when I read the section about not believing in Allah to be the biggest sin.

Developing a richer understanding of Islam is a recurrent theme in this book. In Chapter 2 we will examine the Islamic concepts of justice, equality, and respect and how contemporary Middle Eastern literature draws on these principles as writers critique their societies. In Chapter 3 we will consider Islam and the role of women, and the representation of women in literature. Chapter 9 addresses literature about the experience of Muslim people in English-speaking countries. Chapter 12 will address the representation of Islam in Western literature. Note: In this book I spell the Islamic holy book as "Quran." Blain Auer explains,

> Quran spelling has shifted away from "Koran" which now seems antiquated, though still in use. I prefer Quran because Qur'an, while more phonetically accurate, is not understood by people who have not studied Arabic. The ' symbolizes a glottal stop called *hamza*. However, this is unusual orthography in English. Full transliteration is Qur'ān. The shift from K to Q makes sense to me because these are two different letters in Arabic, Kāf and Qāf. As more and more Arabic words come into the English language the common spelling will be closer to Arabic and full transliteration I assume. Regarding Mohammed or Muhammad, I prefer Muhammad because it is closer to full transcription. Full transcription would be Muḥammad.
>
> *(Personal email, 1 Sep. 2010)*

Fundamentalism

There are groups and individuals often mistakenly referred to in the American media as simply "Islamic fundamentalists" or "Islamists" who, responding to American economic, political, and cultural involvement and intervention in the world, have identified the United States as an "enemy" and are willing to use violence to resist. This book will help readers better understand these groups, as we consider why they exist, and why their anger is directed at the United States. The history of European colonialism and American intervention in Middle East and the Iraq and Afghan Wars and the topic of "terrorism" are addressed in Chapters 5 and 6. The connection between Israel and the United States is addressed in Chapter 7.

At the outset, it is crucial that students come to understand popularly held ideas in the West about "Islamic fundamentalism" and "jihad." Going beyond stereotypes of "Islamic fundamentalism" means recognizing that there is a wide range of religious and political positions within and among Muslim countries and it means attempting to understand the logic and appeal of Islamic piety and revivalism and its social and historical causes. Armstrong situates Islamic revivalism in a global context that also encompasses Christian and other fundamentalisms. I again quote Armstrong at length:

> Fundamentalism is a global fact and has surfaced in every major faith in response to the problems of our modernity. There is a fundamentalist Judaism, fundamentalist Christianity, fundamentalist Hinduism, fundamentalist Buddhism, fundamentalist Sikhism and even fundamentalist Confucianism. This type of faith surfaced first in the Christian world in the United States at the beginning of the twentieth century. . . But when these moderate measures are found to be of no avail, some people resort to more extreme methods, and a fundamentalist movement is born. With hindsight, we can see that it was only to be expected that fundamentalism should first make itself known in the United States, the showcase of modernity, and only appear in other parts of the world at a later date. Of the three monotheistic religions, Islam was in fact the last to develop a fundamentalist strain, when modern culture began to take root in the Muslim world in the late 1960s and 1970s. By this date, fundamentalism was quite well established among Christians and Jews, who had a longer exposure to the modern experience . . . Every single fundamentalist movement that I have studied is convinced that secular establishment is determined to wipe religion out. This is not always a paranoid reaction. We have seen that secularism has often been imposed very aggressively in the Muslim world. Fundamentalists look back to a "golden age" before the irruption of modernity for inspiration, but they are not atavistically returning to the Middle Ages. All are intrinsically modern movements and could have appeared at no time

> other than our own . . . They are all – even in the United States – highly critical of democracy and secularism. Because the emancipation of women has been one of the hallmarks of modern culture, fundamentalists tend to emphasize conventional, agrarian gender roles, putting women back into veils and into the home. The fundamentalist community can thus be seen as the shadow-side of modernity; it can also highlight some of the darker sides of the modern experiment . . . It is not correct, therefore, to imagine that Islam has within it a militant, fanatic strain that impels Muslims into a crazed and violent rejection of modernity. Muslims are in tune with fundamentalists in other faiths all over the world, who share their profound misgivings about modern secular culture. It should also be said that Muslims object to the term 'fundamentalism', pointing out quite correctly that it was coined by American Protestants as a badge of pride, and cannot be usefully translated into Arabic.
>
> *(2002, 165–168)*

This international and ecumenical perspective on fundamentalism is important to bring to American students – as they look at the evolving role of religion in the Middle East they can also look at the increasing role of religion in American politics, the use of religious language by national leaders, and efforts to thwart democratic practices and demonize Islam by extremist Christian groups.

It is important for people in English-speaking countries and the West to better understand this Islamic piety movement; in many ways it represents something precisely opposite of what is portrayed in our media. As Armstrong suggests, the Islamic piety movement is relatively new, starting in the Middle Eastern cities in the 1970s and featuring religious study and regular prayer, modest clothing (hijab for women), beards and sometimes white robes and skull caps for men, modest comportment, and stricter sexual segregation. Also called Islamic Revival or Islamic Awakening (al-Sahwa al-Isamiyya), it has involved the proliferation of neighborhood mosques and institutions of Islamic learning and social welfare, increasing mosque attendance by men and women, increasing numbers of authors in the popular press who comment from a self-described Islamic point of view.

The Islamic piety movement includes a women's mosque movement where women hold public meetings in mosques to teach one another Islamic beliefs and how to behave in a pious and virtuous way, altering a tradition of male-centered Islamic leadership and teaching, and also leading to an enhanced role for women in religious and political life. (Armstrong, Islam 6) For these reasons – despite what many feminists in the West have thought about fundamentalism, and the picture painted by ex-patriot literature – the Islamic piety or fundamentalism has had an important appeal to women. According to Saba Mahmood, professor of Anthropology at Berkeley and author of *Politics of Piety: The Islamic Revival and the Feminist Subject* Islamic revivalism "found active and wide support among the middle classes who increasingly conjoined a critique of their emulation of Western habits and lifestyles with a renewed concern for living in accord with Islamic social mores." (Mahmood, 2005) The connections between social movements, capitalism and consumer culture, and individual or collective resistance are complex.

> Abu-Lughod gives the example of young Bedouin women who wear sexy lingerie to challenge parental authority and dominant social mores. She suggests that instead of simply reading such acts as moments of opposition to and escape from, dominant relations of power, they should also be understood as reinscribing alternative forms of power that are rooted in practices of capitalist consumerism and urban bourgeois values and aesthetics.
>
> *(9)*

Indeed, in another reversal of the Western stereotype, we will see that Islamic revivalism, as portrayed in contemporary Egyptian literature, is tied to calls for openness in government and self-determination. Because of a history of authoritarianism and repression initially established by outside forces and then indigenous governments in many Muslim countries, the Islamic piety movement is connected to efforts at democratization. In *Islam and Democracy* John Esposito argues:

> The processes of democratization and Islamic resurgence have become complementary forces in many countries. The most effective opposition to authoritarian regimes is expressed through a reaffirmation of the Islamic identity and heritage.
>
> *(1996, 16)*

Saba Mahmood argues,

> Islamic political parties have been instrumental in giving voice to popular demands for democratization of the political arena, for an end to single-party rule, and for a more critical stance toward U.S. hegemony in the region. Moreover, Islamic welfare organizations around the Muslim world have increasingly stepped in to fill the vaccum [sic] left by postcolonial states as these states, under neoliberal economic pressures, have withdrawn from providing social services to their citizens.
>
> *(2005, xi)*

The Islamic piety movement is connected to economic and political conditions, and to the role of the United States in the region (see Chapter 5). Loubna Skalli, a Moroccan feminist scholar writes:

> Fundamentalists, then, are a generation of Muslim youth in revolt. They are in revolt against the imposed colonial projects of modernization in their countries and the unfulfilled promises of their postcolonial political regimes and national elites. They are in revolt against the unequal distribution of wealth and resources within and among nations, against their own socioeconomic and political exclusions, as well as against the widening circle of the disenfranchised classes from which most of them come. They are in revolt against their own sense of powerlessness in the face of all the global forces that threaten their religious and cultural identity.
>
> More importantly, perhaps, fundamentalists are in revolt against the traumatic legacy of Western colonialism that continues to destabilize the core of their social fabric – a process kept alive, if not exacerbated, by American hegemony and its perceived homogenizing materialistic values. The West, with America at its head, is unquestionably omnipresent in the vision, discourses, and agendas of Muslim fundamentalists.
>
> *(2004, 43–44)*

The understanding that Muslim fundamentalism is a relatively recent phenomenon similar to Christian fundamentalism, that it is tied to efforts to create greater social justice and democracy in its home countries, and that it resists imperialism may come as a surprise given popular ideas in the West, ideas that undergird stereotypes, media reports, and foreign policy.

Because of the use of the term in the media, it is important that students learn about "jihad." "Jihad" does not simply mean "holy war" or war against Christians or non-believers. Instead, "jihad" means "struggle" in the Arabic language. The word appears frequently in the Quran describing the duty of Muslims to strive in the way of Allah. The term refers to 1) the striving to attain religious and moral self-perfection; 2) the effort to make Islamic societies more just; and 3) defensive military struggle to protect Muslims. A person engaged in "jihad" is a *mujahid*, the plural being *mujahideen*. A well-known Muslim scholar has defined the true goal of jihad: to attain harmony between faith, submission, and righteous living. Ghandi's and Martin Luther King's non-violent struggle for social justice are referred to in Arabic as "jihad." The President of Tunisia has used the word "jihad" to describe the struggle for economic development in his country. Perhaps it is obvious to readers of this book, but let me be clear that neither the religion of Islam nor Muslim people are the enemies of America. As even President George Bush said seventeen days after the 9/11 attacks, "There are thousands of Muslims who proudly call themselves Americans, and they know what I know – that the Muslim faith is based upon peace and love and compassion." ("In His Own Words")

An important film for American and English-speaking students is *Inside Islam: What One Billion Muslims Really Think* (2010). The film is based on a massive six-year study and survey by the Gallop organization that included over 50,000 interviews of beliefs and attitudes of tens of thousands of Muslims in thirty-five predominately Muslim countries worldwide. Representing more than 90 percent of the Muslim world, it is the largest survey of its kind. The results are available first as a book, *Who Speaks For Islam? What a Billion Muslims Really Think* by John Esposito and Dalia Mogahed (2008). The research explodes many myths about Muslims, for instance that they want to be ruled exclusively by sharia law, that they oppose free speech, that they believe women should not have equal job opportunities with men, or that they hate the U.S. While it shows also diversity of belief within the Muslim world it also shows remarkable similarity between Muslims worldwide and Christians in the West. The vast majority of Muslims around the world do not "hate democracy," but, instead, Muslims admire American representative government, even if they question specific American foreign policies and want to develop their own countries in ways consistent with their culture and beliefs.

Trumped up fear and anxiety about Muslims and immigrants motivate political parties in Europe and in the English-speaking world as well. This prejudice has come to be called "Islamophobia." Many Muslim Americans have experienced discrimination because of their beliefs, and bigotry heightened after the 9/11 attacks. A 2009 report by the Pew Foundation noted that nearly six in ten American adults see Muslims as being subject to discrimination, more than Mormons, Atheists, or Jews ("Muslims Widely Seen As Facing Discrimination"). In a 2007 survey 53 percent of American Muslims said it was "more difficult" to be a Muslim after the 9/11 attacks.

Today there are energetic and disturbing groups, some of them self-professed Christians, spreading misinformation, defamatory materials, and unfounded rumor about Muslims in the media, from pulpits, and online. A July 2007 *Newsweek* survey of non-Muslim Americans showed that 45 percent would not vote for a qualified Muslim for political office, 33 percent believed that Muslims were more loyal to Islam than to America, 41 percent believe Muslim culture "glorifies suicide," that 28 percent believed that the Quran promotes violence, and 25 percent do not oppose "mass detentions" of Muslims (Braiker). As teachers we need to pay serious attention to these attitudes. Consider that last statistic. In 1930s Germany what percentage of the non-Jewish population would have endorsed "mass detentions" of Jews? At the same time period how many Americans would have endorsed "mass detentions" of Japanese? Would that percentage have been so different from 25 percent, I wonder? We should find these attitudes deeply disturbing – and energizing to our teaching.

Orientalism

Misunderstanding of Islam is also connected to misunderstanding of the Middle East in general, and to a long history of conflict between the Middle East and Europe. Many of the images we have been given of Islam and the Middle East, from the crusades to the present, are mistaken and inaccurate. In 1979 Edward Said, a leading American professor of literature at Columbia University and a Palestinian Christian, published *Orientalism,* a study of the representation of the Middle East in European – especially British and French – scholarship. Since it was published, *Orientalism* has had an enormous impact in many fields of scholarship. Teachers of Middle Eastern literature need to be familiar with Edward Said's arguments. Said makes the case that rigid categories of "us" and "them," "East" and "West," have created differences that in fact don't exist: "The Orient was almost a European invention, and had been since antiquity a place of romance, exotic beings, haunting memories and landscapes, remarkable experiences" (1).

Over and over again in Europe and the West, the Orient was understood as a location of great "long gone" ancient civilizations but decay, decadence, and corruption in the present. The image was that "An Oriental lives in the Orient, he lives a life of Oriental ease, in a state of Oriental despotism and sensuality, imbued with a sense of Oriental fatalism" (102). Said argues that in European and American discourse and representations of the Middle East Europeans were considered "superior" and "rational" and the Orient "backward" and "sensual." Said identifies attitudes against Arabs with many of the racist depictions of Jews and anti-Semitism. He talks specifically about how views of Islam were influenced by the history of European and Middle Eastern military, political, and economic rivalry.

> Not for nothing did Islam come to symbolize terror, devastation, the demonic, hordes of hated barbarians. For Europe, Islam was a lasting trauma. Until the end of the seventeenth century the "Ottoman peril" lurked alongside Europe to represent for the whole of Christian civilization a constant danger, and in time European civilization incorporated that peril and its lore, its great events, figures, virtues, and vices as something woven into the fabric of life.
>
> *(59–60)*

A leading academic himself, Said argues that Western scholarship, from Napoleon's invasion of Egypt to the present, has been part of the way that Europe exercised power over the Orient. "It has been estimated that around 60,000 books dealing with the Near Orient were written between 1800 and 1950; there is no remotely comparable figure for Oriental books about the West" (204).

The images of the Orient formulated in the West were linked to and legitimated political domination of the region during a period of "an unstoppable European expansion in search of markets, resources, and colonies . . ." (95) so that, by the end of World War I, Europe colonized 85 percent of the earth (123). "From the beginning of the nineteenth century until the end of World War II France and Britain dominated the Orient and Orientalism; since

World War II American has dominated the Orient and approached it as France and Britain once did" (4).

Writing in 1979, 22 years before 9-11, Said commented:

> In the films and television the Arab is associated with either lechery or bloodthirsty dishonesty . . . essentially sadistic, treacherous, low. Slave trader, camel driver, moneychanger, colorful scoundrel . . . the Arab is always shown in large numbers. No individuality, no personal characteristics or experiences . . . Lurking behind all of these images is the menace of *jihad*. Consequence: a fear that the Muslims (or Arabs) will take over the world.
>
> *(286–7)*

Clearly, Edward Said raises issues relevant to students and teachers attempting to understand the Middle East today. He asks powerful questions about developing understanding across cultures:

> How does one *represent* other cultures? What is *another* culture? Is the notion of a distinct culture (or race, or religion, or civilization) a useful one, or does it always get involved either in self-congratulation (when one discusses one's own) or hostility and aggression (when one discusses the "other")? Do cultural, religious, and racial differences matter more than socio-economic categories, or politico-historical ones? How do ideas acquire authority, "normality," and even the status of "natural" truth?
>
> *(325–6)*

In *Orientalism* Said suggests the value of finding new and better ways to understand the Middle East: "Perhaps the most important task of all would be to undertake studies in contemporary alternatives to Orientalism, to ask how one can study other cultures, and peoples from a libertarian, or a non-repressive and non-manipulative, perspective" (24).

Relevant to this book you are reading, Said believes that one of the things most lacking in studies of the Orient is addressing contemporary literature of the Middle East.

> Since an Arab poet or novelist – and there are many – writes of his experiences, of his values, of his humanity . . . he effectively disrupts the various patterns (images, clichés, abstractions) by which the Orient is represented. A literary text speaks more or less directly of a living reality.
>
> *(291)*

As a literary scholar, professor of literature and former president of the Modern Language Association (the professional organization for professors of literature and language) Said makes another argument that is central to this book, that the study of literature needs to be combined with the study of culture and politics. He says, "Too often literature and culture are presumed to be politically, even historically innocent; it has regularly seemed otherwise to me (and I hope will convince my literary colleagues) that society and literary culture can only be understood and studied together" (27).

Though I think the book *Orientalism* is likely too difficult for most secondary students, I have taught it to advanced college students who have made startling connections. Virginia Shedd said,

> This Orientalism business reminds me of slavery and the representations of slaves. Slavery was, at first, justified because of whites' characterizations of blacks as stupid, godless, barely human . . . Even the earliest abolitionists were speaking out on behalf of the slave. Until, that is, the slaves began writing their own letters, articles, and novels and new understandings emerged.

Marie Teitgen points out, "The problem is that we might see the ill in racial slurs for Native Americans, African Americans or even the GLTB [Gay, Lesbian, Bisexual, Transgendered] community here in America, but there seems to be a pass for this same sort of behavior when it comes to anything from the Middle East."

Middle Eastern Stereotypes in Popular Culture

There are so many contemporary images in the news, in film and television, in simplistic political debate, in video games, and online that distort the lives and realities of Middle Eastern people. Reading literature from the Middle East calls for teachers to draw on the ideas of Said's *Orientalism* and help students think carefully about stereotypes. An ideal way to raise issues of Orientalism and to begin teaching Middle Eastern literature with college and secondary students is the film *Reel Bad Arabs* documenting the representation of Arabs in Hollywood. The fifty-minute film is available in its entirety for free online and for purchase in DVD format. The engaging documentary is based on Jack Shaheen's comprehensive study of Hollywood film – the second edition of his book is over 600 pages long – and website with the same title (ReelBadArabs.com). Shaheen is a retired professor of communication at Southern Illinois University and a consultant on Middle Eastern affairs for CBS news. In the film Shaheen makes clear that the racist and violent depictions of Arabs we so often see in popular film at times both become, emerge from, and are used to justify, American foreign policy and military actions. This connection between cultural works and larger political actions marks *Reel Bad Arabs* as both thematically and methodologically related to Said's *Orientalism*, but far more accessible to our students.

Reel Bad Arabs raises profound questions about the way the Hollywood films and popular culture represent people of Arabic descent and students of all ages who view this film will be likely struck by the new perspectives it brings to them on movies they have seen many times, including Disney's *Aladdin, Raiders of the Lost Ark, True Lies, Back to the Future,* and others.

> As the video played on, I was surprised at very large number of movies that involve Arabs and give them the same degrading and villain-like stereotype. They are always portrayed as the terrorists or viewed as lesser compared to the American characters.
>
> *(Lauren Axt)*

> The film *Reel Bad Arabs* . . . made me feel like a hypocrite because I realized how close-minded I was towards this topic. I would be extremely offended if Americans were portrayed in Arab films the way that some American films show Arabs. All of these films plus the tragedy of September eleventh have turned Arabs into the enemy . . . Overall this film inspires me to become more educated on the topic.
>
> *(Rachael Denham)*

> Although Hollywood is responsible to some degree, the blame needs to be placed on many other sources. Educators need to do more to teach children about this rich culture, not just teaching them about the terrorist attacks and burkas. The government must make it clear to all their citizens that Arab- and Muslim-American deserve the same treatment as everyone else, and encourage them to learn more about the culture. Perhaps most important to dispelling stereotypes is the role the media plays. If the only images the national media presents Americans with are of terrorism, repression, and turmoil, is it any surprise it is what comes out in our entertainment?
>
> *(Kristen Felts)*

Of course there are many contemporary films addressing a wide range of issues in the Middle East – many that my students had seen or were watching on their own as the course progressed. Reading Middle Eastern literature, learning about the culture and history, and thinking critically about the representations of Middle Eastern people helped all of us become more savvy viewers. Often after seeing a film we were motivated to do online research about the film and its portrayals.

To ease into the study of stereotyping of Arabs I have even used children's literature with my college students. My students carefully read and compared two picture books set in the Middle East by the same author, Florence Parry Heide. Ashley Auberman commented, "I never realized how much discussion could be generated from two kids' books!" The first book we looked at, *The Day of Ahmed's Secret*, tells the story of a boy who delivers cooking gas in different neighborhoods in the city of Cairo and has a secret to tell his family – he has learned to write his name. In class we especially discussed the illustrations, looking for what John Spreitzer, drawing on our viewing of *Reel Bad Arabs*, called "Arab-land" – people with dark skin, in exotic dress, veils, sand, camels and so on. As we studied the illustrations students argued about whether or not they were stereotyped. We began to see juxtapositions between "modern" and "traditional" clothing, people with a range of skin colors and ethnicities, and a diversity of neighborhoods, some of which seemed to match pictures of Cairo some students were finding on the Internet. Chelsea Leatherman wrote,

> The publisher and the author of both books are Americans. When looking at the pictures in the story, you have to wonder if they are accurate to life in modern day Cairo or if the view we received was a tourist edition.

John Ebbing said,

> This piece of literature is magnificent with its illustrations which give a young reader an idea of what life in Egypt might be like. The faces of the characters are calm and friendly as opposed to what a child may see on television or on the cover of their parent's magazines. My parents raised me to fear people of Arabic decent and that they were most likely no good terrorists living in the United States on a visa to run party stores and gas stations in order to fund their organizations over seas. If I would have been exposed to a story like this as a child I feel that I may have been less fearful of Arab people.

Our discussion of picture books moved to the topic of war when we examined *Sami and Time of the Troubles* also by Florence Parry Heide. This picture book invited my students to consider war from the point of view of an Arab child. Sami lives in Beirut, Lebanon and although the time period is not specified in the book, it may be during the 1993 Israeli attack. John Spreitzer described the book,

> Sami is a young boy who has to spend most of his day in the basement due to gunfire and bombing. We get a glimpse at the casualties of war not shown on the news, the murder of a childhood that should be spend laughing and playing instead of hiding in thick shelters for fear of death. The most chilling and telling scene in this book though is when we see Sami and his friend playing war, discussing when they will get real guns someday.

Rachel Denham stated,

> The pictures displayed the depression that the boy and his family were going through. The hardships of living in a town that was being bombed

> and having to wake up with no house and no city because it has all be burned away.

Reading these children's books led Janelle Mirch to comment, "children understand more than we think they do, and just might perceive things more clearly than adults can through their carefully monitored social lenses." Janelle's description of adults' "social lenses" ties closely to our thinking about how we understand the differences between people.

Difference and Similarity

Middle Eastern literature should inspire us to seek cultural, historical, and political background information. That information may challenge our stereotypes and closely-held ideas about our own society as well as the Middle East, including the past and present role of the U.S. in the region. In teaching literature from today's Middle East be prepared for your own thinking to evolve.

I have traveled extensively on five continents and lived abroad for several years. Before visiting a new place my head is often full of stereotypes and, then, when I get there those stereotypes begin to change. Spain is actually the country that I know best having traveled there repeatedly over a twenty-five-year period and having lived there for nearly two years at separated times. As my initial stereotypes about Spaniards began to fall away, I developed new "theories" and observations about the similarities and differences between Spanish people and Americans. The longer I stayed in Spain, however, the harder even these more "refined" generalizations were to maintain. I would meet people that just didn't fit. I would get to know someone better and realize that they were not the way I, at first, thought them to be. As my language skills and cultural knowledge improved I would develop friendships, friendships that would deepen over the course of repeated contacts over many years. This deepened knowledge has made it harder and harder for me to generalize about Spain. In the end, I have come to think that there really is very little that I can say about the differences between Spaniards and Americans. I can say both countries are full of an enormous variety of good and valuable people.

After reading the Nobel Prize-winning Turkish novelist Orhan Pamuk's book *The White Castle*, my student Ashley Hillyard made some wise comments that I quote here at length:

> This novel questions whether any difference lies between the lives of people who come from different societies. Such perceived differences are the basis for Orientalism and Occidentalism. The idea of "difference" instigates the idea of "identity," or that one person's qualities are unique and therefore better or worse than another person's. This novel breaks down the idea of "difference," and therefore "identity," by building the relationship between

> two men caught in a power struggle and identity crisis. In the end the two men exchange lives, demonstrating that the complex differences in their original cultures are also able to be broken down and exchanged. By doing away with "identity," the novel deconstructs the idea of "power" intrinsic in Orientalism and Occidentalism . . . The narrator realizes the only differences between he and Hoja are those of experience, and the more they share their experiences, the more alike they become. When Hoja decides they must literally switch lives by dressing as each other and adopting each other's pasts, the narrator says, "I felt like saying that his too could have been, my life could have been lived like this," and "I listened in confusion to what 'I' would do in my old world," changing the word "he" to "I" (85). The two men begin to see fewer differences between their lives and cultures, just as countries will begin to break down Orientalism and Occidentalism by sharing experiences. When the narrator tries to escape from Hoja, he is unable to forget him, likening Hoja to his sense of self. He says, "I could almost blame myself for abandoning a man who looked so much like me," (89). Over time the two men develop a need for each other and a sense of brotherhood, just as countries and cultures do . . . The idea that all men are inherently the same contradicts Orientalism and Occidentalism, which like all forms of "othering," have given way to nationalism and colonialism. The borders between people and countries are not inevitable but created to avoid the settling of differences. Peace may be achieved only through self-analysis and shared experience. Not only do the colonized have nothing to gain from being weakened, but the colonizers have nothing to gain from their false sense of security attained through power and separation. The only true security for all peoples may be realized through the understanding that no one is better or worse.

My best friend is an Iranian American who came to America in the 1970s when he was in his late twenties and who returns to Tehran almost every year to care for his aging mother, and also to spend time with his friends and extended family. For at least sixteen years Jahan and I have talked and talked about differences between Iranians and Americans, a topic that, of course – especially because of this book – I am eagerly interested in. After all of these years of conversation, Jahan said to me recently, "Allen, Iranians and Americans are the same." By this I understand Jahan to mean that, in its most important aspects, there is no difference for him between his life there, in Iran, and here, in Michigan. He has friends; they work; they have families; they spend time together. Jahan doesn't mean that there aren't historical, cultural, political, linguistic differences between our countries, but that at some basic level, above all, are the similarities between people.

On the one side, this idea of similarities is actually a bit hard for me to accept. As a teacher dedicated for many years to multicultural and anti-racist education, to recognizing rather than denying differences based in culture, history, race, class, and gender, I resist a leveling of difference that makes inequality invisible. Yet, when it comes to teaching about the Middle East and thinking about stereotypes, I urge us to be profoundly skeptical of cultural generalizations, of knowledge about "them." Edward Said has made it abundantly clear that the Middle Eastern stereotypes of old were deeply linked to a European history of imperial, colonial, military, and economic domination of the region. And, as we will explore later in this book, there are new Orientalisms that stress terrorism, violence, oppression of women, and so on. As teachers it is important that we help students understand and go beyond stereotypes. What our teaching ought to do is to complicate not reproduce generalities, to open up the never-ending basket of differences, to keep refining and deepening our understanding and knowledge, perhaps until we can reach a point where it becomes harder and harder to identify difference.

Further Reading

Women and Gender in Islam by Leila Ahmed (1992) argues that the oppressive practices to which women in the Middle East are subjected are due to patriarchal interpretations of Islam rather than Islam itself. *The Veil and the Male Elite: A Feminist Interpretation of Women's Rights in Islam* (1992) by Fatima Mernissi makes a similar case.

Muhammad: A Biography of the Prophet (1993), *Islam: A Short History* (2002), and *Muhammad: A Prophet For Our Time* (2007) all by Karen Armstrong, one of the world's most popular writers on the subject of religion.

An Introduction to Islam: Third Edition by Frederick Denny (2005). A comprehensive introduction often used as a college text. Used copies are inexpensive.

What Everyone Needs to Know about Islam by John Esposito. (2002). An easy-to-read introductory text that answers almost any question students may have.

Who Speaks For Islam? What a Billion Muslims Really Think by John Esposito and Dalia Mogahed (2008) describes the results of the most extensive survey ever taken of Muslim attitudes.

Islam by Fazlur Rahman. (1979). A text for studying Islam, includes information about the history of the faith and its complexity in the present.

2

THE THEME OF JUSTICE

As with writers the world over, a commitment to justice informs the creative vision of many writers from the Middle East. The theme of justice occurs again and again in today's Middle Eastern literature and many texts with this theme are good starting points for teachers seeking to bring Middle Eastern literature to their students. Issues of social class inequality, corruption, oppressive and unresponsive government, and the struggle for economic and political opportunity are prevalent in literature from every Middle Eastern language and country. This literature is important for English-speaking students to read as it provides a theme they can connect with, and creates a compelling and culturally rich reading experience. North American students discover that while there is oppression, inequality, and lack of opportunity in every country, they also discover that there are powerful forces within the Middle East struggling for justice. Not the least of these forces are the writers themselves. Middle Eastern literature with social justice themes showcases Middle Eastern writers critically examining their own societies, representing and exploring the difficult problems that face everyday people. This literature raises questions about governments and the degree to which they are despotic or fail to address the most crucial problems in their society. It can help our students understand issues, such as the 2011 democracy uprisings in Tunisia, Egypt, Libya, Yemen, Bahrain, and elsewhere, from an Arab citizen's perspective. Rather than call for outside intervention in the region, this literature leads to questions about the role of Americans or Europeans in supporting corrupt and anti-democratic regimes. Often Middle Eastern writers have suffered consequences of speaking out about social justice, and experienced banning and imprisonment. So in conjunction with their writing, students may find the lives of authors also of interest.

In their social critique Middle Eastern writers frequently refer directly or indirectly to ideas of egalitarianism, fairness, hospitality, charity, and social justice that are deeply a part of Middle Eastern tradition and the Muslim faith. Karen Armstrong argues that for Muslims the chief duty given to them by the Quran is "to create a just community in which all members, even the most weak and vulnerable, were treated with absolute respect." (2002, xi) Of course, Judaism and Christianity are religions that also have strong justice threads that influence writers from those traditions. By making this connection between religion and justice I do not mean to imply that all Middle Eastern writers who address questions of justice or fairness are motivated specifically by religious faith. Middle Eastern writers with secular nationalist, socialist, marxist, feminist, or other political or social commitments often write literary works committed to democracy, equality, and social fairness.

An excellent short novel to begin the investigation of social issues in the Middle East is *War in the Land of Egypt* (1997, 192 pages, age 15–college) by Yusuf Al-Qa'id. Al-Qa'id has written eleven novels, and four collections of short stories; *War in the Land of Egypt* is his first novel translated to English. The novel was made into an Egyptian film staring Omar Sherif in 1991. Told from several points of view, *War in the Land of Egypt* describes a series of events that encapsulates class differences and government corruption in contemporary Egypt and goes a long way toward helping our students understand discontent in that country and other dictatorships in the Middle East, including the 2011 revolutionary activities in Tunisia, in Cairo's Tahrir Square and across the country. During the Nasser period (1953–1971) drawing on the principles of Arab socialism efforts were made in Egypt to redistribute large estates to smaller landholders. (See Chapter 5 for a more extended discussion of Nasser.) This novel is set in 1973 during the Yom Kippur War with Israel, after Sadat has come to power and Nasser's reforms are being reversed. A wealthy Umda, village landowner and political leader, corrupts the system and sends the son of one of his tenants (formerly a beneficiary of land reform) to serve in the army in place of his own son. A great text for the study of narrative point of view, the story is told in six chapters from these characters: the Umda (who wants to keep his over-protected son out of the service), a corrupt fixer (a former teacher who has become a genius at bribing officials), the young man's father (a decent, hard-working farmer), his friend, his commanding officer (who admires the young man's courage leading Egyptian troops until his heroic death), and the police officer (who investigates the crime). My students enjoyed viewing the story from varying perspectives that the different narrators provide. Mary Hitt wrote, "This was great because it helped the story truly come alive." Sara Soenen said, "All I can say about this story is wow! I loved it. I think that my favorite part was how the novel was written. It was very clever, and actually did a better job engaging me into the story than most other novels I have read."

We are never directly given the perspective of the young man sent to war – named "Masri" – an outstanding student and dedicated patriot, but too poor to pay the expenses associated with leaving his home town to attend the university, so he is forced to give up his dream of higher education. My student Jen Wiley commented,

> I was able to grow fond of many of the characters simply because of their nature in the tough situation that they were facing, and others I grew an instant dislike for, such as the Umda. What was really interesting to me though was that I grew a big fondness for Masri, the one character that we never got to hear from directly. His situation, the pain brought to his family because of his death and the corruption coming from the classes above him, as well as the government, was striking and I found that I sympathized the most with him.

Since the name "Masri" also means "Egyptian" the story becomes not only one of personal intrigue, but also a broader allegory for the betrayal of the Egyptian people by the abandonment of Nasser's reforms. As Jen subsequently wrote in a paper about the novel,

> I believe that this novel would have held significant importance to the people of Egypt, of all classes and social statuses. The novel addresses all Egyptian people, and makes its point clear: all citizens of Egypt are subject to the corruption that is happening there.

War in the Land of Egypt addresses issues important in many Middle Eastern countries. My students learned about inequality in Egypt and the power of local political and economic elites over the lives of average citizens. Janelle Mirch wrote,

> The title *War in the Land of Egypt* was not talking about an actual war whatsoever. It was talking about how corrupt Egypt is and the small wars that are fought there everyday by the people of Egypt against the government, higher officials, or mayors.

The novel details bureaucratic corruption, failed social and political reform, and the frustration of middle and working classes attempting to use education as a way to improve their situation.

Reading *War in the Land of Egypt* led me to invite my Egyptian colleague and professor of Arabic Dr. Mustafa Mughazy to visit our class and our discussion of the novel with him furthered student understanding. Dr Mughazy's school experiences in Alexandria interested my students. Saralynn Bush wrote,

> When Dr. Mughazy was talking about how much studying he did while in high school, I couldn't believe it was up to 12 hours a day! . . . He also talked about how [as in many countries in the world] the opportunities students have are determined by a final exam in the last year of school.

> A culmination of fifteen subjects are covered in this exam and scores on the exam determine whether the student goes on to higher education, trade school, or no further schooling. To have that much pressure on an exam that determines one's life forever is incredible to me.

My American students are unaware of the structure of schooling and the level of academic expectation in other countries, and even though their own families struggle to send them to college, they tend not to think about similar struggles facing young people seeking education in the Middle East. My working- and middle-class students also tend to be unaware of how unequal educational opportunity is in the U.S., how the experience of young people from wealthy families differs from their own. And they don't consider these differences in America to be matters of "corruption," but, instead, part of the "natural" or "normal" operation of the society. Discussion of the inequality in Egypt portrayed in the novel can, in some measure, be brought home to consideration of the students' own experience.

The corruption portrayed in *War in the Land of Egypt* is direct and brutal and the novel clearly is intended to attack inequality and dishonesty. My student's first reaction to learning about this corrupt system was to declare that the Egyptian people should refuse to participate in it; they should rebel against it. (That was November 2009. January 2011 saw the insurgency in Tahrir Square, an event that, according to the Associated Press (Dozier, 2011), Obama faulted the American intelligence community for failing to anticipate. My students, reading contemporary Egyptian literature, were better informed.) Responding to student questions, Dr. Mughazy talked with us about his perceptions of life under stifling and crushing corruption. Ashley responded,

> Some of the things that Dr. Mughazy brought up in class struck me as being extremely important. The first thing is that he said there are only three options for those affected by a corrupt system, but who are not strong enough to overthrow it: 1) die in the attempt to change it, 2) run from it and their fellow citizens, or 3) join it. This is a powerful statement, especially when we are analyzing a different culture and are prone to judging it for the choices its people make. How do people in Egypt fight corruption in their government? Yes, it is up to individuals to take a stand against corruption, but what about when their family suffers from their choice to stand up? And what if their choice to stand up simply does not make any difference in the grand scheme of things? . . . So corruption is a self-continued and self-contained system, starting from the top-down. And the "fixer," like the one in the book, is needed not to get what you want, but what is yours that someone has taken from you. We may judge Masri's choices, but I wonder if any one of us would have chosen differently if we were put in his situation.

Ashley's projection of herself into the situation of the literary character she is reading about is enriched by additional information from our speaker. This careful consideration of the actions of characters in *War in the Land of Egypt* helped the young people in my class see some of the complexities of life confronted by people in other cultures, and specifically the challenges of Egyptians and others in the Middle East living under repressive governments.

A similar theme is found in the writing of Yusuf Idris, one of Egypt's best-known authors of short stories and plays. His haunting short story "The Chair Carrier" (Trans. 1983, 4 1/2 pages, age 14–college) offers a brief allegory of the mindset and predicament of Egypt's poor and working classes. The story has been anthologized and can also be found online. On a modern Cairo street the narrator sees an enormous and elegant chair carried by a frail man, dressed like an ancient Egyptian laborer. The magical realist suggestion is that the man has been carrying the chair since the age of the pharaohs, and, indeed, the frail man explains that he was ordered to carry the chair by Ptah Ra (in Egyptian mythology Ptah is the primordial deity). Despite the best efforts of the narrator to convince the laborer to set down the chair, the laborer refuses: he must follow the orders he was given. Since he is illiterate he can't read the instructions attached to the chair that allow him to put it down. The story champions the importance of the Egyptian poor learning to read and taking action to end an ancient and ongoing exploitation.

Two recent works from Egypt address the topic of justice and are also great reads for English-speaking students, *The Day the Leader Was Killed* (1988, 103 pages, age 16–college) and Alaa Al Aswany's *The Yacoubian Building* (2002, 272 pages, age 17–college). Although the 1998 Nobel Prize winner Naguib Mafhouz' novels are difficult for English-speaking young people, *The Day the Leader Was Killed* is an exception. This short novella narrates, again from different points of view, questions facing all young people, including problems living with their parents, finding employment, and marriage. The novel depicts an Egyptian middle-class family struggling to make ends meet in a difficult economic time – again helpful to understanding the 2011 rebellions and ongoing tensions. In the 1970s Anwar Sadat – Egypt's president – at the urging of Americans and the World Bank, instigated a number of reforms supporting the "free market," reduced the role of government and fostered domestic and foreign investment in the private sector. Called "Infitah," Sadat's approach was widely understood in the country to eviscerate labor laws, and benefit a small class of people already wealthy, decadent, and corrupt. During this period Egypt became increasingly dependent on richer Arab countries, Europe and the U.S., and the gap between rich and poor significantly widened.

The situation for the characters of *The Day the Leader was Killed* is increasingly familiar to American young people: there are simply not enough well-paying jobs available. It is difficult for the main characters, Elwan and Randa, to leave their parents' apartments, marry, and start a life of their own. Narrated in alternating chapters by Elwan, Randa, and Elwan's grandfather – Muhtashimi Zayed – the novel creates an interesting juxtaposition of generations. While the title of the novel refers to the assassination of Sadat, that event is not directly related to the events of the story. My student John Novak says,

> The book is curious in that [despite the title] many of the themes and topics of the book are focused on the family. It would not be difficult to write a paper and focus on the role of extended family, the difficulties with branching off and starting a new family, or marital decisions made for financial security instead of love. The book is also "cool" in that the story is multi-generational. We see things not only from the perspective of the main character, but also from the grandfather's perspective. The book is short, but seems deep with symbolism and themes that are more than meets the eye.

Talented students who enjoy *The Day the Leader was Killed* can be encouraged to explore additional works by Mahfouz, who published over 50 novels and more than 300 short stories.

The novel *The Yacoubian Building* (Arabic 2002, translated to English in 2004, 246 pages, age 17–college) is a best-seller in the Arab world and was made into both an Egyptian television series, and the highest-budgeted movie in the long history of Egyptian film (2006). Both *The Day the Leader was Killed* and *The Yacoubian Building* depict the frustrated ambitions of the younger generation of Egyptians in a society that is corrupt, dictatorial, and fundamentally unjust. An exuberant, sexy, and engaging text, *The Yacoubian Building* traces the intertwined

FIGURE 2.1 Talat Harb Square, Cairo, Setting of *The Yacoubian Building*

lives of the inhabitants of an apartment building in downtown Cairo in Talat Harb Square – a short walk from Tahrir Square, the focus of the 2011 protests. The proximity in the building of characters of different backgrounds and social classes allows the building to become a metaphor for contemporary Egypt. The depiction of a gay romance in the novel and film caused some controversy in the Arab world.

A particularly powerful and disturbing example of the frustrations of younger Egyptians is the character Taha el Shazli. The impoverished son of the building doorman living on the roof, he is an outstanding student who sets his heart on becoming a policeman. Like Mazri in *War in the Land of Egypt*, corruption cuts short Taha's career and potential. Despite the fact that Taha has appropriate grades, the generals conducting the character interview for admission to the police academy reject him because they consider his father's profession of doorman unacceptable. Frustrated, Taha enrolls instead at the university where he finds himself alienated from the closed social groups of the wealthier students and joins with an earnest, good-hearted, and pious group of young men from rural areas, whose Islamic devotion emerges as an island of honesty and authenticity in a dishonest world. These young men are understandably drawn to pray together at a mosque where the Sheikh preaches against corrupt leaders dedicated to the pursuit of money and pleasures of the flesh. The first sermon Taha hears has powerful resonance with the reality of Egypt, many Middle Eastern countries, and the concerns of Islamic social justice,

> The supposedly democratic state is based on the rigging of elections and the detention and torture of innocent people so that the clique can remain on their thrones forever. They lie and lie and lie, and they want us to believe their revolting lies. We say to them, loud and clear, "We do not want our Islamic Nation to be either secular or democratic. We want it Islamic-Islamic, and we will struggle and give up our lives and all we hold dear till Egypt is Islamic once more . . . My children, the task before Muslim youth today is to reclaim the concept of gihad and bring it back to the minds and hearts of Muslims. It is precisely this that terrifies America and Israel and with them our traitorous rulers . . . A handful of warriors from Hezbollah and Hamas were able to defeat Almighty America and Invincible Israel, while Abd el Nasser's huge armies were routed because they fought for this world and forgot their religion.
>
> *(95–6)*

After a non-violent anti-government protest, Taha is captured by the police and violently and humiliatingly tortured. He determines to avenge this torture and eventually joins a militant organization modeled upon Jamaa Islamya, an Egyptian Islamist group dedicated to the overthrow of the government. Eventually Taha is involved in a secret plan to murder the very military officer who oversaw his torture, and, at the end of the novel, during the attack, Taha is mowed down in the street by a hail of bullets.

While *The Yacoubian Building* traces the stories of a diversity of Egyptian characters from different social classes, sexual orientations, and genders, the story of Taha, in particular, is likely to interest English-speaking readers. This thread of the novel illustrates how a fine, ethical young man living under a corrupt and despotic regime becomes frustrated, drawn to extremist Islam, and converted to – depending on your perspective – freedom-fighting or terrorism.

These Egyptian works provide insight into life in contemporary Egypt, but for English-speaking readers they also raise subtle questions about American policy in the region, particularly the support for corrupt and undemocratic regimes, such as that in Egypt. Egypt is the second largest recipient of American foreign aid (after Israel) and two-thirds of that aid is military assistance – aid that is explicitly given without expectation that there will be progress toward democracy. As a lead editorial in the *Washington Post* has indicated,

> Mr. Gates, like Secretary of State Hillary Rodham Clinton before him, heaped praise on Mr. Mubarak [President of Egypt] while making clear that the new administration will not trouble him about his systematic and often violent repression of the country's liberal politicians, bloggers and human rights activists . . . Mr. Mubarak and his fellow Arab autocrats are widely despised across the region—and the United States is blamed for unconditionally propping them up. ("No Questions")

If teachers want their students to understand daily life in the Middle East and the thinking of the average Middle Eastern person about the U.S., it is important that these questions become open topics for student research and discussion.

The struggle for social justice against corruption and greed is a central and recurrent theme in literature from the Middle East from different countries, languages, and traditions. *Memed, My Hawk* (1955, 395 pages, age 13–college) by Yasar Kemal is one of the great novels of modern Turkey and addresses the struggle of a young man and his community against a powerful rural landlord. (The novel was adapted to film in 1987, *The Lion and the Hawk* staring Peter Ustinov.) Alain Bosquet writes, "For over four decades Yasar Kemal has been Turkey's greatest and best-known writer. His works have been translated into every major language, and he has been short-listed several times for the Nobel Prize in Literature." (Bosquet, cover) Of Kurdish origin, Kemal has spoken out in favor of Kurdish rights, for which he has spent time in jail. Growing up in an impoverished village in the agriculturally rich Cukurova region of south central Turkey ("chuk" meaning "hollow" and "ova" "valley," in the valley formed by the Taurus mountains), the violence of Kemal's own life is paralleled in the novel. As a young man Kemal lost his eye in a knife accident and saw his father stabbed to death. Raised by his widowed mother, he worked for a rich landlord controlling the flow of water from a dike, but secretly opening it for poor farmers at night. His uncles were outlaws and bandits. A remarkably bright child, Kemal's village raised money to send him to college. At thirty he married a member of a prominent Jewish family in Istanbul and she eventually translated seventeen of his novels into English. Greatly admired in Turkey, it is said that Kemal "smells of soil" ("*toprak korkuyor*") meaning that he is "of the people." (In contrast might be the 2006 Turkish Nobel Prize winner Orhan Pamuk from cosmopolitan Istanbul and a wealthy European-oriented family, whose writings are better known outside of Turkey.)

Some background on Turkey, on rural land ownership and ideas of honor, is important to understanding this novel – and many other works from the Middle East that address life in the countryside. Under the early Ottoman Empire efforts were made to prevent the development of powerful, large landowners. Land was Allah's and the Sultan had sole authority. In effect, the central government owned most of the land and it was permanently leased to farmers where tenure was known by tradition and marked by landmarks, including the planting of mulberry trees. Villages also often paid a certain portion to the local aristocratic lord, or "*Bey*." (See definition of terms in Chapter 11.) During the later years of the empire, changes in land policy, the implementation of "*tapu*," title deed ownership, in the 1860s led to small numbers of people owning huge estates. In the 1920s and 1930s, the new Republican government established by Ataturk made efforts to break up large estates and set minimum and maximum sizes for land holding. This situation sets the stage for the struggle between the *Aghas*, the new large landholders famous for their ruthlessness, and the villages and peasants.

Although *Memed* is a long novel, it is a captivating adventure story on the lines of Robin Hood. Indeed, Robin Hood is an important parallel to help English speakers understand *Memed, My Hawk*, and the tradition of the outlaw in the Middle East. Of course, in England, Robin Hood has been a heroic and honorable outlaw figure and folk hero since medieval times. In the early legends Robin Hood is a yeoman (commoner) who takes the side of the poor, honors women (Maid Marian), and authentic religion (Friar Tuck). An outstanding archer and swordsman Robin Hood attracts to him a band of wronged "merry men" who live a life of freedom in the woods and skirmish against usurping bureaucrats and land owners (the Sheriff of Nottingham is a landowner and an appointed regional administrator, not simply a policeman) as they "rob from the rich and give to the poor." In some later, perhaps domesticated, versions Robin Hood is a supporter of the King, Richard the Lionhearted, and, while Richard is on crusade, Robin Hood is driven to banditry by Richard's evil brother John.

In Turkish the outlaw or brigand is an "*eşkıya*" or "*hajduk*." During the Ottoman period throughout the Middle East this kind of bandit took arms against and in opposition to corrupt or oppressive central powers – the more powerful the dominant force the more the *eşkıya* was respected. The *eşkıya* is obligated to bring protection from oppression emanating from outside of the village or community, and, in a reciprocal way, the community has the obligation to hide and protect the *eşkıya* from the central authorities. (Students reading *Memed, My Hawk* can consider how this long-standing "Robin Hood" historical tradition comes into play when America invades Iraq or Afghanistan, and Osama Bin Laden, Saddam Hussein, and other "insurgents" are recognized by the common people as an *eşkıya.*) The *eşkıya* goes back also to the traditions of pastoral peoples, the way of life of many Middle Eastern people in the not so distant past and, for Kurds and Bedouins, into the present. Pastoralists, concerned with the raising of animals, camels, sheep, goats, etc. often must be on the move to new sources of pasture and water. When traveling pastoralists need people to protect the group, people who restrict their movement are the enemy. For the pastoralist a complementary ethic of hospitality, and respect for others and their property is crucial. Oral traditions are important to maintain histories and group identification. For some pastoralists, intermarriage with people from the villages they regularly pass creates deep relationships, kinship ties, and the circulation of stories, culture, and values between those on the move and those that are more sedentary.

One of my student comments on *Memed, My Hawk*:

> I thought *Memed My Hawk* written by Yashar Kemal, was a very intriguing and adventurous story. I would disagree when people in class thought of it to be a 'boy' novel because I enjoyed reading it as well, but I also like reading novels that have a lot of action in them and are exciting to read. Although it was a bit longer of a book I thought it did a good job of keeping the reader's attention. There were not many parts that were slow and boring. Memed is talked about in different reviews as being the Turkish 'Robinhood' and I would have to agree. Although he was a bandit he was seen as a hero by many. Memed and his mother were treated poorly during his whole childhood. In the novel Memed seeks justice and vengeance upon the Agha, who has done many things that has made Memed's life more difficult. This novel is full of action, yet also has a softer romantic side to it when it talks about his relationship with his love Hatche. Which is why I think the novel would appeal to both males and females that are looking to read a good story.
>
> *(Rachel Denham)*

Students who enjoy *Memed, My Hawk* might also find parallels in the account of growing up in the same region in a Kurdish storytelling family by Mustafa Mirzeler, "The Legends of Kurdistan."

Another wonderful novel for English-speaking students on theme of struggling against a corrupt government is *Rooftops Over Tehran* (2009, 343 pages, age 14–college) a best-selling first novel by Mahbod Seraji. Seraji has lived in the United States for many years, but he grew up in Iran before the Islamic Revolution. The novel, originally written in English, combines a moving coming-of-age story of a 17-year-old high school student in a middle-class neighborhood in Tehran with a narrative of political repression and coming revolution. Although the novel is relatively long, it is an easy read, fast paced, and appealing to teenage readers who can identify with the characters. Pasha Shahed, the main character, is 17 and falls in love with his beautiful neighbor Zari, betrothed to another young man who Pasha greatly admires, an intellectual and activist whom he calls "the doctor." Pasha's loving family and spirited friends certainly humanize Iranians for North American readers and make it difficult to think of that country as a part of an "Axis of Evil" (as George Bush memorably called Iran in 2002) or a threat to the United States. In many ways their lives seem "American" – Pasha loves old movies, watches *The Six Million Dollar Man* and *I Dream of Jeannie* on television and puts up with overbearing teachers. As the novel develops there are increasing signs of the Shah's repressive rule. The doctor is arrested by SAVAK (the feared secret police of the Shah). A friend of Pasha's father, Mr. Mehrbaan, a political prisoner, is released with stories of torture. The reader learns that the American CIA that overthrew the elected prime minister and put the Shah in power in 1953 (see Chapter 5) is still, in the 1970s, widely suspected of controlling events in Iran. My student Lisa Anderson states, "This book was amazing!! It was so easy to get lost in the story and it was a really quick read. I was fascinated by the representation of the U.S. in this book. The U.S. was everything from an ideal disciplined nation to the very demon Persians needed to fight against." Without giving away the dramatic conclusion to the novel, suffice it to say that we discover the depth of Zari's character and her willingness to take public and dramatic political action. My student, and aspiring secondary school English teacher, Carly Fricano says of *Rooftops Over Tehran,*

> While becoming one of my favorite contemporary novels of all time, this book taught me a great deal about Iranian life and culture. I found the language to be beautifully romantic and appropriate for the seventeen year-old protagonist/narrator. I could picture the houses and the rooftops upon which Pasha and his friends would sit and dream. The relationships that develop throughout the novel are relevant to any adolescent in modern-day America, making this an excellent novel to teach at the secondary level. Although the characters in the novel share a great many similarities to the modern American student, the differences are what play a key role in making this novel teachable. Pasha, Zari, and their friends not only have to deal with hormones, new love, and strict parents, but they are under a regime that dictates what kind of books can be read and what opinions can be expressed in a school essay. The punishment for breaking these rules is not to get the car keys revoked, but imprisonment and possible death. For me, this book did an excellent job balancing the similarities of the characters that make them sympathetic to the modern young reader as well as highlighting the differences that teach about Persian life, specifically in the 1970s.

FIGURE 2.2 Protestors During the Iranian Revolution

When teaching *Rooftops Over Tehran* it will be important to update information about Iran to the present. In my efforts to do that my students watched a number of YouTube clips and films about Iran. Combing visual images with texts seems especially important when students don't have many mental pictures of the landscape or cultures described – particularly useful when teaching about the Middle East. I showed my students segments of a famous 1969 quazi-documentary about the geography of Iran, "*The Lovers' Wind*," available free online. As the website explains,

> A well-known French filmmaker, Albert Lamorisse, under the auspices of Iran's Ministry of Culture and Art, produced the poetic film "Lovers' Wind" (1969). Eighty-five percent of this dramatically visual film is shot from a helicopter, providing a kaleidoscopic view of the vast expanses, natural beauty, historical monuments, cities and villages of Iran. The "narrators" of the film are the various winds (the warm, crimson, evil and lovers' winds), which according to folklore, inhabit Iran. They sweep the viewers from place to place across the Iranian landscape, introducing the incredible variety of life and scenery in Iran.

Be alert that this film doesn't portray the modernizing of Iran, or contemporary life there. One vehicle my class examined to better understand the present in Iran was Rick Steve's PBS program, *Iran: Yesterday and Today*, about his visit to the country in 2009. During a period of tension between the U.S. and Iran, Steve sets out to learn what the Iranian people are really like. My students had mixed and interesting reactions:

> Aside from those interesting facts and observations, the biggest thing that I paid attention to throughout the documentary was how the Iranian people viewed America, America's government, and America's people. First, I was not surprised to learn that most people in the country are bilingual, speak English, and are well informed about the West. As far as I know, it seems like most cultures are far more "worldly" than we are here in America, and Iran seems to be no exception to this.
>
> Within the first ten or so minutes of the documentary, Rick Steve mentioned that the Iranian people "loved Americans." Frankly, I was a little surprised to hear this and found myself quite skeptical of the comment, wondering if perhaps that was a biased statement or if there was some selective film editing to show mostly positive opinions about the U.S. The documentary continued on, and proceeded to show murals throughout Tehran saying things like "Down with the USA" or showing images that depicted the United States as some evil, unwanted force. Yet despite the substantial number of negative images seen on the murals, most of the people Rick Steve interviewed seemed to have mostly positive things to say about America. One woman seemed to put it into perspective quite nicely, saying, "Government has a lot of war with each other, because they have benefits. But there is no war between people."
>
> *(Amanda France)*

> I found the PBS mini series, *Iran, Yesterday and Today*, hosted by Rick Steve, both informative and problematic. On one hand, it provides a brief (helpful for the unfamiliar viewer) political and cultural history of Iran. On the other hand this history is littered with commentary comparing Iran with western European countries, using the latter as the standard. Steve approaches Iran from the admittedly bias viewpoint of an American, and to his credit, he reacts well to anti-American murals. His bias becomes problematic as he attempts to react to Iran as his country's "other." He says things like, "This shopping district could be in Paris or London." It left me wishing that he could just present this country without calling attention to the pre-existing negative stigma it gets in the U.S. By constantly declaring how surprised he is that parts of Iran are "modern" and even that women attend college, Steve orientalizes Iran. His way of defending and befriending Iranians is to show their similarities to Americans and Europeans. Their differences, in turn, are treated as "advancements only of Iran's past." Steve looks at Iran with a strictly American definition of advancement.
>
> *(Ashley Hillyard)*

In addition to these depictions we looked at in class, I also directed students to Iranian films. Iran has a substantial film industry and many titles are available with English subtitles. Many can be found on Netflicks or under "Iranian Film" on Arab Film.com.

One of the most taught novels from the region is *The Kite Runner* (2004, 400 pages, age 15–college) a work that makes a natural comparison with *Rooftops Over Tehran.* A compelling read, immensely popular, and adapted to film in 2007, *The Kite Runner* addresses issues of social justice particularly the unequal relationship between Pashtun and Hazara ethnic groups in Afghanistan, and the repression and violence of the Taliban. Students are caught up in the relationship between two boys, Amir and Hassan, who turn out to be half brothers, and in the guilt that Amir feels for failing to defend Hassan from a homosexual assault. Thinking about both novels, I agree with Jennifer Donovan, who in her Amazon.com blog post "Literary and Suspenseful" on *Rooftops Over Tehran* states,

> The comparisons to *The Kite Runner* are inevitable – although they are set in different countries, they both deal with events that precipitate a coming of age, set in the backdrop of a totalitarian regime. *The Kite Runner* is a wonderful book, but I think that *Rooftops of Tehran* has more heart, more range (since in addition to being touched, I laughed aloud a time or two), and is overall a better story.

Students reading *The Kite Runner* learn about Afghanistan from the point of view of an enormously privileged and Americanized family. They learn about Taliban extremism. However they learn little about the historical, cultural, or political background to the conflicts in Afghanistan, the efforts of the socialist movement to improve rights for women and break up huge rural estates, America's involvement in originally supporting the Taliban, or the impact and consequences of the American-led invasion – all topics that students could investigate. (*The Kite Runner* is also discussed in Chapter 5.)

That the struggle for justice can be seen to have an environmental as well as a cultural dimension can be seen in the writing of the North African novelist, Ibrahim Al-Koni. Al-Koni is Libya's best-known living writer and one of the most prolific in the Arabic language; he has published over eighty books. Al-Koni grew up in the Libyan Desert as a member of the Taureg, nomadic Berber/Bedouin pastoralists that for 2,000 years have led camel caravans through the Saharan Desert. Although his novels are clearly Islamic they also include elements from pre-Islamic animist traditions and mythologies. The Taureg resisted both French and Italian colonialism in North Africa and those events provide a backdrop to the novels. Their society is hierarchical, divided into separated classes of nobles who have developed highly ritualized poetic, sport, and courtship traditions, and vassals treated almost as slaves. In Tuareg society women do not traditionally wear the veil, whereas men, once they reach manhood keep their faces covered.

FIGURE 2.3 The Tuareg

I have taught two of Al-Koni's novels, *The Bleeding of the Stone* (2002, 135 pages, age 15–college) and *Gold Dust* (2008, 144 pages, 10–college) and both captured the fascination of the desert, the pride of desert people, the close relationship between humans and animals, and the fragility of the natural environment. Here I focus on *The Bleeding of the Stone*, which traces the story of a solitary Bedouin who knows where a rare wild sheep, the *moufflon* lives in the mountains of the Libyan Desert. Two foreign hunters, Masoud and Cain, who have already killed off many of the desert's gazelles, demand that Asouf, the solitary main character, takes them to hunt the wild sheep. The interaction in the novel between Islam, Sufism, and traditional African animist beliefs, practices, and religion is fascinating, and there are often elements of magical realism.

> He'd become wary of hunting the *waddan*, and would never venture to the majestic heights until he'd recited all the Quranic verses he'd memorized, repeated, in Hausa, all the spells of the African magicians, then hung around his neck all the snakeskin amulets he'd bought from soothsayers traveling in caravans.
>
> *(23–4)*

My students had a variety of reactions to the novel. Sarah Pollard commented, "This book has turned into one of my favorites of the semester. I found this novel to be a bit confusing at times with the mixed up timeline and the unusual names. Asouf, the main character, was my favorite and the life he led was inspiring." Anne Morgan was also intrigued by Asouf,

> The first thing that stood out to me after reading this book was how alone Asouf seemed to be . . . Asouf is a "desert man," but he has plenty of memories of his family and comes in contact with the outside world a significant amount . . . Another thing about Asouf that stood out to me was his direct contrast to Cain – Asouf does not eat any meat, but Cain literally lives for meat (and how disgusting was his character? Ew.)

Craig Downer, a hunter himself, was also troubled by the portrait of Cain,

> As an avid outdoorsman I was quite disturbed by the character of Cain. Nature is a precious resource that must be protected and people like Cain are disrespectful and merciless. I have always wanted to move away to a desolate area of the world and live off of the land so I was able to relate to Asouf and his father and the way in which they took care of their family. I was also happy to see that Asouf was finally able to stand up to Cain and not take him to the Waddan.

Social justice in the novel revolves around respect for nature and the strong, independent life of the Bedouin people, both violated by the Italian interlopers.

Some Middle Eastern literature has strong postcolonial themes, addressing the experience and aftermath of European colonialism particularly of the British and French. Since the invasion of Egypt by Napoleon in 1798 the French made repeated efforts to colonize and control North Africa, culturally close to the Middle East. (European colonialism, and its aftermath, is addressed in Chapter 5.) Morocco was one of the last regions to fall under their authority in the late nineteenth and early twentieth century. A fascinating text for examining the anti-colonial struggle in North Africa, and Morocco in particular, (1956), is the *Year of the Elephant* (1989, 70 pages, age 16–college). The author, Leila Abouzeid, became well known in Morocco as a journalist, writing and directing a popular radio talk show and serving as an anchor on Moroccan television. Leaving journalism for literature in the 1980s, she refused to use the French language and wrote instead in Arabic. She is the first Moroccan woman, and one of the first Moroccan writers, translated into English. As well as addressing the anticolonial struggle, Abouzeid discusses the experience of women. (I recommend her novel *The Last Chapter* in Chapter 3 addressing women in Middle Eastern literature.)

Year of the Elephant is a historical work set in the 1950s during the struggle against the French. It was first published in magazine installments, and used an interesting technique of combining classical, formal Arabic with the local Arabic dialect actually spoken in Morocco. The title of the novel refers to a well-known battle at the time of Muhammad's birth, when Ethiopian tribes riding elephants attacked Mecca; they were defeated not by powerful arms, but by a cloud of small birds which bombarded the elephants with rocks leading to their defeat. The main character in the novel, Zahra, is a young, female, working-class revolutionary participating in a variety of insurgent activities including burning the shops of French sympathizers, smuggling guns and resistance fighters, and supporting prisoners. The French are defeated by the various activities of the insurgents, just as the Ethiopians and their elephants were defeated by the birds. Yet, after the war is over, we see that many of those who fought for a free and just Morocco decide to enrich themselves. Zahra's husband is the prime example. He takes over a sumptuous home, built and lived in by the French, loses sympathy with the common people, and becomes corrupt. This problem of the class that leads the independence movement stepping into the former colonizers shoes and establishing "neo-colonialism" has been all too common, as described by Frantz Fanon's famous essay (available online), "The Pitfalls of National Consciousness" in *Wretched of the Earth.* Soon after moving into the French house, the husband divorces Zahra in favor of a younger wife, leading to her loss of social status, and a personal and spiritual struggle to become independent. In the introduction Elizabeth Fernea argues that in the novella, "One woman's experience becomes a metaphor for society, a view that has less to do with western ideas of individualism than it does with Middle Eastern ideas of the value of the group" (xxv).

The classic expression of anti-French resistance in North Africa is the film, *Battle of Algiers* (1966), chronicling the bitter Algerian revolution that lasted from 1954–1962 with likely over a million dead. This black-and-white film is not a documentary, but is considered to offer an even-handed portrayal of the conflict. The vivid depictions of torture by the French led the film to be banned in that country for five years. The film may have something to say about the American presence in Iraq – it was shown in 2003 at the Pentagon as a useful illustration of the problems that American soldiers were facing. The film has been re-released and can be found online.

Literature from the Middle East with justice themes also raises questions that North American and English-speaking students can and should bring home. As I have suggested, these questions include how the policies of their own governments have supported corrupt or despotic regimes in the Middle East. Careful attention to the issues these works raise also can draw attention to the West. Rather than drawing clear distinctions between their society and those in the Middle East, students can explore how issues they encounter in Middle Eastern literature, issues of inequality, class difference, corruption, lack of economic opportunity, and so on, impact their own lives and societies. It may be instructive to turn around the usual question, "What do these texts teach us about the Middle East?," and also ask, "How can we learn from Middle Eastern writers about how to understand, address, and improve the failings of our own societies?"

Further Reading

The Other Place by Ibrahim Abdel Meguid (2005), a challenging novel addressing the inequality of resources and opportunity based on the experience of a middle-class Egyptian living in one of the oil-rich states of the Persian Gulf.

Fragments of Memory by Hanna Minah (2004), an autobiographical novel about the life of a boy born to a poor family in the north of Syria under the French mandate.

Memory in the Flesh is the first novel written by an Algerian woman, Ahlan Mosteghanemi (2003), and treats the Algerian struggle for independence from France and disappointments of the independence era.

3

MUSLIM WOMEN IN THE MIDDLE EAST

One of the topics of greatest interest to our students about the Middle East is the status and life experience of women. If there is anything that our students know from the mass media about contemporary culture in the Middle East it is that, in the Middle East women are oppressed. Islam condemns women to a subordinate role. Women must wear veils, headscarves (hijab), and full coverings (chador). They are forced to marry against their will. They are dominated by men, who are allowed to marry more than one wife. In some countries women can't drive cars or even leave their homes. Some are subject to barbarous acts of female circumcision and others, still worse, to "honor killings" by their own family members.

When it comes to teaching about women in the Middle East, I think our most important job as teachers is to complicate this simplistic and distorted picture of female oppression and domination. This is not to deny that women in the Middle East are oppressed – as women the world over are oppressed. Of course, there is domestic violence and spousal abuse in the U.S. a woman dies as the result of spousal abuse every six hours in the U.S. ("Most Recent"). Students need to learn about the oppression of women in the Middle East – and draw on that knowledge to consider how women are oppressed in their own country and culture. In this way we help our students go beyond the polarized, binary thinking fostered by the one-sided stereotypes proffered by the mass media and popular culture. But teaching in a thoughtful and balanced way about women in the Middle East is complicated.

First, there is no one common woman's experience in the Middle East. Instead, as in the rest of the world, there is an enormous diversity of experiences that depend on country, social class, geographical location (rural vs. urban), religious practice, social group, and individual families. Throughout the Middle East, as in other parts of the world, there are struggles between liberal and conservative factions over women's rights and freedoms. In Saudi Arabia, women are required to wear an abaya (full black cloak), but in Turkey it is illegal for public school or college students, government employees, or doctors to wear even a headscarf. Afghanistan under the Taliban – where women were excluded from school – is completely different from Iran, also an officially Muslim nation, where 70 percent of the college students in the country are women. Although abortion is illegal in most Arab countries (it is legal in Turkey and Tunisia) women in the Middle East often find ways to obtain abortions. While most Muslims view the Quran as allowing a man up to four wives, if all can be financially supported and equally treated, polygamy is actually uncommon in the Middle East. It is illegal in Turkey, Tunisia, Israel, and the former socialist countries of Tajikistan, Turkmenistan, Kazakhstan, and Kyrgystan. Even in countries where polygamy is legal, it is typically practiced by only 2–5 percent of the population. (And remember that polygamy is not unknown in the United States, as the popular television program *Big Love*, about renegade Mormons, demonstrates! Not to mention issues in the West of frequent divorce, women with children in poverty, marital infidelity, and so on.)

There is no one yardstick by which to measure oppression, and many of the cultural practices that might at first seem to symbolize oppression, may, in fact, provide women with increased freedom. In Islam, women pray separately from men, either in separated parts of the mosque or at home. Since Muslim prayers involve kneeling and bending over in an open room without pews, women feel more comfortable praying in separate spaces rather than in front of men. Depending on the country, many Muslim women do not wear veils or headscarves. Some Islamic feminists reject the veil, and their protests go back at least as far as Egypt in the 1920s where there was an organized feminist movement whose leaders threw their veils into the sea. Muslim women who do choose to wear headscarves do so not only as a sign of piety and modesty, but so they will be judged by their personality, character, and morality – not how they look. There are a great variety of types, styles, and ways to wear veils and hijab, such that, perhaps ironically, in many contexts the headscarf itself becomes a fashion statement. On the other side, the headscarf may reduce the costs of clothing for working women. During the period of direct European colonial domination of the Middle East, the veil was, at times, a symbol of anti-colonial resistance. Today, the veil in certain contexts continues to be a statement of Islamic self-assertion in the face of invasive Western culture. Recently in some European countries the veil has been banned in schools or public places, leading to claims of discrimination against Muslims and protest by Muslim women. Obviously, the veil has become the center of a complex discourse, and an interesting topic for students to investigate. A good discussion starter is the essay "The Burka and the Bikini" by Aziz Poonawalla (available at AltMuslim.com). Poonawalla describes different types of clothing for Muslim women, distinguishes Muslim and tribal practices, and argues that both bikini and burqa, depending on how they are used, "can serve to reduce women from a person to an object."

Throughout the Middle East there are many powerful, vibrant women, and Middle Eastern people will tell you that women have an important say in family and community affairs. In the region, women often play significant roles in politics, government, business, and the arts. Women have served as government ministers in Syria, Jordan, Egypt, Iraq, and Tunisia, as vice president in Iran, and prime minister in Israel. Women are members of parliament in the Middle East in numbers roughly parallel to the U.S. and Britain (Iran 25 percent; Egypt 12 percent; Turkey 10 percent; U.S. 17 percent; England 20 percent). While in some countries a woman cannot obtain a passport without permission of a male relative

FIGURE 3.1 Hijab

or her husband – and women do not enjoy equal rights under Muslim Sharia law statutes governing divorce, inheritance, and child custody – many predominately Muslim countries do not follow these laws and there is general agreement that, at the time of Muhammad, the Quran represented a significant advance for women. (Discussed more fully in Chapter 1.) Female genital mutilation and honor killings are not sanctioned by Islam, but have their origins in cultural practices in specific regions and among certain ethnic groups.

As in the English-speaking world there is an active debate among Muslims about sexism, discrimination, and the roles and rights of women. Some argue that women in the Middle East are no more oppressed than women elsewhere. Others recognize oppressions, but argue that the oppression of women is not intrinsic to Islam and the Quran but that inequality and oppression have their roots in non-Islamic cultural practices. Nawal El Saadawi, an Egyptian medical doctor, novelist and well-known feminist has argued:

> I've noticed that many people including professors of religion and Islamic studies, pick up one verse and say that in the Quran, God allowed men to beat women. They don't compare it to other verses. They also don't compare the Quran to the Bible. If you do, you will find the Bible more oppressive to women.
>
> *(quoted in Kamguian)*

Indeed, in regard to the position of women, conservative Islam has much in common with Orthodox Judaism and Eastern Orthodox Christianity, other religions with origins in the Middle East long before Islam. Interestingly, some historians believe that the seclusion and veiling of women came to the Arabic world from Christian Byzantium. Of course, certain orders of Catholic nuns still wear veils and the Virgin Mary is rarely depicted with her head uncovered. Indeed, many protestant Christian women wear veils on their wedding day: an elegant wedding dress fashion as well as a symbol of modesty and chastity.

In the first chapter we examined Edward Said's critique of Orientalism. One dimension of Orientalism is a tradition in Western thought of identifying the Orient with the oppression of women. "The colonialist logic attributed the backwardness of Muslim societies and the inferiority of their cultures particularly to two main observed practices: veiling and seclusion of women"(Kincheloe, 47).

This "backwardness" is often used as a justification for bringing "civilization" or "democracy" to the region in the name of protecting women. Indeed, there are racial and sexual dimensions to this discourse, with white men coming to the rescue of brown-skinned women, saving them from brown-skinned men. Yet, the facts relating to European and American actions in the Middle East often tell a different story. Colonial and neo-colonial interventions have been about strategic geopolitics and access to resources, not protecting women. For instance, throughout the 1970s and 1980s, U.S. foreign policy in the region was guided by a concern about the rise of Arab nationalism and socialism – movements which called for national rights to control oil exports. At the same time, those Arab movements took large strides in obtaining rights for women in education, the family, and the workplace. As a counter force to Arab nationalism, groups that opposed women's rights – conservative religious elements in Islam – were supported by the American government. The same story was true in Afghanistan, where a socialist government created more rights for women than at any point in the history of the country. When the Russians intervened to support that government, the U.S.' "secret" arming of the Mujahidin brought to power the Taliban and drastically curtailed rights for women. As'ad AbuKhalil writes,

> Ever since the 1950s, successive American governments have supported Saudi Arabian Islam and have funded and armed Islamic fundamentalist groups, which have tormented Middle Eastern women and frustrated their efforts at emancipation.

A polarizing discourse between East and West, talk of crusades, of "Evil Empires" or an "Axis of Evil," military interventions, support for Israeli domination of Palestine – all of these play into the hands of the conservatives in the Middle East who use American and European involvement in the region as their justification for a narrow interpretation of the Quran and curtailment of women's rights.

> Strict policing of women' bodies and lives and a retraditionalization of the Muslim family, both taken as major features of religious ethical and moral law, are considered by virtually all fundamentalists among the viable strategies for countering Western imperialism and curbing the impact of its powers.
>
> *(Kincheloe, 44)*

The desire to signal rejection of Western imperialism may well be part of a woman's decision to wear a veil or headscarf, not necessarily something imposed by the men around her. My point is that teachers of literature from the contemporary Middle East need to recognize the complexity of the issue of women's rights in the region, the problematic history of American and European involvement in regard to women's rights, and the pitfalls of prescribing, from America or Europe, solutions to women's issues in the Middle East.

Teaching in a thoughtful way about the Middle East, it is vital for teachers and students to learn more about Middle Eastern women, to identify authentic, realistic, and balanced literature from the Middle East that features women, and to examine stereotypes prevalent in the West. While there are many books published about Middle Eastern women, identifying the best and appropriate materials is surprisingly difficult. Be alert that there are groups, including certain fundamentalist Christians, who go out of their way to attack Islam and present, on the Internet and in published books, inflammatory and distorted stories and images; our students often encounter these materials and it may be important as a class to examine and critique them. Even more responsible sources should be treated with care. American and British publishing houses have found that writing by women from the Middle East that provides images of oppression can generate sales, appealing to women's reading groups, teachers and students, and others eager to learn about women in the region. This literature is important, but needs to be understood in a balanced way.

The Iranian scholar Fatemeh Keshavarz, now a professor at Washington University in St. Louis, has published a book combining scholarship and personal narrative that I recommend to teachers interested in the topic of women in the Middle East. *Jasmine and Stars: Reading More than* Lolita *in Tehran* addresses this outpouring of recent publications about the oppression of women in the Middle East, books such as *Reading Lolita in Tehran*, *Lipstick Jihad*, *Nine Parts of Desire*, *The Bookseller of Kabul*, *The Kite Runner*, *Persepolis*, and so on. Written as non-specialized, autobiographical narratives, first person novels, or eyewitness accounts for non-expert Western readers, these recent books are effectively marketed yet can, while they point to important issues, also, like any representation, reproduce stereotypes. Keshavarz calls this literature "the New Orientalist narrative" and describes it in this way,

> The emerging Orientalist narrative has many similarities to and a few differences from this earlier incarnation. It equally simplifies its subject. For example, it explains almost all undesirable Middle Eastern incidents in terms of Muslim men's submission to God and Muslim women's submission to men. The old narrative was imbued with the authority of an all-knowing foreign expert. The emerging narrative varies somewhat in that it might have a native – or semi-native – insider tone. Furthermore, as the product of a self-questioning era, it shows a relative awareness of its own possible shortcomings. Yet it replicates the earlier narrative's strong under current of superiority and of impatience with the locals, who are often portrayed as uncomplicated. The new narrative does not necessarily support overt colonial ambitions. But it does not hide its clear preference for a western political and cultural takeover. More importantly, it replicates the totalizing – and silencing – tendencies of the old Orientalists by virtue of erasing, though unnuanced narration, the complexity and richness in the local culture.
>
> *(3)*

Keshavarz is not the only one making this observation. Mitra Rastegar, for example, makes a similar argument in her essay "Reading Nafisi in the West: Authenticity, Orientalism, and 'Liberating' Iranian Women."

> While Nafisi [author of *Reading* Lolita *in Tehran*] challenges a wholly monolithic understanding of contemporary Iran, she ultimately reframes the predominant Orientalist binary – of the "West" as modern, rational, and dynamic and opposed to an "East" that is static, irrational, and antimodern – into one of promodern Iranians versus antimodern Iranians. Nafisi's representation of women as victims of state violence in Iran becomes a key component of asserting this binary, opposing a monolithic and barbaric Iranian state to the democratic ethos that she argues is implicit in the (Western) novel and appreciated by her female students.
>
> *(108)*

So images of oppression need to be complicated, and literary and autobiographical narratives need to be read carefully and with balance. Saba Mahmood describes the contribution of feminist scholarship: "Feminist scholarship performed the worthy task of restoring the absent voice of women to analyses of Middle Eastern societies, portraying women as active agents whose lives are far richer and more complex than past narratives had suggested" (6).

One of the most popular books from the Middle East, focused on the experience of women, and rapidly become known to secondary and college teachers and students, is Marjane Satrapi's graphic novel *Persepolis*. Written in French (2000–2001) and translated to English (2003, a portion was first published in *Ms. Magazine*) *Persepolis: A Story of a Childhood* (2001, 153 pages, middle school–college), it has a sequel volume (French 2002/03, English 2004) *Persepolis 2: The Story of a Return* (2003, 192 pages, age 17–college) and was made into a fascinating black and white animated film (2007). This autobiographical narrative in the first volume apparently traces the author's life from her girlhood in an intellectual, privileged family in Tehran during the Islamic Revolution in 1979, and in *Persepolis 2*, her teenage years studying abroad in Switzerland, and her return to Tehran as a young woman in 1991.

Original, engaging, and appealing, *Persepolis* facilitates American students' connection with the main character who likes American music (Iron Maiden and Michael Jackson), dancing, and rebels against the oppressive efforts of the Iranian revolutionary government to enforce "Islamic" behavior and wearing the veil. My students are passionate about the work – and quick to view it as *the* story of contemporary Iran and Iranian women.

> As a young girl, Marjane is a good student who only begins to rebel when her formerly secular school becomes strictly religious. She can't help but point out the irony of religious rules and punishments. Her parents, who share and encourage her liberal political views, are very proud of the strong woman their daughter has become. But Marjane's strength under Iran's new fundamentalist regime, where women are discouraged from having a voice, becomes her weakness, and her parents begin to fear for her safety.

> Marjane Satrapi's graphic novel, *Persepolis*, is not only a story of a childhood, but the story of a people and a nation. Her consistent wit and humor in the face of traumatic violence drew me in as a reader, opening my mind to more dry political subjects.
>
> *(Ashley Hillyard)*

> Her story gives tons of perspective on the history of Iran, it's relationship with Islam, the struggle between the ideals of the West and East, exile, and repression in her own country. The story is very accessible through vivid images. I was completely moved by this book. I don't think one can read this book and not feel a sort of compassion for the Iranian people and their struggles. For anyone who wants to begin to understand Iranian people, I believe this graphic novel is a fantastic first step.
>
> *(Marie Tietgen)*

Persepolis is such an engaging text that it is a valuable resource for classroom teaching, for learning about the Iranian revolution, and for considering the diversity of women's perspectives. Students are drawn to *Persepolis* first by the intriguing graphic format. Teachers will want to help students learn to read graphic texts and examine how panels use detail, proportion, angle of view, visual clues, sequence, language bubbles, etc. to convey meaning, and how the "gutters" between the panels allow the reader's imagination to fill in action. Because of their appeal and interesting working together of images and texts, graphic novels, autobiographies and other forms are increasingly popular for instruction. Resources for teachers working with the medium include *Understanding Comics* by Scott McCloud, *Graphic Novels* by Paul Gravett, and *Building Literacy Connections with Graphic Novels* edited by Bucky Carter (to which I contribute a chapter on the subject of teaching about anti-Semitism in *Oliver Twist* using the graphic novel *Fagin the Jew* by Will Eisner).

Readers of *Persepolis* will be attracted to a loving family with wise, caring parents who do their best to support each other and their daughter through times of change and even violence. Students should note that this is an extremely privileged family. The great grandfather was apparently the Iranian Emperor; the grandfather was the Prime Minister to the Shah; they have a maid; drive a Cadillac; take vacations in Europe; and the daughter – the narrator – is enrolled in an elite French language school in Tehran. Highly educated intellectuals, the parents are not religious, but sympathetic to Marxism and critical of the Islamic revolution. The centrality of the family to national events does add interest to the story and provides readers with information about Iranian politics. It is difficult for English-speaking young people to put these events into perspective. Unless teachers provide students with additional background information or encourage them to do more research, young people are likely to find more memorable the scene where women from the Guardians of the Revolution stop Marjane because she is wearing a

Michael Jackson pin, rather than other more historically significant scenes exploring the 1979 revolution, friends of the family tortured by CIA trained secret police, the coming to power of the Islamic fundamentalists, and the devastating war between Iran and Iraq.

Persepolis portrays a variety of women characters and clearly demonstrates that Iranian women, and by extension women of the Middle East, are by no means a demure or submissive group. Examining the diversity of portrayals of women in this text creates important possibilities for student writing and learning. At the center is the narrator Marjane, an independent and flamboyant girl who challenges the authority of her teachers, loves American heavy metal music, mocks and resists wearing the veil – and is enormously appealing to Western students. Marjane's mother is a loving wife and parent, a protestor who takes to the street to defend women's rights, and a thoughtful person who carefully weighs the risks and dangers of opposing the regime. Marjane's grandmother is perhaps the most free-thinking, liberated character in *Persepolis* with a bawdy sense of humor and a commitment to honesty and fairness. We see other independent, yet tragic, young women including Niloufar, a communist girl who helps make fake passports and is killed by the secret police, and a Jewish girl, Neda, who lives next door to Marjane and is killed in an Iraqi bomb attack.

Persepolis 2 focuses in the first half on Marjane's stay in Austria and in the second half on her return to Tehran. In Europe Marjane develops a number of rebellious friendships, continuing struggles with teachers and authority figures, and experiences a period of homelessness. Back in Iran she is depressed and makes an unsuccessful suicide attempt. She finds that in her group in Tehran in the 1990s the young people lead defiant social lives, privately ignoring narrow religious authority, to party and drink behind walls. Marjane starts an unhappy marriage at twenty-one, divorces, and, at the conclusion of the story, leaves Iran to live in France because, as she explains, she "can't take" the restrictions on women any longer. While continuing the interesting narrative, *Persepolis 2* may not be as useful to students as the first text. (It does include drugs and sexual experimentation and some secondary teachers may be uncomfortable assigning it to all students.) There is also a third volume, *Embroideries*, set entirely in one scene in the Satrapi home sometime after *Persepolis 2*. After dinner with friends, the men go off into one room and the women into another. Since Marjane is an "experienced" divorcee the other, older women freely discuss past marriages and sexual experiences. An interesting and explicit read for college students, the text once again breaks stereotypes about Middle Eastern women as modest, reserved, or demure.

While *Persepolis I* does not center the viewpoint of the "average" working-class or rural Iranian citizen, it does include an important side story about the family's maid, Mehri, who apparently at the age of ten was "given" to the narrator's parents because her parents couldn't afford to feed her. Mehri lives in the family home, takes care of Marjane, and has no chance of an education. Even the ten-years-younger Marjane thinks she is "not very talented." After developing a crush on the boy neighbor, Mehri is told by Marjane's (supposedly Marxist-leaning) father that she can't marry the neighbor because "in this country you must stay within your own class" (37).

There are also any number of conservative, apparently conformist, female figures, including women protestors who support wearing the veil; the frightening female guardians who enforce dress codes in the streets; and women teachers who repeat the various orthodoxies of the regime. Written from Marjane's point of view, the autobiography has little or no sympathy with these women, likely of poor or working-class backgrounds. We learn from *Persepolis* about how boys from poor families are given "keys to paradise" and taken as cannon fodder in the war with Iraq. There are clearly many teachers, soldiers, and citizens who support the measures that appear repressive to Marjane, but the reader doesn't get a sense for much of anything potentially positive about the Islamic revolution, about the benefits it may have had for sectors of the population. The hints in the graphic novel about working-class people and those with other perspectives are intriguing, and could be used by teachers to open the door for students to explore a fuller range of Iranian and women's perspectives.

Two additional and wonderful resources for the classroom that enrich the picture of women in Iran after the revolution, and that would make a good match with *Persepolis*, are the film *Two Women* and the collection of ethnographic stories by Erica Friedl, *Women of Deh Koh: Lives in an Iranian Village*. *Two Women* (1999, 96 mins., age 16–college), by the leading Iranian female film director Tahimine Milani, was filmed entirely in Iran and addresses the experience of two architecture students during the early years of the Islamic Republic. Niki Karimi is the most famous and internationally acclaimed actress and filmmaker in Iran. She plays the role of Fereshteh, a brilliant student from a working-class family in Isfahan, a provincial city. Marila Zare'i plays Roya, a girl from a wealthy, urban family in the capital Tehran and Fereshteh's best friend. The contrast of their experiences is dramatic, as Fereshtah is stalked, pushed into marriage with a controlling husband, kept from finishing school, and trapped in her home, while Roya is able to pursue a career as an architect directing teams of men in the construction of major office buildings. The film is unsparing in its criticism of the treatment of women, of their inequality in the home and before the law. At the same time it shows the women as self-reflective, making careful choices, and working together to support each other.

> It was really interesting to see the relationship of Roya and Fereshteh develop and how the two women coped with different aspects of their culture . . . Fereshteh's marriage was anything but a fairytale. Her husband was controlling and manipulative. Fereshteh lost all respect for herself and found herself stuck at home with no means of communication. Her only hidden pleasure was her books that she had to keep from her husband . . . The

> movie ended with Fereshteh contemplating different scenarios for her life. But how was she going to manage? How was she going to live for herself and for her children after being confined for so long? The movie left you wondering and that's what a truly liked about it.
>
> *(Chelsea Leatherman)*

The film doesn't paint a simplistic portrait of Iranian men either. As another of my students Saralynn Bush notes,

> What I thought was most interesting was the different types of men portrayed in this film. There were . . . men who stop and stare at women in the middle of the road. Men who are stalkers. Men who stick up and defend women. Men who are traditional fathers. Men who are controlling husbands. Men who are distracted doctors who won't give women the time of day. Finally, there are quality, caring men such as Roya's husband who want the women in their lives to succeed.

While *Two Women* is a well-made film, students might be forewarned that it doesn't have production values or special effects of a Hollywood blockbuster and that it is in a foreign language (Farsi) with English subtitles. (I was surprised to learn that some of my small-town, Midwestern college students had never seen a film with subtitles before; they needed some help learning to read subtitles and watch the film at the same time.)

Erika Friedl's *Women of Deh Koh: Lives in an Iranian Village* (1991, 256 pages, age 16–college) offers a rich way to further extend the understanding of women in Iran after the revolution. Friedl is a German anthropologist and a former colleague of mine who spent 20 years off and on living in a small town in the mountains of Iran. The *New York Times Book Review* describes the book as "enthralling" convincing" and "remarkable,"

> A single brilliant description of a visit to "the city," seen as it were through the veil of a village woman, serves to emphasize the centrality of the community of families whose members, and whose mud houses and courtyards, are so intricately related to one another among the poplar-lined watercourses of the village.
>
> *(Glazebrook)*

Teachers can chose to use these stories either individually or as a set. Taken together they remind us that most woman of the Middle East are undertaking the tasks of everyday life, providing for themselves and their families, often under the difficult conditions of developing nations. We see jealousies and rivalry between families, an intense social life among the women, as well as evolving social practices.

Examining together this graphic novel, film, and ethnographic short stories, we have discovered an enormous range in the representation of women's experience in one country at a particular historical moment, illustrating the importance of considering women in the context of the diversity of historical periods, cultures, societies, and nations of the region. The Iran of the 1980s depicted in these works is not the same as the Iran of the present day. While the country has achieved substantial economic and educational development and passed through several liberalizing movements and repressive backlashes, teachers and students will need to find ways to continually update their assessment.

Another text that would be interesting for students to complexify their understanding of women in the Middle East would be *Girls of Riyadh* by Rajaa Alsanea (2007, 304 pages, age 16–college). Tracing the life of four wealthy college-age women in conservative Saudi Arabia over six years, the book might be called an epistolary novel, since it is made up of a collection of email letters sent anonymously to a large circle of Saudi Arabian readers. The use of email, the informality of style, and the inside perspective on the hidden lives of these young women navigating school, college, and marriage will interest young people. Reviewers frequently describe the book as "Sex in the City" for Saudi Arabia. One element the work chronicles is how the changing technology and economy is rapidly evolving life, even in this most conservative country. Although women are not allowed to date, be alone with men, or be seen in public without full burqa covering them from head to toe, the young women in this book all visit modern shopping malls, access the Internet, use Instant Messenger, carry cell phones, and spend extensive time talking with prospective boy friends. This book caused a sensation when it was first published in Arabic in Saudi Arabia, and was initially banned, but now has led to an outpouring of literature by women from that country.

While the women have similar backgrounds and social situations, they take different approaches to trying to negotiate their strict society and the power of family obligations. The young men portrayed in the novel are disappointing. The men submit to family pressures and enter into arranged marriages that they have no interest in. Although they pressure girls for sex, if the young women succumb they lose interest. They are more attracted to younger, weaker, less educated women than strong, independent ones. In short, while the upper-class world of Saudi women is unique, readers will likely find elements they may identify with or find familiar from their own society.

The other end of the spectrum of literature addressing the experience of Middle Eastern women is the best-known feminist work from the region, the short novel *Woman at Point Zero* (1975, 108 pages, age 16–college). The novel was written by Nawal El Saadawi and translated into English in 1983. My student Kendra Matko describes the novel this way,

> The book opens with a confident, concerned woman psychologist and author trying to learn the story behind quiet, death row inmate Firdaus, a

> mysterious, ex-prostitute who killed her pimp and refuses to speak with anyone in or out of the prison. She at last agrees to speak to the woman psychologist/author, and slowly unravels her tragic life history . . . her turbulent childhood, abused and witnessing the abuse of her mother by her father, her female circumcision as a young woman, twisted molestation by her uncle, betrayal by lovers, and on to bitter exploitation by pimps, and last and possibly most ruthless – the persistent taunting of men, women, and law enforcement – as she struggles to live an adult life she has no tools for.

Firdaus' father is a *fellah*, a poor peasant farmer and the lowest social class in Egypt. Although Firdaus manages to obtain a secondary certificate and thus middle-class status, she finds herself in a cruel arranged marriage to an older man and is often beaten both by her husband and uncle. The author, Nawal El Saadawi, is a medical doctor who served as director of public health in Egypt and has written nine novels. In Egypt Saadawi is a controversial figure, and she and her husband were imprisoned for their political views by Anwar Sadat (Sadat is remembered more fondly in America than Egypt). *Woman at Point Zero* traces the darkest underside of women's oppression. My student Heather Winowiki decribes it in this way,

> From a female perspective, there are a lot of things that hit close to home for me. In no way am I comparing my life and situations to Fidaus', but her pain and suffering at the hands of men is still something that can be seen splashed across the headlines of newspapers today. Women abused, battered, raped and prostituting themselves out as a profession is still common today in our own country. It made me angry, the further into the book that I went, not only at the men who abused Firdaus, but at Firdaus herself for not fighting harder for respect and self dignity. The book was very powerful and I would recommend it to anyone looking for a book that shows the struggles of a woman in modern Middle East culture.

Linda Cross responds,

> I agree with you that Firdaus is so abused and used she can only see the bad in men. But in a situation where women are abused many don't understand that what is happening to them is abuse. The abusers make their victims feel they deserve what is happening and it's a very hard cycle to break free from. Many fear for their lives if they leave their abuser and for good reason too.

Woman at Point Zero is an important narrative but far from the only perspective on women from Egypt or Islam. I caution teachers to not use this as the *only* text their students read from the region. (For a dramatic contrast on perspectives on Egyptian women, *Woman of Egypt* (1987, 466 pages, age 16–college) by Jehan Sadat, Anwar Sadat's widow.)

Reading Middle Eastern texts carefully reveals complexities in the role of women that may alter the stereotypes students bring to the works. A case in point occurred when I was teaching the short and wonderful Egyptian novel, *Aunt Safiyya and the Monastary* (1996, 115 pages, age 13–college) by the male writer Bahaa' Taher. (So popular in Egypt that it was made into a TV soap opera!) The full text is available free online from the publisher University of California Press. Reading this novel my students were quick to see the oppression of women, and blame them for their situation. Many initially viewed the mother of the family as oppressing her daughters. Before class discussion Ashley Auberman wrote,

> The mother's relationship with her son, her daughters, Safiyya [an adopted daughter], and her husband was quite shocking. The fact that she openly favored her son over her daughters, and was even slightly abusive to her daughters when they did anything wrong, took me by surprise! I expected that the mother would have had sympathy toward her daughters, I guess like my own mother has toward me. Also, she favored Safiyya over her own daughters, because of her beauty and prospect of advancing the family's honor by a prosperous marriage.

During discussion, still wrestling with the role of the mother, Ashley herself brought up an interesting point. Was the mother's harshness toward her daughters part of ensuring that they will be successful in the village in which they live? Ashley wondered. There were other elements of the story that emerged during discussion. After one student pointed out that education was not encouraged in the village for the girls, another pointed to the father's insistence on his daughter's education – and argued that this broke his own stereotype of Arab fathers. At first students noticed that the mother submitted to the father's wishes regarding the daughter's education, then other students pointed out that the mother got her way in the case of Safiyya, so that the decision making in the family was actually more balanced than it at first appeared. Students were disturbed that Safiyya marries a much older man, but as they examined the text more closely they noticed that her parents, though they may have had objections, allowed Safiyya to make her own choice and supported what she wanted – especially after they learned that the man they thought she was going to marry endorsed the union. John Ebbing wrote, "An arranged marriage may seem unfair to me and you, but Egyptian fathers do not do this because they like to be cruel and torture their daughters; they do it out of love and because they want what is best for their families."

Students were also surprised to see that Safiyya, even as a young woman in her twenties, ends up having enormous power once her wealthy husband dies. As we further discussed the novel, and they wrote papers about it, my students began to see that the roles for women were not as limited as they initially thought, and they came to recognize how those roles are rapidly evolving in Egypt as new forms of communication and transportation link village and urban life. At the same time there is something attractive about even the traditional village.

> While reading *Aunt Safiyya and the Monastery*, you begin to realize that the customs of the Middle East are greatly valued and respected by the villagers. Everyone has a purpose in the village and everyone works together to achieve harmony. Their religion and their beliefs are their motivators. Everything they do is done with respect for their fellow neighbors and relatives. They treat each other like they would treat a close family member.
>
> *(Chelsea Leatherman)*

Aunt Safiyya also offers an interesting introduction to many other important themes, such as father–son relationships; respect and hospitality in Arabic society; class distinctions between villagers and land owners; relations between Egyptian Muslims and Coptic Christians; distinctions between Upper and Lower Egypt; issues of honorable brigandage and "outlaws" somewhat in the mold of Robin Hood; the vendetta system as a form of justice in a region without legitimate authority; the mobilization of Egyptians in the 1967 war with Israel; and so on.

The changes in women's experience in the Middle East are also a central theme in the novel *The Bastard of Istanbul* (2008, 368 pages, age 16–college), Elif Shafak's second novel in English. The best-selling female author in Turkey, Shafak has an MA and PhD in women's studies and international relations from Middle East Technical University in Ankara, one of the most prestigious universities in the region. *The Bastard of Istanbul* is told from the point of view of an American girl, Armanoush Tchakhmakhchian, with Armenian parents and a Turkish stepfather. She travels to Turkey to live with her stepfather's family in an effort to better understand her roots. The novel examines the intimate relations between Turks and Armenians before, during, and after the Armenian genocide. (Because the word "genocide" appears in the text, Shafak was charged in Turkey with "public denigration of Turkishness" – the charges were later dropped.) My students were fascinated with this story.

> I haven't read a book that was so difficult to set aside when my evil demon told me to get back into reality and the duties of everyday life, in a long time. Elif Shafak does beautiful work in telling an exciting story, providing cultural insight, making bold statements, and creating a need to learn more about two cultures that seem so distant, but in actuality aren't.
>
> *(Maria Benson)*

> *The Bastard of Istanbul* by Elif Shafak resonated deeply on many different levels. I found myself unable to put it down! The text weaves a scintillating

> tale, alternating between past and present narratives in order to ultimately divulge a horrific family secret.
>
> *(Megan Carlson)*

In addition to addressing the important topic of Armenian–Turkish relations, the novel presents a wonderful variety of women living in contemporary Turkey. There is: Banu, a devout head-scarf-wearing mystic with powerful abilities; Cevriye, an atheistic high school history teacher; Feride, who changes her hair color and style "at each stage of her journey to insanity," and is variously diagnosed as "depressive," "borderline," and "schizophrenic;" Zeliha who has a string of lovers, uses foul language, and runs a tattoo parlor for the *avant garde*, urban and secular Turks; and her daughter, Asya, a cigarette-smoking rebel, obsessed with Johnny Cash, who hangs out in a cafe with a group of alienated philosophy types. What's striking is that all these women are in the same family, live together under the same roof, and share their meals – so much for stereotypes of Turkish or Middle Eastern women!

One of the most memorable and helpful things I have done as I have taught Middle Eastern literature and addressed the experience of women, has been to invite women from the region to speak in my class. Students welcome visitors who can talk about their cultural background and answer questions. Of course, since there is no one experience, I have found it valuable to have panels of speakers when possible. My student Jennifer Wiley commented,

> I really enjoyed hearing from our guest speakers on Tuesday. To get a firsthand account from women who practice Islam and can understand the way that Islam is applied to woman and Middle Eastern society is a treat, and I particularly enjoyed hearing from two different women of varying ages, from different regions and with different methods of practicing Islam. I though that the presentation that was given to us was very useful in helping us to understand the place that women have in Islam and that, much like our ideals in Christianity, women are to be treated with respect and it is acknowledged that woman are created from men and are to be considered equals with them. I like how she made the distinction between what Islam says about female treatment and what is actually practiced. There is a discrepancy there, but this is the kind of pattern that one would find in any society, under any religion. We tend to associate violence against women with a problem concerning Islam, but she made it clear to us that this was not the case; rather it is caused by a problem with society not obeying the laws of Islam. I found this presentation very helpful in understanding divisions between religious and societal standards in the Middle East.

Teachers should not feel awkward reaching out to invite speakers from the Middle East to their classes – my experience is that people welcome the opportunity.

FIGURE 3.2 Turkish Basketball Player Nilay Yiğit

The experience of women in the Middle East is an enormous topic and the focus of a corpus of teachable works translated into English. While I have addressed works from Iran, Egypt, and Turkey, there is no shortage of additional materials that may come to hand. As we teach about women in the Middle East, just as with the theme of justice, I believe it is important for students to break down categories of "us" and "them" and begin to see that while there is progress, there are also women the world over, including in Europe and America, who face challenges, discrimination, abuse, and even violence because of their gender. Women in the Middle East, like people everywhere, are focused on critical issues of obtaining education, employment, quality food and housing, and so on. There are progressive women working for change and equality and there are conservative movements seeking to restrict women's rights and freedoms. The recognition of this kind of commonality is important to help our students make personal connections with the experience of women in the Middle East that they encounter in literature and face-to-face.

Further Reading

The Last Chapter by Leila Abouzeid (1989) tells the story of a young woman high school student in Morocco who wonders if it is OK to be single.

Salwa Bakr's *The Wiles of Men and Other Stories* (1993) – Powerful short stories from Egypt focusing on the experience of women.

West of the Jordon by Laila Halaby (2003) portrays the coming to age of four young Arabic women in Jordan, Palestine, and the United States. (Described in Chapter 7.)

A Thousand Splendid Suns by Khaled Hosseini (2003), a powerful and disturbing novel that examines the experience of women in Afghanistan before and under the Taliban. (Described in Chapter 5.)

Zaat by Son'allah Ibrahim (2004). Zaat is the name of a typical middle-class Egyptian woman. The chapters alternate between her everyday life and the headlines of the Egyptian newspaper that she works for in the late 1980s and early 1990s.

Dreams of Trespass by Fatima Mernissi (1994), a well-known sociologist and feminist in Morocco. Her memoir of a childhood during the 1940s explores women growing up in a traditional Muslim household, crossing boundaries, and developing solidarity.

Daughter of Damascus by Siham Tergeman (1994) is a collection of nostalgic related stories about a young woman growing up in Syria.

4

A NEW HIGH SCHOOL SOCIAL STUDIES CLASS

The Middle East, Beginning with Turkey

Monica Mona Eraqi[1]

In the school curriculum in English-speaking countries there is a gap in regard to the Middle East, a region where particularly the U.S. is playing an ever-increasing role. To address this gap, I developed a semester-long curriculum for a new high school level course, and, after a year and a half of proposal writing and curriculum review, the "Modern Middle East," received final approval from the school district. This one-semester elective social studies class is in its second year of operation; so far I have taught six sections – a definite sign that students are fascinated by the Middle East and have a desire to learn about the area. Teaching the first ever high school course devoted to the Middle East in our school district (and perhaps in America!) I found few resources and materials specifically for secondary teachers. Of course, I realize that not all teachers will be able to teach a whole course on the Middle East, but I hope that what I can offer of my experiences, and the resources I suggest, will help both history and literature teachers – in whatever classes or levels they teach – begin to bridge the divide between American, Middle Eastern, and Muslim cultures.

Addressing such a historically rich and culturally diverse region as the Middle East, it is difficult to know where to begin. In my classes I start with Turkey. Located between Europe and the Middle East, Turkey can serve as a bridge between Western and Eastern cultures. I have found that knowledge of Turkey helps students' transition to cultures such as Saudi Arabia and Iran. There are so many aspects of Turkish history and culture that might be covered that it can be overwhelming for teachers to decide where to start or what resources to use. I focus on the development of the modern Turkish state and its current bid to join the European Union. Themes that organize my teaching include Turkey's minority issues, religious balance, and Turkish militarism/patriotism. I use these teaching points to explore democratic values and invite my students to compare and contrast issues that Turkey and the U.S. both face in the twenty-first century. Even though I am of Middle Eastern heritage, I am not Turkish, nor have I ever had Turkish students in my classes, although some of my students' ancestors have had experiences with the Ottoman Empire in the Balkans and Middle East.

My students, if they have any prior knowledge of Turkey, may bring to the class stereotypes or negative perceptions. For some, Turkey is ruled by a Sultan, who lives in a harem, where women are veiled. People shop in bazaars, drink Turkish coffee, and eat Turkish delight. My students may not know that Turkey is one of the earliest members of NATO, one of the United States' closest allies, and a nation becoming an active partner in Europe and playing an increasing role in world affairs.

To create an accurate picture of modern Turkey, I need to draw on a multitude of resources. I try to use teaching materials that students will find appealing and interesting, and that will appeal to a variety of learning styles. The book *Teaching About the Middle East: A Teacher's Resource Guide* (Chill, 2002) provides individual lesson plans on the Ottoman Empire and the formation of the Turkish state that were effective in my class. I've also used online lessons from Ithaca College's *Media Construction of the Middle East* (Sperry, 2010). Both of these resources include speeches from Ataturk and the Young Turks (the founders of modern Turkey), excerpts from historical documents including the

FIGURE 4.1 Galata Bridge in Istanbul Connecting Europe and Asia

Treaty of Versailles, the Balfour Declaration, and the Sykes-Picot Agreement that have helped me establish a historical background for modern Turkey. (These documents are also readily available in full text online.) I often bring to the class articles from CNN, BBC, Al-Jazeera, and the *New York Times* found through the Internet. I used current news articles, journals, and texts by Turkish authors such as Orhan Pamuk's *Istanbul: Memories and the City*.

I not only want to introduce my students to Turkish history, but also show them visual images of contemporary Turkey. I created a PowerPoint presentation that includes many images found easily on the web, as well as pictures I took on a trip to Turkey. (For teachers addressing the Middle East, information-gathering trips to the region are likely tax-deductible!) I have also used videos from other popular travel experts, including *Rick Steve's Turkey* and Anthony Bourdain's *No Reservations: Istanbul*. These travel guides, though narrated by Americans, are candid, recap local history, visit historic landmarks, emphasize local culture and cuisine, and attempt to provide insight from Turkish points of view. In addition to their comprehensive coverage, both were created for American television and thus are easy for our students to understand and for teachers to fit within a one-hour class period. Students particularly enjoy Anthony Bourdain's open mindedness and blunt comments, as well as his fascination with local cuisine. Bourdain's and Steves' videos are easily accessible. Rick Steve has his own website where DVDs, travel guides, and commentary can be downloaded and purchased and many can be accessed for free from the PBS website. Anthony Bourdain has a page on the Travel Channel website where viewers can read his journals as well as blog with Bourdain and other viewers. All of Bourdain's episodes can be purchased through the iTunes store.

To address Middle Eastern and Muslim stereotypes, I have used *Allah Made Me Funny*, and *Inside Islam: What One Billion Muslims Really Think* (free DVDs for teachers are available through Unity Productions, an educational organization that produces films on a number of cultural sensitive issues, via its website www.upf.tv). This helps the students see life from a Middle Eastern and Muslim perspective, something that is important for the students when they study Turkey. I also frequently use news report videos and articles on issues currently facing Turkey, issues such as honor killings, women's right to wear headscarves in the university, and Turkey's relations with Kurds, Israel and Armenia. The *60 Minutes* program recently presented a newscast titled *Battle Over History*, focused on the debate between Turkey and Armenia over the Armenian Genocide, a genocide that Turkey has repeatedly denied. Equally important was the connection between this issue and the U.S. This hits close to home for the students and is a sharp reminder that what happens "over there," directly affects what happens "over here."

In addition to these resources, my students have a chance to experience Turkish culture through Turkish music videos, TV shows and a Turkish food day known as Turkish Thursday. After seeing Bourdain's video in particular, students were excited to try the same foods that Bourdain eats during his travels. I use classical Turkish food that many of my students from the Balkans and Middle East are familiar with because of the exchange of cultures through conquest and trade with the Ottoman Empire. These include foods such as pita, borek, Turkish delight, Turkish coffee and lahmacun (Turkish pizza). These dishes are easy to make, even if you're not Turkish, with recipes available online. They are also easy to serve in a classroom, can be made ahead of time (with the exception of the coffee) or even bought in local stores (as is the case with Turkish delight). They also come in vegetarian forms, which many students with food restrictions appreciate. In the past my Albanian, Syrian, Bosnian, and Macedonian students have helped to make and prepare these dishes for the classes. Doing so allowed these students to make a connection with the class and show how their families have individualized these dishes by adding their own cultural flare.

Finally, I try to emphasize the more modern aspects of Turkish culture in a way that the students can appreciate through the use of Turkish music and music video clips. These video clips help dispel my students' misconceptions and are easily accessible through YouTube with English translations. Students are surprised to see that Turks have their own punk rock, heavy metal, hip-hop, and even rap bands. They are surprised to see expensive cars, elaborate video sets, males and females intermingling, and the numerous similarities between American and Turkish life and music. Even my Middle Eastern students are excited to recognize Arabic words in Turkish songs and the links between the two languages. The music videos help show Turks for who they really are: energetic, enthusiastic, and in love with life. These are not words that my students might typically associate with the Turkish people. When used in context, all of these sources help students experience Turkey's transition from the Ottoman Empire to a new nation and modern republic. They illustrate that although Turkey is a Muslim nation that borders the Eastern and Western worlds, it is a contemporary in its own unique way. Certainly, students recognize that Turkey is not America, and that is OK. Part of what I hope students understand is that a country can be considered "modern," but that does not mean that it has to be just like the U.S.

In addition to bringing these resources to my students, both as a whole class and for their independent study, there are several activities that I have developed to help my students better understand Turkish history, some of the current controversies in Turkey, and decisions that contemporary Turkish people face. Many of the activities are written pieces that allow students to express their beliefs and reasoning. I have had students write an acrostic poem, a form of poetry that my students had used in their English classes, about a historic Middle Eastern leader, Ataturk. Students use the poem to interpret the life of Ataturk and the reforms he made as president of Turkey. At the very end of the poem students write a paragraph explaining what made Ataturk such an important figure in Turkish and Middle Eastern history. Was he successful in making a modern Turkish state and what is his legacy? To do this, the students had to synthesize and analyze class notes and discussions, handouts, the class text, their group projects, and speeches that Ataturk made regarding his dreams for the new Turkey.

Next I have a group activity where students play the role of Turkey's Foreign Relations Minister. In their groups students determine which factors, if any, supported Turkey as state ready to join the European Union (EU) and which factors hindered that goal. As a group the students try to come to a consensus and draft a proposal describing how Turkey can improve its global image and, if necessary, take steps to appease European demands in order to join the EU. Each group presents their ideas, in writing to me, as I take the role of the Turkish president. I read each group's suggestions anonymously and, as a class, they vote on which proposal should be accepted. In a similar activity I have students assume the role of a Turkish representative and individually write a persuasive letter to the EU Parliament explaining why Turkey should or should not be allowed to enter the EU. Drawing on their independent research, students include details supporting their views, and the opposing view. The persuasive letter allows students to voice their opinion on the topic, give the assignment personal meaning, and develop their thoughts for the final activity – the class debate.

A class debate also helps the students consider issues in the controversial decision for Turkey to enter the EU. The debate encourages students to be aware of an important current world issue, to consider the relations between East and West, and calls for group research using a plethora of resources. Once they conclude their research, students weigh the pros and cons of each option, take a stand and finally defend that position, thus developing life skills important for active citizens in a democracy. By the end of the debate students decide, as a class, if they think Turkey should be granted EU status. Students could do an essay, but I use this debate because the format encourages teamwork, communication, the exchange of ideas, and provides another avenue for students to express themselves. The debates themselves are memorable.

In the debate students put themselves in the position of Europeans looking at Turkey from the outside, as well as in the position of the Turks, both those who want to be in the EU and those who would prefer not to join. Many of Turkey's historical events and current issues surface during the debate and class discussion. I begin by placing students into two teams: those in favor of Turkey joining the EU (Team B) and those who oppose it (Team A). Teams opposing Turkey's ascension into the EU frequently reference the at least half a million Armenians killed in the Armenian Genocide, a genocide that is not documented in Turkey nor legal to discuss, and Article 301 of the Turkish penal code, which prohibits anyone from insulting Turkish history, culture, or Ataturk, and limits freedom of speech in Turkey. These teams also reference the thousands of Turks who feel culturally threatened by the EU and are concerned that they are being forced into an image that doesn't fit them. These Turks feel that the EU threatens their religious and cultural values and look at the EU and Europe as anti-Islamic.

Still other Turks view the EU as a political machine that exploits Turkey political and economically as merely the trading center between the East and West. Teams in support of Turkey joining the EU bring forward many interesting points as well. Students realize the political message that would be sent to the Arab and Muslim world if Turkey was accepted by the European community and the economic benefit of allowing Turkey into the EU for both Turks and Europeans. Students often mention that Turkey is also a member of NATO and long-time ally of the U.S.

After opening statements I open the floor for rebuttals. To keep the debate running smoothly, I allow each side equal opportunity to state several facts, before moving to the next group. This helps ensure that all students have a chance to state their opinion and that no one is overlooked. I also focus on a particular group, rather than just one person, to prevent the students from feeling singled out. Sometimes I specifically invite students who are less apt to participate, but whom I know through their writings are passionate and knowledgeable. Although I typically do not participate in the debates, there are occasions in which I find myself playing the devil's advocate. This helps to deepen the level of analysis and opens up additional discussion. Sometimes I bring up topics or questions that have not yet surfaced, but that I want students to respond to.

In our last debate on Turkey, after discussion of the economic benefit of allowing Turkey to enter the EU, I noticed the debate begin to slow and students seemed unsure of direction. I decided to turn the focus to human rights, since that was one topic that many students were passionate about and one that we, as a class, could build from. I knew that one student on Team A, Spencer, had recently read an article focused on Germany's attempt to move forward after the Holocaust, to eventually become the leading economy in Europe. I asked the class about Germany and their image after the Holocaust, which led Spencer to participate. Spencer brought up the Armenian Genocide, connected it to the Holocaust and continued to debate the topic with Dillon, a member from the opposing team. Spencer's comparison of Turkey and Germany launched the class into its next part of the debate.

Dillon, a member from Team B, was frustrated that Turkey has not recognized the Armenian genocide. In Dillion's opinion, Germany was able to move forward because they had admitted to genocide and dealt with the consequences, so how could Turkey move forward when they had not accepted their past? Spencer rebutted this comment by distinguishing between a government-planned genocide, such as that carried out by the Nazis, and actions carried out by individual citizens, like the Young Turks, who, Spencer argued, were, in fact, acting as leaders of the former Ottoman Empire, not the current Turkish nation state. As the debate continued, Nicole, Spencer's teammate, came to his aide and connected human rights to the honor killings that take place in Turkey. Nicole said, "It's the people that are doing these things, not the government. It's not the government's fault."

As students continued to debate the issue of honor killings, the Armenian Genocide and Turkey's human rights record, I notice two of my ESL students, Romina and Silvana, both of Albanian background, whispering about facts on their debate paper. Silvana spoke up mentioning that Albania has honor killings as well. Romina chimed in that several neighbors in her hometown were killed in honor killings. Another student, Courtney, brought the issue closer to home, by saying that Turkey's human rights issues can be compared to human rights issues in the U.S., including the genocide of Native Americans, slavery, and civil rights abuses. The debate provided students with rich, memorable, and personal discussion requiring high level thinking to make connections to their lives, to people in the Middle East, as they engaged in complex, cross-cultural analysis.

The resources and activities I mention here are not meant to serve as any kind of rigid, step-by-step guide to teaching about Turkey or the Middle East. While I use similar assignments, debates, and food days with Egypt, Saudi Arabia, Lebanon, Syria, and Iraq, including, travel videos, news reports, articles, and video clips to help the students make cultural connections to the region, I remain flexible and open to current events and additional materials. I believe that these assignments can be adapted at different grade levels, elementary through college, and in different courses including global studies, world religion, or current issues classes, as well as English and literature courses where they can provide essential historical background and cultural context. As teachers, we can work together to prepare a generation of active citizens who better understand their diverse classmates, neighbors, and other citizens with which they share this world.

Note

1. Monica Eraqi has done pioneering work in interdisciplinary teaching about the Middle East at the high school level. In this chapter focused on Turkey, Ms. Eraqi reports on approaches to establish historical and cultural themes and contexts that can be used with any Middle Eastern region or country.

5

EUROPE AND AMERICA IN THE MIDDLE EAST

Colonialism, Neo-Colonialism, Intervention, Terrorism, and War

The terrorist attacks of 9/11/2001 were not only a shock to most Americans, they were incomprehensible. The news media and even national leaders did little to help us understand why the attacks took place. In a speech to congress on September 20 President Bush said,

> They hate . . . a democratically elected government . . . They hate our freedoms – our freedom of religion, our freedom of speech, our freedom to vote and assemble and disagree with each other.
>
> *("Why")*

At a press conference a month after the event President Bush stated,

> I'll tell you how I respond: I'm amazed. I'm amazed that there's such misunderstanding of what our country is about that people would hate us. I am – like most Americans, I just can't believe it because I know how good we are.
>
> *("Why")*

Apparently, the President, the press, and most of the American people seemed to have little idea about why people from the Middle East might have animosity toward the U.S. Clearly they are not well informed about the history of European and American involvement and intervention in the region. There are serious consequences for failing to understand the events of 9/11, not the least of which is the risk that such an event might happen again. Providing students opportunities to explore that history, to read and view literature emerging from these conflicts, is vitally needed in secondary and university curriculums. In the *Christian Science Monitor*, two weeks after 9/11, Peter Ford argues,

> Muslims and Arabs . . . do not share Mr. Bush's view that the perpetrators did what they did because "they hate our freedoms." Rather, they say, a mood of resentment toward America and its behavior around the world has become so commonplace in their countries that it was bound to breed hostility, and even hatred. And the buttons that Mr. bin Laden pushes in his statements and interviews win a good deal of popular sympathy – the injustice done to the Palestinians, the cruelty of continued sanctions against Iraq, the presence of U.S. troops in Saudi Arabia, the repressive and corrupt nature of U.S.-backed Gulf governments – win a good deal of popular sympathy.
>
> The resentment of the U.S. has spread through societies demoralized by their recent history. In few of the world's 50 or so Muslim countries have governments offered their citizens either prosperity or democracy. Arab nations have lost three wars against their arch-foe – and America's closest ally – Israel. A sense of failure and injustice is rising in the throats of millions.
>
> *(Ford, "Why")*

Clearly, a deeper understanding of the relations of the Middle East to the West does not require advanced degrees in Middle Eastern studies. Basic information about colonialism and Western intervention in the Middle East provides a starting point.

A History of Colonialism and Intervention

While people in the Middle East have great respect for the people, culture, and technology of Europe and America, as mentioned in the discussion of Orientalism in Chapter 1, there is a history of European and American intervention in the region that has damaged relations. The history of intervention is widely known in the Middle East and by Middle Eastern writers, but tends to be unknown, forgotten, or generally overlooked outside the Middle East, particularly in America and Europe. Understanding this history is critical for teachers and students who seek to learn about the Middle East today, including attitudes, politics, literature, and culture. Certainly Europeans and Americans are aware of the Crusades, those religiously sanctioned military assaults by Europeans primarily against Muslims in the Middle East that lasted from the eleventh to the thirteenth century. Many in the West are less aware of more contemporary European and American colonial, imperial, military, and economic domination of the region. The lack of knowledge fosters misunderstanding about contemporary events. This chapter attempts to provide some of this history as important for teachers of Middle Eastern literature. My intention is not to present a comprehensive history or a "balanced" perspective, but to fill in areas where teachers are likely to be less informed, to help teachers understand as much as possible from a Middle Eastern point of view some of the contemporary issues between the Middle East and the West, and to facilitate education of English-speaking students and citizens so that the unequal relations of the past need not continue into the future. The global "War on Terror," including the Afghan and Iraq Wars, is certainly the most prominent contemporary illustration of the history I am addressing. Strategies for addressing these conflicts and teaching literature emerging from them are an important focus of this chapter.

European Control of the Middle East

In 1798 Napoleon, with dreams of imitating the empire of Alexander the Great, invaded Egypt and inaugurated the present period of Middle Eastern history, one increasingly dominated by Europe and, more recently, the U.S. As the European powers, especially England and France, gained influence over the Middle East and North Africa during the nineteenth century, the Ottoman Empire weakened. Part of the "scramble for Africa," the French established colonial rule over Ottoman, Arab, and Berber-speaking states in Algeria, Morocco, and Tunisia, and the British ruled Egypt, Sudan, and Somalia. Since 1911 the Italians ruled Libya. Thus it should not be surprising that in World War I the Ottoman Empire aligned itself with Germany against England and France. While Europeans and Americans know that Germany and the Central Powers were defeated in WWI, they might not know that 3 million Turks died from violence, starvation, and disease in this war. This was also the period of the Ottoman genocide of the Armenians that claimed at least half a million lives, ostensibly based on a fear that Armenians were conspiring with the Allies. During the war the British and French fomented Arab revolts against the Ottoman Empire (the subject of the film *Lawrence of Arabia*) and promised self-rule to Arab leaders, while, at the same time secretly planning to divide the Middle East between themselves (Sykes-Picot Agreement, 1916). The British also promised a national homeland in Palestine to the Jewish Zionists (Balfour Declaration, 1917) inaugurating the most long-term and tenacious conflict in the region.

At the end of World War I the victorious British and French, already rulers of vast global empires, took charge of the former Ottoman territory, dividing it up into separate states and establishing "mandates" or districts of colonial rule that were approved by the new United Nations (UN). These actions created the nations found on maps today. Christian regions of the former Ottoman Empire, including parts of Southern and Eastern Europe, Greece, and the partly Christian Balkans were made into separate nations. England took over regions that would become Palestine, Jordan, Iraq, and Kuwait – they already possessed Egypt, Bahrain, Qatar, Aden, and Oman. France took control of the region that became Lebanon and Syria.

BOX 5.1 EUROPEAN IMPERIAL EXPANSION IN THE MIDDLE EAST PRIOR TO WWI

- 1830 French conquer Algeria
- 1838 Unequal trading conventions favor Europe
- 1839 Britain takes Aden in Yemen
- 1881 French army occupies Tunisia
- 1882 Britain takes over Egypt, controls Suez Canal
- 1890–1910 Europeans build railroads in Middle East for economic "concessions"
- 1899 England controls the Sudan
- 1901 British "concessions" in Iran
- 1904 Spanish and French partition Morocco
- 1908 Founding of Anglo–Persian Oil Co. (Now BP – British Petroleum)
- 1911 Italy invades Libya

At the time the English and French openly acknowledged that one of their goals was to ensure that, long term, no Middle Eastern or North African state could rise to global prominence and threaten the position of the European empires. Smaller states, they believed, would be less powerful, and would likely be pitted against each other. This went against promises made to Arabs and to Arab nationalists who envisioned an Arab nation comprising Iraq, Syria, Lebanon, Jordan, Palestine, and Saudi Arabia. The establishment of independent states in the Middle East after World War I by the victorious British and French was a classic case of the imperial practice of "divide and rule," and the strategy was effective because it also drew on existing differences and animosities. The people living in the region had no say in how the lines that defined their nations were drawn, or in who their rulers were going to be. These decisions were made for them by Europeans, in collaboration with local elite families and groups who stood to benefit from the arrangement. The monarchial dynasties that were put in power were not democratic. They were dedicated to keeping their positions, which meant keeping the countries of the region separate, and for the most part cooperating with the British, French, and Russians (and, later, the Americans) in foreign policy and the exploitation of their resources. The ruling families were often not even originally residents of the countries they were put in charge of. They gained wealth and the distance between them and the people they ruled increased, leading to one of the most critical issues in the region today: a lack of democracy combined with profound economic inequality.

The behavior of the Europeans in the Middle East has had long-term consequences. By dividing up Arab-speaking peoples and forming non-democratic nation-states in many ways different from the European model, Europeans left lasting memories that continue to shape attitudes and identity. Magda M. Al-Nowaihi writes:

> The admiration for European civilization was tempered, if not sometimes actually reversed, by the way actual Europeans behaved in the Arab countries, with arrogance and ruthlessness that were in such stark opposition, or so it seemed, with the ideals of liberal humanism which symbolized European culture. This "superior," infuriatingly aggressive and oppressive West, with its master narratives of nationalism, democracy, individualism, and modernity, its schools of thought and intellectual giants, and its material power over the Arab world, in the various guises that this material power takes, is at least one of the crucial parameters within which, and against which, a sense of identity: individual, collective, and national, is negotiated.
>
> *(2007, 286–7)*

Having to negotiate individual and collective identities in a framework created by someone else is certain to create lasting animosities. The case of Turkey offers something of a counter example. In 1920 the Treaty of Sevres simply divided Turkey between England, France, and Italy. British, French, and Greek armies quickly moved to occupy the terrain, but the Turks, with their developed military left over from the Ottoman period, were in a better position to resist the Europeans than other Middle Eastern countries. Led by a rebellious general, Mustafa Kemal (Ataturk), the Turks fought a successful insurgency against the Europeans and established a new state dedicated to republicanism, secularism, populism, reformism, nationalism, and self-development of resources and industry. In years to come other states in the former Ottoman Empire looked, in some ways, to Turkish nationalism as their model.

Nationalist movements followed in many of the European-created states including Algeria, Morocco, Egypt, Syria, Iran, and Iraq. These nationalist movements often had progressive agendas, including the creation of economic infrastructure – such as the famous Aswan Dam in Egypt – the development of political, juridical, and medical institutions, and the establishment of public education, including the education of women. The pre-eminent Middle Eastern nationalist, and an important world leader, was Gamal Abdel Nasser in Egypt. Nasser sought to create an Arab Nationalism that would draw back together the different Arab-speaking regions that had been separated by the European colonial powers; at one point Egypt even formed a union with Syria. (Nasser's land reforms in the countryside are discussed in Chapter 2 regarding the novel *War in the Land of Egypt*.) Nasser significantly extended secondary and university education and addressed chronic under employment and unemployment. He also unified Arab resistance to the State of Israel (see Chapter 7). An important Arab nationalist organization was the Ba'aths, a secular political party dedicated to unifying all

Arab countries and combating Western colonial rule, especially strong in Syria and Iraq. Nationalists typically repressed and were opposed by conservative Muslim groups such as the fundamentalist Islamic Brotherhood in Egypt. During the Cold War, Nasser and other nationalists in the Middle East came into conflict with Britain, France, and, increasingly, the United States over ideology and access to resources, when they sought a larger share for their countries in the infrastructure (Suez Canal) and profits, principally of the corporations extracting their oil. A foreign policy that basically followed the Arab proverb, "the enemy of my enemy is my friend," led the U.S. to support fundamental Islamic governments and movements to oppose Arab nationalism.

Oil and American Foreign Policy

From World War I forward, oil has become of increasing necessity to the world economy and the presence of vast oil reserves in the Middle East has made the region immensely strategic. Oil and oil products not only fuel cars, trucks, airplanes, boats, and trains, but also are used in agriculture, all forms of manufacturing, provide light, heat and cool our homes, and are found in almost every product we consume. One measure of the value of gasoline is that one gallon has been considered roughly equivalent to 500 hours of human work. Obviously, access

FIGURE 5.1 King Abdullah with Dick Cheney and George Bush (2005)

to oil is critical for any modern industry – and modern warfare. One third of the entire domestic American oil supply was spent in World War II, and, at the end of the war, Hitler and the Allies raced to grasp oil resources in Iran. Control over this awesome resource is extremely unequal. Some citizens of the world have far more access than others to oil, and at cheaper prices. Since America came to pre-eminence as a world power at the end of World War II, energy supply and oil have been of primary consideration in American policy toward the Middle East, a policy that has been marked by undercover and high-handed diplomacy, intervention, and war (see Box 5.2 for some highlights of this history).

Awareness of American actions in the Middle East may be closely tied to literature students will read. For instance, the American CIA, with the help of the British, organized the overthrow of Iran's democratically elected Prime Minister Muhammad Mosaddeq in 1953 in order to install the authoritarian monarch Shah Reza Pahlavi who ruled Iran for the next twenty-nine years until the revolution in 1979. Once in power, Shah Pahlavi quickly arranged for the Americans and British to control 80 percent of Iranian oil output (at that time Iran was the world's largest oil producer). Every Iranian knows this history. Most Americans do not, though Americans may know about the takeover of the American Embassy during the Iranian revolution and wonder why that happened. To comprehend the ongoing tension in Iranian–American relations, or to read with understanding Mahbod Seraji's *Rooftops Over Tehran* (see Chapter 2), the history of American involvement in ending the Iranian democracy is an important starting point. Teachers may sometimes simply provide important background

BOX 5.2 HIGHLIGHTS OF AMERICAN INTERVENTION IN THE MIDDLE EAST

- 1928 Red Line Oil Agreement between America and Britain to share Middle East oil. Standard Oil and Mobil get shares of Iraq Petroleum Company.
- 1944 The Anglo-American Petroleum Agreement divides Middle Eastern oil between the U.S. and Britain. Roosevelt says: "Persian oil . . . is yours. We share the oil of Iraq and Kuwait. As for Saudi Arabian oil, it's ours. (Between 1948 and 1960, Western companies earned $12.8 billion in profits from the production, refining and sale of Middle Eastern oil, on investments totaling $1.3 billion.)
- 1949 CIA back military coup in Syria, overthrows elected government.
- 1953 CIA organizes coup in Iran, overthrows elected government putting Shah in power.
- 1956 CIA coup in Syria aborted.

continued . . .

- 1957 Marines land in Lebanon to prepare invasion of Jordan.
- 1958 U.S. Navy and Marines to Lebanon, threat of nuclear attack if Iraq invades Kuwait, invasion of Iraq planned with Turkey.
- 1957–8 Plots to overthrow Nasser in Egypt, not successful.
- 1960 U.S. tries to overthrow government of Iraq.
- 1963 U.S. supports coup led by Ba'ath Party in Iraq, Saddam Hussein (on CIA payroll) comes to power.
- 1973–5 U.S. supports Kurdish rebels in Iraq, then abandons them.
- 1978–79 U.S. supports Shah and tries to organize a coup to keep him in power.
- 1979: Carter designates the Persian Gulf a vital U.S. interest and declares the U.S. will go to war to ensure the flow of oil.
- 1979: U.S. begins arming and organizing Islamic fundamentalist "Mujahedeen" in Afghanistan, Brzezinski writes, "This aid was going to induce a Soviet military intervention," drawing the Soviets into an Afghan quagmire.
- 1979 Soviet Troops enter Afghanistan at invitation of Afghan government, American "secret war" begins, over $3 billion spent on arms, funding of Osama Bin Laden and others, by 1989 over 1 million casualties, 1/3 of population refugees.
- 1980 Iraq invades Iran with U.S. support, U.S. supports both sides, 1.5 million dead.
- 1983 U.S. troops to Lebanon.
- 1983 CIA involved in murder of general in Morocco.
- 1985 CIA attempts to kill Shiite leader in Lebanon.
- 1986 U.S. bombs Libya.
- 1987 U.S. shoots down Iranian airplane, all 290 passengers killed.
- 1990 Iraq invades Kuwait after American "green light."
- 1991 "Desert Storm" 200,000 Iraqis killed.
- 1992 Marines land in Somalia.
- 1992 Department of Defense official plan "In the Middle East and Southwest Asia, our overall objective is to remain the predominant outside power in the region and preserve U.S. and Western access to the region's oil."
- 1993 U.S. Missile Attack on Iraq.
- 1995 Oil and Trade Sanctions against Iraq, UN says 4,500 children die per month, 280,000 sorties flown over Iraq in 10 years.
- 1998 Congress funds "secret" attacks against government of Iraq; U.S. launches missiles against Afghanistan, Somalia, and Iraq.
- 2001 Invasion of Afghanistan.
- 2003 Invasion and occupation of Iraq, by 2011 over one million (?) dead. (See Box 5.3 on p. 95)

information for the works they teach, or, better still, they can invite students to research historical contexts and share with classmates.

It is appropriate that the study of contemporary literature of the Middle East help students understand events in the news and recent history of the region. Often "protecting oil supplies" has been a publicly acknowledged justification for American interventions in the Middle East. At the same time there have been other justifications. In the case of the 2003 Iraq War, for example, oil was not supposed to explain the invasion. Instead there were other reasons Americans thought that Iraq was invaded: revenge for 9/11 (but Saddam Hussein had nothing to do with 9/11, in fact he and his Ba'ath Party were traditional enemies of Osama Bin Laden); to eliminate weapons of mass destruction (but Scott Ritter, Republican head of the UN inspection teams in Iraq made it clear *before the invasion* there were no such weapons there); to free Iraq from Saddam's brutal despotism (but there are other despots in the world, why this one?); to create a democracy (by an invasion? at the point of a gun?); and so on.

My students and I watched the compelling film *Blood and Oil*. (The DVD can be bought or viewed online.) In the 53-minute documentary based on Michael Klare's book of the same title, Klare explains that 5 percent of world's population consumes 25 percent of petroleum. He discusses the role of oil in American foreign policy in the region, from Roosevelt to Bush, and shows that American administrations – Republican and Democrat alike – supported the Saudi royal family in exchange for special rights to Saudi oil. The CIA-organized coup in Iran in 1953, Operation Desert Storm, Osama Bin Laden's war against the United States, the wars against Iraq – all tied by the film to control over oil resources. *Blood and Oil* raised this question for my student Janelle Mirch: "In the movie there is a soldier that tells the camera crew he was sent to guard the oil refinery. Are we sending our men over there to guard potential oil or to find peace in the Middle East?"

The American military has a substantial history and presence in the Middle East closely tied to the mission to "protect energy resources." Even after the "withdrawal" of combat forces, many troops and bases remain. Looking at a map of American military bases in the Middle East (Figure 5.2) can raise a number of interesting questions and help students understand attitudes toward the U.S. Not all of my students agreed that America should not be at war over oil. Katie stated on her blog,

> George W. Bush, following 9/11 stated that the United States was going to take on a policy of preemptive action, and we did! And that is good. Does anyone stop and think that maybe protecting the oil that the U.S. military, and that U.S. society relies on, may not be such a bad thing? And if it is a bad thing (and I do believe we can argue both ways) how come everyone in the U.S. drives a fuel driven car? And they could definitely call our class hypocrites because almost 100 percent of the class drives fuel driven

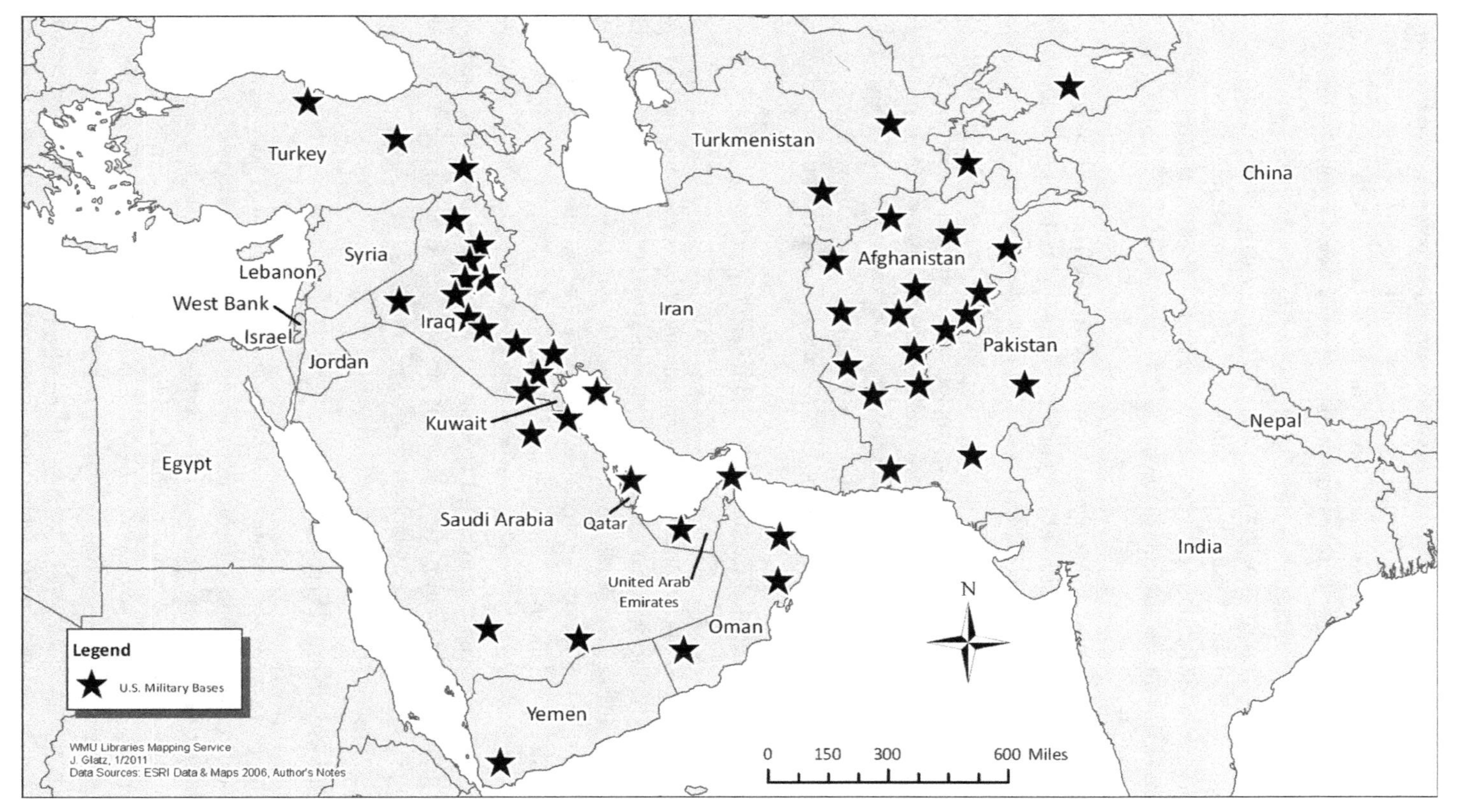

FIGURE 5.2 Map of United States Bases in Middle East

> cars. Some people will argue that there is no other choice since an alternative fuel source has not been discovered. Welllll maybe we should go and discover it? Sitting in a classroom arguing about how selfish America is does not change the fact that without oil, our society won't run.

Clearly, it is sometimes difficult for students to put themselves into the position of people in another country and think about how Americans and American policies are viewed from abroad. One day I created a hypothetical situation about Saudi Arabia for my students to discuss:

> Imagine you are an average citizen of Saudi Arabia. The royal family controls the wealth created by the country's immense oil resources, wealth it gets from American oil companies that pump and process the oil. Princes of the royal family receive $100,000 per month, but your income is $6,000 per year. There is 30 percent unemployment. An alliance between the royal family and the most conservative religious leaders means that there are very strict rules in everyday life. Even though your country is the keeper of the holiest shrines of Islam which non-Muslims are not allowed to visit, by the will of the royal family the U.S. stations troops on bases in your country.

I had students write individually about a number of questions:

> What kind of laws, mass media, religion might the royal family favor? How does it affect you that there is high unemployment? What might you think about the royal family? What views might you have of the U.S.? What might you try to do to change your society? How does this hypothetical situation influence your views of the events of 9-11?

The class discussion that followed brought up few answers, but many questions my students could further research, and it provided information that would put into perspective reading literature from the region.

Teaching about Terrorism

In the 1950s there was a communist hiding under every bed. Today we are led to believe we are under threat from Islamic terrorists determined to destroy democracy and our way of life. We frequently hear about terrorism, or the threat of terrorism, in the news and fictionalized in movies and television programs. A recent TV program I saw involved Middle Eastern terrorists taking over American shopping malls; this kind of portrayal has become a standard feature of daily programming. Many years after the 9/11 attacks, the country remains on alert at the border and in airports, where announcements remind us that no one is to leave a bag unattended for fear that a bomb will be planted in your suitcase. Politicians use the threat of terrorism to garner votes and pass a wide variety of legislation, some of it curtailing freedoms. Fighting terrorism has become the primary public justification for American involvement in the Middle East, in wars in Iraq and Afghanistan and in relations with Israel and Iran. Phillip Cryan says, "'Terrorism' may be the most important, powerful word in the world right now." (Cryan) For all these reasons, students and citizens need to study "terrorism" – and think carefully about how the way we allow this word to be defined creates enemies, justifies political and military actions, and legitimizes state authority. Quite an opportunity to examine the power of language.

I abhor terrorism in any form, be it by individuals, organized groups, or nation states. The suffering of the families of the victims of the 9/11 attacks is still fresh in my mind and was recently brought home by a visit I made to the 9/11 museum and memorial, near the site of the twin towers. The 14-year old Israeli girl Bat-Chen Shahak was killed on a bus in Tel Aviv by a Palestinian suicide bomb. In a letter she wrote to the family of Yizhak Rabin just four months before her own death (Rabin was killed at a peace rally by a right wing Orthodox Jew who opposed the Oslo accords), she asks, "Who has the right to take the most beautiful gift of all – of life?" Bat-Chen's question is one that must be asked about any and all acts of violence. (See Chapter 7 for discussion of a collection of Bat-Chen Shahak's writing.)

If terrorism is to be stopped it must be understood, and this is where education comes in. Although religion and ideology can be abused to justify terrorism, terrorism does not come from religion, race, or culture. Terrorism by individuals or organized groups is usually the expression of extraordinary desperation by disempowered people, and the sources of that desperation – most often economic and political – need to be examined and addressed. In *Holy Terrors: Thinking about Religion after September 11* Bruce Lincoln contends most conflict is caused by competition over scarce resources. He argues,

> Would-be aggressors become able to define their violent acts as not just greedy, but morally justified. The discourses they develop and circulate toward that end may be intended to persuade others, but above all they help overcome their own subjective (i.e. moral) inhibitions. Certain kinds of religious discourse can assist in this task, specifically those which recode otherwise problematic acts as righteous deeds, sacred duties or the like, as when killing is defined as sacrifice, destruction as purification, or war as Crusade. In principle, no religious tradition is more inclined than any other to make arguments of this sort. All people are capable of this move and the canonic texts of all religions include passages that can be put to such purpose. . . When social groups constitute their identity in religious terms and experience themselves as a sacred collectivity (the faithful, the righteous, or God's chosen people, for instance), as a corollary they tend to construe

> their rivals in negative fashion (heretics, infidels, apostates, evil, bestial, demonic, satanic, etc.). Under such circumstances, the pursuit of self-interest—including vengeance for slights to one's pride (a.k.a. "honour")—can be experienced as a holy cause, in support of which any violence is justified.
>
> *(94)*

Terrorism sponsored by states – the terrorism that has killed the most people by far – also entails failure to abide by international law, exhaust diplomatic options, and think of others as fully human. Citizens in a democracy have a high duty to make careful judgments about their government's actions and to reject terrorism by their leaders. I believe that the teaching of literature, particularly humanizing contemporary literature from the Middle East, has an important role in this kind of civic education.

I have found it helpful to start conversations about "terrorism" with students by having them consider whether or not they believe the following actions to be "terrorist:"

- Native Americans attack a frontier fort (or a frontier settlement).
- John Brown attacks the federal armory at Harper's Ferry to end slavery (seventeen dead, including ten raiders).
- Al Qaeda members fly airplanes into the World Trade Center to oppose the presence of American troops in Saudi Arabia and U.S. support of Israel (2726 deaths).
- Americans drop an atomic bomb on Hiroshima to force an unconditional surrender by the Japanese (200,000 deaths, including from radiation).
- Americans use a bombing campaign of "shock and awe" in Iraq as a response to Al Qaeda attacks. (Hundreds of thousands of Iraqis dead as a result of the American invasion.)

These examples raise powerful questions and illustrate for students that the word "terrorism" has a lot to do with perspective. As Michael Kinsley has stated, "One person's terrorist is another person's freedom fighter." To foster a thought provoking perspective different from the mass media, I have had students look at information about the long history of American military and political intervention in the Middle East before 9/11. My students have found it interesting to compare and contrast the official definition of "terrorism" in the American legal code vs. that issued by the British government:

- "The term 'terrorism' means premeditated, politically motivated violence perpetrated against noncombatant targets by subnational groups or clandestine agents." United States Legal Code (Zalman).

- Terrorism is "The use of violence for political ends, and includes any use of violence for the purpose of putting the public, or any section of the public, in fear." British Government ("What is Terrorism").

Which of the acts listed above are considered "terrorism" by the American definition? By the British definition? Why is the difference significant?

The question of terrorism is also certainly relevant to direct American actions against "terrorists," whether that be the wars fought; the escalation of security measures; the dedication of security, police, and espionage forces; the capture, trials, and extraordinary rendition of terrorists; and, of course, the infamous Guantanamo prison. My student Molly White, a freshman from a conservative small town near our university, recommended that our class read the autobiography *Five Years of My Life: An Innocent Man in Guantanamo* (2008, 256 pages, age 15–college) about the story of Murat Kurnaz. When Kurnaz was 19 he was heading home to Germany from a trip to Pakistan when he was arrested by the Pakistani police and sold, for $3,000, to Americans in Afghanistan as a "spy." Held and tortured for five years in Kandahar and Guantanamo, in August of 2006 he was finally released. Three American officers who reviewed his case asserted that they had classified evidence that established his guilt, but never disclosed this evidence to Kurnaz, his attorneys, or to the public. Both German and United States Army investigators failed to find any evidence of a tie between Kurnaz and Al-Qaeda or any involvement in any terrorist activities, yet, apparently, the U.S. Army has refused to admit the "mistake." In 2008, the CBS news program *60 Minutes* investigated the story, "Nightmare At Guantanamo Bay." The actress Vanessa Redgrave is quoted inside the book jacket,

> I thank God that Murat kept his sanity in the hell of injustice and torture of nearly five years in Guantanamo so he could tell his story. May it be studied in every school and college in Europe and the USA. May it help to close down all the illegal and secret prisons and camps, as well as Guantanamo, and restore the prisoners to their families. I am sure Murat's book will educate a whole generation about justice and the defense of human rights.

To many people around the world, the prison camp at Guantanamo has become a symbol of American violation of international law. During his election campaign, Barak Obama promised he would close Guantanamo within a year; however, the United States Congress refused to provide funds to close the camp. As of this writing approximately 250 prisoners – never tried, never found guilty – are still held there. Molly wrote about Kurnaz's book,

> One of the torture treatments that disgusted me was one I shared in class: prisoners were hung up by their wrists from ceiling rafters for hours and for days; they would only be let down so that doctors could check to see

> if they were still living and if they were, the prisoners would be raised up back into the rafters. Much like Nazi doctors, the doctors at Guantanamo used the prisoners as experiments. Prisoners were even tortured and beaten into admitting to being a terrorist, and then for admitting to it they were beaten and tortured more. Originally I picked this book out because I thought it would be interesting to look at the reactions of the innocent who were accused of being terrorists, just as another point of view in war, but I didn't know I would be so interested in Kurnaz's story. I also learned that most of the prisoners in Guantanamo were nowhere near terrorists. In fact most were victims of the United States paying bounties to countries for people that they could use in the media to pretend that they were capturing terrorists. I would definitely recommend this book to those who are pro and anti-war. How can this cruelty be humane and legal?

Responding to the autobiography future secondary teacher Carly Fracano said,

> It is interesting that the majority of secondary students would recognize the name "Guantanamo" without knowing what actually happens there. I think this is another way in which the media and Hollywood have provided a diluted version of such an important issue.

This discussion of "terrorism" is relevant to the literature emerging from the Afghan and Iraq Wars discussed in this chapter as well as Chapter 6 and to the Israel–Palestine conflict in Chapter 7, as well as to examination of the news, popular culture, and current politics.

Teaching Literature from Afghanistan and Iraq

From *The Red Badge of Courage* to Mark Twain's "War Prayer," from Wilfred Owen's "Dulce et Decorum Est," to *All Quiet on the Western Front*, from *Hiroshima* to *The Diary of Anne Frank*, teaching the literature of war has been for generations an important part of the curriculum. In *Illumination Rounds: Teaching The Literature of the Vietnam War*, a book written in 1992, 17 years after the Vietnam conflict ended, Larry Johannessen writes, "I have been amazed by students' interest in the war and the lack of knowledge about it, and I have been equally amazed by how what little they think they know is so distorted" (1).

Johannessen's experience teaching the literature of the Vietnam War squares with my experience teaching the literature of the – then still ongoing – wars in Afghanistan and Iraq. My students have been fascinated to learn about the experience of American soldiers, and having several soldiers speak in class was one of the highlights of the semester. "By far, my favorite set of speakers to date," said Heather Winowiecki. Students were engaged by delving into the variety of literature, autobiography, film, and online materials that address not only the experience of American soldiers, but also, and importantly, the experience of the citizens of Afghanistan and Iraq. My students have been confused, as many Americans, about some of the most basic information about these wars. When we talked in class (in 2009) before the unit about what we knew about the Iraq War, I asked, "How many students in this class believe that there was some kind of link between Saddam Hussein and 9/11?" Fully half of the class raised their hands.

Part of student confusion about wars in the Middle East is the way that these wars are portrayed in popular culture. One of the most important mediums addressing war is video games. My graduate student Andrew Taylor gave a presentation for secondary teachers at the 2010 NCTE conference on a panel I organized on the theme of teaching about terrorism. Andrew spoke specifically about the game Call of Duty, Modern Warfare Series. Call of Duty is one of the most popular video games in the world, by 2009 surpassing 55 million units and $3 billion in retail sales. Nearly all of the 40 or so secondary teachers at the presentation indicated that they had students who played this game. Andrew argued that Call of Duty is one of the most culturally visible texts on terrorism and that it should be critically examined in schools along with other texts about war. He suggested that, like literary works, video games have plot, setting, characters, and dialogue and that the tools of literary analysis can and should be brought to video games. Andrew pointed out that video games also call for a medium specific analysis that looks closely at their powerful immersive quality and the fact that in the game the player kills others, but when shot or even killed himself, is able to be resurrected and returned to battle and move to higher levels in the game. Andrew said that, "The only solution (if any solution is suggested) to terrorism in these worlds is violence. Often protagonists must murder thousands of innocents for the greater good. Students might compare the game's plot to other works on terrorism and the reality of the War on Terror."

He also described a "hidden narrative:"

> Beneath the game's exterior, the mechanics of game play tell another (potentially unintended) story. Terrorist-occupied locations (including the Middle East) are a shooting gallery with black-and-white morality. And counter-terrorism operatives are hardy, one-man death squads fighting an army of toy soldiers.

Andrew showed us fascinating clips from YouTube that recorded the game play in Call of Duty that teachers could use with their students (www.youtube.com/watch?v=lMkl6g7sCHE and www.youtube.com/watch?v=xAscuD4loh8). The second clip was from a helicopter gun ship that the player pilots in the game and fires at ground targets. Andrew then showed us a portion of a U.S. military video also found on YouTube, made available by Wikileaks, and titled "Collateral Murder"(www.youtube.com/watch?v=5rXPrfnU3G0, also at www.collateral murder.com) This video clip is actual footage and recorded dialogue of American soldiers in an Apache helicopter on July 12, 2007 firing on and killing Iraqi citizens including a Reuters reporter and children in a van. Much about this juxtaposition was disturbing. It was shocking to move from fictive killing in a video game to actual killing in the real helicopter recording. The video game was clearly a distorted version of war, yet the actual footage was also a distortion. In the footage the soldiers were so distanced by their overwhelming technology and fire-power that their actions and chatter, including congratulating each other on "good shooting," made what they were doing look and sound like a game – and profoundly dehumanized the people they killed.

From either perspective, our students must learn that *war is not a video game.* Clearly, bringing video games like Call of Duty into the curriculum and analyzing those games thoughtfully, both in terms of what they do and don't depict about war raises relevant and important questions. These games and the American military video lead us to ask about how citizens of the U.S. learn about and understand war; how the Iraq and Afghan wars are actually fought; the effects on Iraqis and Americans; and why such violent events are taking place.

This war is close to my students and it is critical that they come to recognize its real world consequences. Teaching in a working-/middle-class university, when I ask my students how many know someone – either a family member or a friend – who has served in the Armed Forces in Afghanistan or Iraq, nearly every student puts his or her hand in the air. Indeed, some of my students are returning war veterans. Matt, recently returned from Iraq, was still haunted by the experience. He told me about how in Iraq he could only leave his base at night, how he had sent a fellow soldier to a town where that soldier was hit and killed by a random rocket. Matt himself had shot and killed insurgents. He told me he was having a hard time making the return to civilian life. He missed several classes to be with a friend, another soldier who was going through depression. Matt felt out of place among the other students who were, in fact, his age or only a couple of years younger. As the semester came to a close it was hard for Matt to finish the work for my class. Finding himself alienated from school and life back home, he decided to drop out of college and re-enlist.

The experience of American troops in these wars, and the representations of their experience, present important topics for teachers to address, and there is a wealth of engaging materials that will allow us to do so. There are an increasing number of compelling accounts by soldiers and journalists about their experiences in the invasions and occupations. Some of these accounts focus on the rigors of battle – such as *Black Hawk Down* (during the American occupation of Somalia in 1993) or *Generation Kill* described below. Others look at more solid perspectives on occupation and war crimes such as *What Was Asked of Us: An Oral History of the Iraq War by the Soldiers Who Fought It* by Trish Wood or *Winter Soldier: Iraq and Afghanistan: Eyewitness Accounts of the Occupations* written by members of the Iraq Veterans Against War. For younger students from middle school to high school an excellent choice is the novel *Sunrise over Fallujah* (2008, 300 pages, age 13–17) by the outstanding young adult fiction writer Walter Dean Myers. My student and future secondary teacher Virginia Shedd describes the work:

> *Sunrise Over Fallujah* portrays a young soldier's coming of age in the current Iraq War. Robin encounters battle, and Myers describes piles of body bags, soldiers killing and being killed, soldiers being dismembered, even attempted rape. He provides a pretty clear picture for adolescents, but not in such a graphic way that it will cause controversy as a school reading. It is a toned-down-yet-realistic picture of what soldiers encounter.
>
> Through Robin, Myers brings to light issues young people likely to be enlisting in the near future may not have considered, issues that aren't often discussed with adolescents, especially by recruiters. Robin is dedicated to his country and his job, but he is conflicted because he now sees that war isn't as cut and dry as he imagined. It's difficult to tell the good guys from the bad guys. He wants to feel safe and protect his fellow soldiers, but really doesn't want to kill anyone. He is often scared and sometimes cries. He doesn't always understand the U.S.'s policies or logic . . . Robin serves with women, blacks, whites, Hispanics, young people, older people. And while the U.S. soldiers are primarily presented in a positive light, those who condemn all Iraqis are disliked by other soldiers. Those who seem to enjoy war are, through tone and imagery, presented in a somewhat negative light.
>
> The book gives adolescents an idea of the plight of Iraqi citizens; the myriad tribes and factions present there, the local violence, lack of hospitals and drinking water. It shows how the soldiers help the people as well as how the invasion has brought strife to the area. It would be a great book to use in a literature class, current events class, or social studies class for high schoolers or beginning college students.

In 2006 one of my literature classes studied, along with more traditional works, the poetry of contemporary American soldiers and their families, found in digital form on sites such as the League of American Poets, Author's Den, War Poets.co.uk, and Poets Against War. (Rozema and Webb, 12–14) The fact that much of this poetry was absolutely contemporary, written in the last few weeks or months before our class, and dealing with immediate and vital personal issues and experiences relevant to a war that was under way, made the study of poetry more relevant than usual. It would simply not be possible to find this kind of material in even the most recent literature textbook or anthology. From the poetry we turned to soldier's blogs. The students found these sites and shared them with the rest of the class. The blogs represented a great variety of points of view on the war, but all were certainly current. Some included photographs and short videos. My student Sara Keeler recommends a published collection of solider blogs by Matthew Burden, describing the difficulties soldiers face yet supportive of

American policy, *The Blog of War: Front-Line Dispatches from Soldiers in Iraq and Afghanistan*:

> It's definitely heart wrenching. Hearing what the soldiers have to say about different topics such as living conditions in their FOBs (forward operating bases), their feelings on the Iraq War and Bush, their reactions to and interactions with the Iraqis, and how they feel about what they are doing in the Middle East . . . One of the most memorable to me would be one that talked about the first democratic elections that took place in Iraq. The viewpoint of this particular soldier was inspiring, and his experience with the Iraqis really makes you think about what we are doing and why we are there.

FIGURE 5.3 American Soldier in Iraq (2008)

An important question for teachers and students to ask about soldiers' blogs, including this collection, is were they written under "registration orders" or subject to "operational security" and thus their authors limited or prohibited from writing critically about the U.S. military or mission?

Teachers and students who want to better understand the Iraq War will find many excellent resources. One useful book is Phyllis Bennis' *Ending the Iraq War: A Primer* (2009, 203 pages, age 16–college). The text is as much about the historical background, reasons for and conduct of the war, and implications for the region as it is about ending it – so it will remain a useful resource. Bennis structures the book around a series of simple and important questions such as: "Didn't the Iraqis want the U.S. to overthrow Saddam Hussein?" "What are the costs of War for Iraq and the Iraqis?" "Does the Iraq War make us safer against terrorist attacks?" "How does the Iraq War effect global terrorism?" etc. For those who wish to understand the high level strategies for the occupation of Iraq, the Academy Award winning documentary film *No End in Sight: Iraq's Descent into Chaos* directed by Charles Ferguson is an exposé of mistakes made by the American civilian and military command narrated in their own words. Ferguson has followed the film with an extensive volume of source materials and analysis.

It is valuable for students to develop their critical thinking by examining contradictory perspectives, perhaps especially when they go beyond American soldiers' experience and toward perspectives of people from the region. A powerful discussion took place in my class when my student Andrew Parent drew our attention to the Al Jazeera news service website in English (www.aljazeera.com). Just as with any close reading assignment we began to compare different versions of the same news story. Treating the stories as digital texts, the students studied the language of three different online news stories. We were astounded by the dramatic differences in perspective and word choice.

As it so happened, the day we were comparing sites, a lead news item was a horrific story reported by *Al Jazeera* ("11 U.S. Soldiers Court-Martialed for Crimes in Iraq."), the *BBC* ("Court Martial in Iraq Rape Case."), and *CNN* ("Four U.S. Soldiers Charged with Rape and Murder") about the assault, rape, and murder of an Iraqi girl, her parents and her five-year-old sister by a group of American soldiers. I asked the students what differences they could find in the different versions of the events. Looking at the details of the language one student noticed that while the *CNN* article stated that there was "confusion about the girl's age," "A Justice Department affidavit in the case against Green says investigators estimated her age at about 25, while the U.S. military said she was 20." However, the *Al Jazeera* report provided a photograph of the girl's identity card showing her age as 14. "How does the different information about the girl's age affect our sense of the crime?" this student asked. Another student noticed that information in the *BBC* report provided "explanation" for the soldiers' rape and murder, and "blaming it on the Iraqis" by mentioning that the soldiers were suffering "intense combat stress . . . left demoralized and emotionally drained by frequent insurgent attacks." The student noticed that even though 11 American soldiers took part or were present at the event, the *CNN* report seemed to blame just one soldier with "an anti-social personality disorder." On the other hand the *Al Jazeera* site quotes the Association of Muslim Scholars "an influential Sunni organization in Iraq" as issuing "a strong condemnation over the rape of the Iraqi girl and the brutal killing of her family by U.S. troops," referring to the Americans as "invaders," and claiming that the rape and killing, "show the truth of the ugly American face and shows that their claims of supporting humanity and liberation are false."

The close reading of detail, word choice, and nuance of meaning of our previous comparative study of poetry was directly transported to our examination of the language of these online news reports. The Internet was making possible the inclusion of texts, information, and news sources not usually available to students or in the classroom. In this case the class was able to study information from an Arabic news source and point of view and, by comparing it to American and British sources, raise basic and important questions about the information they customarily receive through more traditional media. Of course our class discussed potential bias on all sides, why *Al Jazeera* might want to quote the Association of Muslim Scholars and why such a quote and words for the Americans such as "invaders" might not be found in the *CNN* and *BBC* reports. But it was the inclusion of the *Al Jazeera* reporting that most prodded students to think critically about the language and detail of media coverage of the war and how U.S. actions might look different to other people around the world.

Moving beyond a focus on American and coalition soldiers and toward the experience of Afghan and Iraqi citizens is critical if we are serious about having our students understand the Middle East. Such a move isn't always easy, especially when there is such a flood of American perspectives, and finding Middle Eastern perspectives requires research.

A step in this direction, again one that will appeal to and raise important questions for younger students, is the young adult novel *Under the Persimmon Tree* (2005, 288 pages, age 12–14) set in Afghanistan at the time of the American invasion in 2001. This book is not an indigenous perspective, but the author Suzanne Fisher Staples, an American who worked for UPI (United Press International) and U.S. AID in the region, narrates the terror caused to civilians both by the Taliban and by the American bombing. My student Diane Hall describes *Under the Persimmon Tree* as,

> primarily about two characters, Nusrat and Najmah. Najmah is a young shepherd girl in Afghanistan and Nusrat is an American woman who converted to Islam, married an Afghani doctor and moved with her husband to Pakistan. The story takes place just after 9/11. Najmah's father

> and oldest brother are taken by the Taliban and forced to fight. Her mother and newborn brother are killed shortly after her brother and father are taken by a bomb that hits their house. Najmah makes a long dangerous journey to a refugee camp in Pakistan and eventually meets Nusrat.

Under the Persimmon Tree is a good choice to help younger students understand the impact of the war in Afghanistan and the mixed reception that coalition troops experienced there.

There are also works that can help provide historical and cultural background to the conflicts. Afghanistan has become known to Americans through two popular works, the best-selling novel *The Kite Runner* (2004, 400 pages, age 15–college), by Khaled Hosseini and the film *Charlie Wilson's War* directed by Mike Nichols and staring Tom Hanks – both works set before the American invasion in 2001. *The Kite Runner* has also been made into a popular film directed by Mark Foster. A compelling story about the relationship between an elite Pashtun boy and a poor Hazara boy, presumably the son of his father's servant, though we eventually discover the boys are half brothers, *The Kite Runner* may well be the most taught contemporary work from the region and it certainly engages reader interest as my student Dan Brim confirms,

> This book is, so far, beyond fantastic, and is quickly becoming one of my favorites. If I'm in another class, I'm thinking about this book – if I'm hanging out with my friends, I catch myself wondering what's going to happen next. I find myself having to take breaks after each chapter to deliberate the intended meaning of certain passages, as well as taking a break emotionally because the story has the tendency to become quite heart wrenching.

Secondary teachers who want to use this novel are supported by the recent National Council of the Teachers of English publication, *Middle Ground: Exploring Selected Literature From and About the Middle East* by Finkle and Lilly, which has a chapter on the novel that provides lesson plans, discussion questions, and assignments. I applaud the fact that novel and film have fostered interest in Afghanistan and the author Khaled Hosseini has developed a foundation to support important humanitarian causes in the country. At the same time I recognize that as cultural and historical background, the novel and film are only partly helpful. They certainly portray the oppressive Taliban regime at its most extreme as sadistic, engaging in pedophilia and drug abuse. There is little subtlety about the portrayal of life before the Taliban, which comes across as longing to return to a lost world of childhood. Perhaps that is not surprising considering that the author was the child of an enormously privileged family that appears in the novel to lead an American lifestyle including driving around Kabul in a Ford Mustang. In fact, this American connection may be part of the appeal of the novel to American readers – they can identify with this Americanized family. Hosseini only spent eight years of his childhood in Afghanistan, growing up instead in Paris, France, and San Jose, California. Perhaps this explains the nostalgic childhood portrayed and the lack of attention to the full story of the Russian presence in the country, the role of America and Saudi Arabia in arming the mujahideen (creating the Taliban) and welcoming them to power. Hosseini's second novel, *A Thousand*

BOX 5.3 COUNTING DEATHS IN THE IRAQ WAR

Any death in any conflict or war is tragic. Counting them up, whether the number is small or large, can trivialize the human impact of any one death. Yet it is important to have some idea of the toll of war. We have precise information about the numbers of Americans and coalition soldiers that have died, as of this writing over 4,000 in Iraq and over 2,000 in Afghanistan. Those tragic numbers are frequently in the news. However, there is scant attention in the mainstream media to the number of Iraqis killed as a result of the 2003 American-led invasion. Different sources come up with widely varying numbers. The American Department of Defense has not released a composite estimate of Iraqi civilian deaths during "Operation Freedom." The Iraq Body Count Project uses reports from English-language news media, NGO-based reports, and official English language records to assert that (as of July 2011) the number is between 101,000 and 110,000. Yet a study by Burnham et al. published in the prestigious medical journal *The Lancet*, estimated that over 600,000 Iraqis had been killed as a result of the invasion as of July 2006. In 2007, Opinion Research Business, an independent polling agency located in London, published the number 1.2 million as the total number of war casualties ("More than 1,000,000 Iraqis murdered"). Certainly many Iraqis have died since 2006 or 2007. Clearly, a relevant question is how deaths are counted, and which deaths are attributed to the conflict. Is a death resulting from the invasion counted only when it results from direct violence, or should deaths from disease, malnutrition, and chemical pollution caused by the war also be counted? What about deaths from civil unrest? What about refugees? The UN indicates that 5 million Iraqis have fled their homes during the war, but that number, too, is surely hard to verify. In putting the war in perspective, it matters, doesn't it, whether the number of the dead is 100,000, or 12 times greater, 1,200,000? As students attempt to understand the death and suffering in the Iraq and Afghan wars, they should be invited to look into these numbers and consider both the politics and the human suffering they involve.

Splendid Suns (2007, 372 pages, age 15–college) does a better job describing both the oppression of women by the Taliban and the opportunities for women under the socialist and Soviet periods, and ends soon after the American-led attack against the Taliban. It is based on interviews Hosseini conducted on his first return to Afghanistan after twenty-seven years, and after writing *The Kite Runner*. Both novels contain disturbing passages. After reading either novel students should learn more about America's role in the "covert" war against the socialist government in Afghanistan and the Russian troops that sustained it, and about the most current situation in the country. The film *Charlie Wilson's War* is also a valuable, though partial resource. Staring Tom Hanks and Julia Roberts the film purports to tell the true story of Texas congressman Charlie Wilson. Wilson is presented as a womanizer who is converted to passionate action to fight the soviets in Afghanistan after visiting an Afghan refugee camp in Pakistan (a scene actually filmed in Morocco). The terms of the film are simplistic: us vs. them Cold Warism. The CIA program Wilson helped foster became one of the longest and most expensive in American history. The U.S. government spent, and convinced Saudi Arabia to match, billions of dollars on arms and the insurgency that funded the mujahideen (including Osama bin Laden) and drove out the Russians but also entailed the death of hundreds of thousands of Afghans and the creation of 7 million displaced refugees. The powerful conclusion of the film, where the American congress refuses to fund rebuilding the country after fostering this kind of devastation, sets the stage for the tragedy of the Taliban and 9/11, and makes the film an important contribution to understanding the background to the more recent Afghan War. It is tempting to ask what would have happened in Afghanistan had American not intervened in the first place.

Especially when addressing controversy, I believe it is important for students to encounter a variety of opinions about the topics they are exploring. Sometimes students are able to bring forward important material for the whole class. In one of the introductory literature courses I taught about the Middle East, students wanted to explore the justification for invading Iraq that Saddam Hussein was such a ferocious dictator that he had to be removed from power. To begin this we read, at Katie's suggestion, the memoir, *Escape from Saddam: The Incredible True Story of One Man's Journey to Freedom* by Lewis Alsamari (2008, 320 pages, age 15–college), a book that tells the story of a young man drafted in to the Iraqi army in 1994. The brutality of the Iraqi military intelligence is shown from the inside, and the majority of the text describes the author's perilous journey to escape the country. On her blog Katie stated,

> Lewis (Sarmed) Alsamari's *Escape From Saddam* tells of his endurance of tyranny, and struggle to escape it and paints a dark and contrasting picture of what life is like when a dictator rules a country while the rest of the world stands by idly . . . Through his story a strong case for American intervention can be made.

Later Katie adds,

> In *Escape from Saddam* at the end . . . Sarmed talks about the U.S. invasion of Iraq and says that though he is happy to see Saddam's reign come to an end, he knows the U.S. had ulterior motives for their invasion. I believe it would be naive to say that we invaded solely on the grounds of protecting human rights.

Considering life under the Saddam Hussein's dictatorship is appropriate to studying the Iraq War, and doing so can raise questions about the appropriate response of the world community to despotism.

From looking at conditions in Iraq before the American invasion it makes sense to look at literature from Iraq during the occupation and insurgency and doing so is a natural and relevant part of reading Middle Eastern literature. To explore Iraqi perspectives teachers and students can look at the new collection of short works in the anthology *Contemporary Iraqi Fiction* (2008, 202 pages, age 16–college) edited by Shakir Mustafa. Younger students may find inspiring *Thura's Diary: My Life in Wartime Iraq* (2004, 112 pages, age 12–17), by Thura Al-Windawi. A non-fiction work, *City of Widows: An Iraqi Woman's Account of War and Resistance* (2007, 160 pages, age 16–college) by Haifa Zangana offers a more mature perspective we don't often hear. Blogs have been a vital way for ordinary Iraqis to express their perceptions of the occupation and two books published from blogs and written under pseudonyms are high interest, educational, and appealing to students: *Salam Pax: The Clandestine Diary of an Ordinary Iraqi* (2003, 288 pages, age 16–college) and *Baghdad Burning: Girl Blog from Iraq* (2005, 303 pages, age 14–college) by Riverbend. All of these works can be excerpted for class reading and discussion. Two excellent films can make important connections with young people in Iraq. In *The Boys from Baghdad High* four high school students in Baghdad were given video cameras by *BBC* and told to film their lives – with powerful results (shown on and available through *HBO*). *Heavy Metal in Baghdad* is a long-term study of a heavy metal group before and after the American invasion – allows students to make a connection to Iraqis and see consequences of occupation (nine parts, www.youtube.com/watch?v=QTJ1Ki4OM-g).

I shared with my students a powerful series of three five-minute 2008 YouTube clips titled "Baghdad Five Years On" created by British *Guardian* newspaper reporter Ghaith Abdul-Ahad that portray contemporary life in Iraq as a result of the American occupation. The first clip, "City of Walls," examines the division of Baghdad neighborhoods into sectarian ghettos, the loss of basic services, and the degradation of everyday life. (www.youtube.com/watch?v=TTMp-YNaDdg). The second clip, "Killing Fields," show the effects on Iraqis of the deaths created by the war, and includes interviews with grieving parents and visits to grave sites. (www.youtube.com/watch?v=Woxu5dwCSX0&NR=1). The third clip, "Iraqis Lost Generation", is about the experience of children in

Baghdad, including the homeless and orphans created by the war. We see one boy crying about the death of his father. We see a charity school and the frightened and hardening attitudes of the children toward America. (www.youtube.com/watch?v=GRA3QdvY9rQ&NR=1). The series was extended and updated in 2009 (www.guardian.co.uk/world/series/baghdad?intcmp=239). These clips humanize the suffering of the people of Iraq and, from a teaching standpoint, are important to pair with any of the other materials on war, including the video games and American military footage "Collateral Murder" released by Wikileaks.

Teaching the history of European and American involvement in the Middle East addresses a central topic of life in the region, a topic that brings up issues that are, from the perspective of our students, both familiar and far away. Recently I realized that the entire time my students have been in high school and college their country has been at war in Afghanistan and Iraq. I posed a question to several classes of college seniors: during all of this time you have been in school and our country has been at war have you had, in any of your high school or college classes, significant time devoted to addressing those conflicts or understanding the perspective of people in the region? Sometimes one or two students raise their hands, and mention a social studies class in high school. Often no student indicates that they have experienced any such study. Certainly, I have not yet had a student indicate that reading literature from the Middle East was part of one of their literature classes. I believe this should profoundly concern us. Should our country be *at war* and the topic never, or almost never, come up in school? Isn't the most fundamental purpose of our educational system, and especially of our classes in English and social studies, to prepare students for democratic citizenship? How can schools and universities perform that function if the major events in the world where their own country is the primary actor are not addressed in the curriculum?

Further Reading

Translated from Persian, *Journey to Heading 270 Degrees* (2006, 180 pages, age 16–college) by Ahmad Dehqan is one of the most popular novels in Iran about the Iran–Iraq War (1980–88). The memoir-like novel uses spare language to narrate the brutal violence of the front lines, the camaraderie of the troops, and the impact on soldiers, family, and friends. Students who are intrigued by war fiction will find an Iranian perspective interesting to compare.

The Breadwinner by Deborah Ellis (2001, 170 pages, age 10–13). Written before the 9/11 attacks, this engaging young adult novel describes life in Kabul for an educated family under the oppression of the Taliban. A young girl, Parvana, must dress as a boy so she can go into the street and help her family survive. The role of the United States in bringing the Taliban to power is not addressed. Compare to the disturbing *Osama*, the first film produced in Afghanistan after the fall of the Taliban in 2003.

Inside Fallujah: The Unembedded Story (350 pages, age 16–college, 2009) is an account of one of the bloodiest battles in the Iraq War written by an Egyptian journalist, Ahmed Mansour, who was in the city during a an American bombing of residential neighborhoods resulting in many civilian causalities. It provides a counter perspective to that of journalists embedded with American troops.

In Brian K. Vaughan's graphic novel *Pride of Baghdad* (2006, 130 pages, age 16–college), four lions – Zill, Safa, Noor, and Ali – escape from the Baghdad Zoo after an American bombing in 2003. While this novel is actually based on a true story of a pride of lions being freed from the Baghdad Zoo during an American bombing, the story is also quite metaphorical to the culture and experiences of the Iraqi people, living in a continuous state of war and change. (Amanda France) Contains violence and sexuality.

In *Generation Kill* (2004, 380 pages, age 16–college) an embedded journalist – Evan Wright – writes about the experience of reconnaissance Marines at the spearhead of the 2003 Iraq invasion. Cited by soldiers as an accurate portrayal and used by HBO to design a TV mini series, the book illustrates the challenges American soldiers had distinguishing innocent Iraqis from combatants, questions the competence of leaders and commands, and the challenges and camaraderie of ground warfare from the viewpoint of American troops. My students found the account compelling and it generated discussion about the nature of warfare in the Middle East.

6

EMBEDDED

Teaching the Iraq War

Jeffrey A. Patterson[1]

A Starting Point

The husband of one of my grade 12 English students (aged 17–18 years) recently witnessed a fellow soldier stationed in Iraq shot in the head by a sniper. My student brought this up during a class discussion about the war – her husband told her the story the night before, while they were talking to each other on Skype. I knew that Stacy's husband was serving in Iraq, along with the husband of Jen, another student in the same class. Stacy had mentioned her husband's military assignment at the beginning of the school year, and, at that time in September, I asked her how her husband described being in Iraq. Josh had told Stacy that the situation wasn't as bad as it had been in the past, that soldiers were now just "cleaning things up" and "getting people back home." Stacy told me that she had found comfort in his assurances. Now, for Stacy, the sniper story had changed things.

Stacy and Jen are seventeen years old and students in the alternative school where I teach English in a small town in south west Michigan. Students attend our school for a variety of reasons: some have been expelled from their traditional school; some are transitioning from being home-schooled, some attend because they didn't fit in at their previous school; and some come to our school because they've heard good things – energetic caring staff, small numbers of students per classroom, and creative teaching methods for non-traditional learners. So we have an interesting mix of students: an honor student from a small rural school who has been expelled for having weed in his locker, sitting next to a sub-literate gang member from a large semi-urban school expelled for hitting a teacher, sitting next to a shy, formerly home-schooled girl who has been sort of bug-eyed since opening day, but is now starting to find that these people actually have thoughts and values in common with her. Some are teen parents; a small number like Stacy and Beth are already married, to husbands the same age or only a year or two older. The young people

FIGURE 6.1 Recruiting Officer Helps High School Student

in my classes are frequently recruited to join the military, and often they do, as options like attending college or finding a high paying job are remote.

Because of the heavy military recruiting at my school, I have become increasingly concerned about the war in Iraq and conflicts in the Middle East, about the impact it has on Iraqis, on America's image in the world, and the impact on my students, their family, and friends who are serving there. So precisely because I am dedicated to exceeding state standards, rigorous education, and serious student engagement with reading and writing, I decided this last year to put our traditional textbook on the shelf for a while, and start with a new unit addressing literature from the war in Iraq.

Still I wasn't sure how to respond to the heightened fear that Stacy was experiencing, and the powerful realities she was helping the other students attend to. What is the right way to deal with these traumatic feelings in the classroom? I was prepared to teach a lesson on war, but I had been thinking of war in some measure in an abstract sense – war as literature. I was prepared to push my own agenda and call for tolerance and understanding, but this incident left me at a loss. What was I going to teach these girls, and the rest of my students, about what was happening on the other side of the world that was, at the same time, so connected to them and their isolated, but not so sheltered, lives in middle America?

Further, this event forced me to acknowledge my limited knowledge of the situation in Iraq. I was prepared to walk the students through *Sunrise Over Fallujah*, a young adult novel written by Walter Dean Myers about a young soldier's experiences in Iraq. The novel showed us that some of America's soldiers in Iraq are scared and confused, and that war is bad, often unnecessary – the novel is a fine example of the kind of war literature we should be teaching today. But even still, the time we had together in this class was precious and the need to address the topic urgent. Once the subject was opened, students wanted to find answers: why were we there? Is the war worth the staggering amount of debt and deaths? The reality check that Stacy was giving us meant I needed to rethink my approach to dealing with the conflict in my classroom. We just couldn't simply read a couple of books and move on to the next topic.

I realized that I was not capable of being the one with all the answers in this class; I decided that we would need to engage in research together. As a class, we set out to develop a better understanding of the situation in Iraq. The idea was to attack the topic from many different angles. Students would become experts in their chosen area. For example, the two military wives expressed an interest in researching the effect of war on the soldiers; another student wanted to examine stereotypes of Iraqis; another wanted to research war profiteers. I discovered that some students – students who had lost interest in traditional schooling – were in fact eager to investigate this issue that was in the news and touched some of their lives.

Sadly, not everyone was on board: the class seemed divided. There were more than a few students who didn't find relevance in researching the conflict in Iraq.

In fact, I soon discovered that they couldn't care less about the war. It didn't matter to them. The war was something that they were able to turn off whenever it was on television and shut it out of their mind. Or, if they did have an opinion about the conflict, it was something ignorant, along the lines of, as one student put it, "we should kill all the towel heads."

Some of my students see no problem in using a term like "towel head," or even worse, to describe a person from the Middle East. When I asked why students feel that it is OK to use terms like this, the response is often the same: they attacked us; we are at war. The more I pressed students to articulate reasons behind their views, the more I began to realize that many students had created or adopted a sort of mythology connecting to the little they know about the events of September 11, 2001. For many of my students the war and the current global situation could be summed up in one sentence: Saddam Hussein and Osama Bin Laden led a team of terrorists who were out to kill every American citizen. This mythology has perpetuated fear-based racism toward Arabs among many of my students.

What was also disconcerting was my realization that students are being raised in a culture where developing negative attitudes towards Arabs has become acceptable. In mainstream American media, Arabic people have been vilified. From movies, to video games, to comedy routines, Arabs continue to be presented in a negative light. Citizens of our country are being conditioned to fear, suspect, and even hate people from the Middle East.

I decided that the first step in this research project would be to confront stereotypes associated with Arabs. First, I gave a brief, open-ended survey about Arabs, 9/11, and the Middle East. The results were what I had expected. Students responded in the following ways:

> The girls wear veils and the men wear turbans.
>
> They look like dirty people.
>
> Women are treated like crap.
>
> They are short, have brown hair, talk with phlegm, and wear turbans.
>
> The Arabs, towel heads, Al-quida (sic), and Saddam Hussein were responsible for 9/11.

It was evident that the students knew close to nothing about Iraq or its people, even though our country has been involved in a war there since before some of them were born. It was clear that the students' preconceived ideas about the Middle East included an idea that Iraq is an emerging nation filled with primitive people. One student remarked that the citizens, "dressed like Aladdin." I had students generate a list of questions about the people of Iraq. Students had a variety of inquiries: Do they live in huts? How do they cook their food? What sort of sports do they play? What are their homes like? What kind of clothes do they wear? Their "prior knowledge" and simple questions made it evident that dismantling stereotypes should be the next step in our research process.

An Iraqi on YouTube

The first resource for dismantling stereotypes came from the Showtime series *This American Life*. Ira Glass heard the story of Haider Hamza, a former Iraqi citizen who travels the country and sets up a portable booth with a placard reading simply, "Talk to an Iraqi" – short clips my students could watch were available on YouTube (www.youtube.com/watch?v=GPEX0PnV-LU). In the clips, curious Americans approach Hamza's booth and have conversations with him. Watching Americans talk with Hamza, it quickly becomes evident that most American citizens, of all ages and backgrounds, know precious little about the people, politics, or daily lives of Iraqi citizens. My students are astounded to find that many Iraqis live in homes with possessions similar to their own: televisions, stereos, video game consoles, even Oprah's magazine.

In the segment, viewers see news reports from Hamza's life before and after United States occupation. They see Iraqi students at college, families relaxing at home, and female Iraqis with freedom and jobs – Hamza's mother was a software developer for twenty years. Even with this first step, my students' preconceived notions of life in the Middle East were beginning to crumble, and their responses to this clip were starting to become more thoughtful:

FIGURE 6.2 Talk to an Iraqi

> I learned that they lost jobs after the invasion, just like we are losing jobs. This could lead to crime and selling drugs. It's not their fault it's the government's fault.
>
> I thought that people in Iraq were different than us. He seemed calm. I was expecting an Iraqi to be angry. Americans are rude and they think that they know stuff that they don't.
>
> Maybe Iraqis aren't all that different from us. They're just trying to make it like we are.
>
> He is answering questions that the media isn't answering. It is brave of him to get outside of his comfort zone.
>
> I didn't know that women could get jobs. I also thought everyone in Iraq was raised to be in the war.
>
> They don't live in mud huts. We didn't see any camels. They have colleges.

Iraqi Blog

The second resource was a collection of blogs by the anonymous blogger, Riverbend. Riverbend was living in Baghdad during the 2003 U.S. invasion. She used her blog to vent her frustration and terror during that time, and also show her sense of humor. Students had the opportunity to see, again, the realities of life in Iraq. Riverbend listens to Nirvana, goes to the cinema to see American films, and even uses Google. After my students started to develop a real sense of life in Iraq, they were able to connect with the humor in a section of one of Riverbend's blogs. One blogger, commenting on one of Riverbend's posts, stated that she could not be an Iraqi because Iraqis didn't use computers or speak English (Riverbend, 6). The ignorance of the comment became a joke among my students, who were beginning to develop a more educated view of Iraqis. After reading blogs from Riverbend, students wrote the following responses:

> They don't have confidence in their government. She was antiwar. The war is draining her. I thought all Iraqis supported the war.
>
> Iraqis have computers and Google. I didn't think that they had technology, jobs, and clothes like we do.
>
> I didn't know that they had our music and movies over there. She said she listens to Nirvana.
>
> Riverbend is upset about her country being ruined. I would be, too if someone tried to take over America.

I could see that my students were starting to change their ideas about the people of Iraq. The citizens of Iraq went from a cross between Aladdin and a Hollywood terrorist, to someone with whom they might find life similarities, common interest, even agreement on a variety of social and political issues.

Recording and Organizing our Thinking

Along with the reading, writing, and viewing, in my class I had students videotaping themselves discussing their emerging knowledge about the situation in Iraq. At first the video sections were awkward, but after a while, continuing their discussions while the camera was running became almost second nature. My students were raised with technology and the idea that cameras are everywhere, at the convenience store, on the street corner, on the school bus, even in school hallways.

At the beginning of the first quarter, students were asked to look into the camera and explain what they know about the situation in Iraq and how it affects them. A majority of the students claimed that they didn't know much about the war in Iraq and that the events in the Middle East did not affect them. Of course, a few of the students had opinions:

> The economy is affected by the war and my dad has lost his job.
>
> I feel unsafe because of the war.
>
> The war affects me because gas prices keep going up.

As this process of filming continued, I noticed something that happens when students know that they are presenting for the video camera – they seem to take things more seriously. A student who may say something thoughtless or nonsensical during camera-less class discussion will take time and structure his remarks for film. One student, who is usually the class clown, became serious and focused while presenting for the camera. There is something about the permanence of video; they are on record and able to look into the mirror to see themselves saying something. I have found this makes students more thoughtful and articulate as they realize that they have a potential audience beyond their immediate group. Writing about the experience in front of the camera, students created the following responses:

> It will be good to see how much we changed.
>
> You get nervous, you start to get more stage ready. You prepare more because you don't want to sound stupid.
>
> Other people see this instead of informal conversation. We need to think about what we are saying.

As we moved forward, I realized that I needed to structure my student's research process, so I developed a class Ning in an effort to create a publicly accessible pool of research. The Ning emerged as a great resource for many reasons. A Ning is an enhanced social networking tool, so in this format students were able to communicate with me, and with each other, share a wide variety of writing, images, resources, and links. They can keep this information in a central location in cyberspace, where they – and anyone – can have access to it at any time. Plus, simply, my kids like technology, and the Ning, like the filming, was another way to capture their interest, develop their speaking, writing, and research abilities – and their confidence. (In 2010 Ning suspended its free service. Teachers could set up something similar where students could share writing using a wiki site, such as Wikispaces.)

Multigenre Research

When the class became more thoughtful in their perception of the conflict, some students started to investigate the situation outside of the classroom, on their own time. They returned to class armed with Internet-searched accounts of events, statistics, and graphs. Wikipedia was a source for information about events starting with the first Gulf War, September 11, then the second Gulf War. One student brought in a timeline. I was glad to see these beginnings, but it seemed to me that to really understand what is happening in Iraq and how it is affecting people, we needed to look past the typical maps and graphs. I wanted students to make connections to the people involved in the conflict.

After looking over the timelines and viewing the conflict from a historical perspective, the students were asked to choose individual texts to use as a start to their research. I didn't want them to simply regurgitate the Wikipedia information. I wanted them to find a way in for themselves and to take ownership of what they were studying. Multigenre research seemed like something that would help students explore the various issues related to the war in a way that would help them understand multiple perspectives on the issues. Students found texts that covered a variety of issues associated with Iraq, from the history of the region, to the food, to American soldiers' experiences in Iraq, to the story of a librarian in Baghdad trying to save her collection of books. They were supposed to read these choice texts and then present information to the group. We would be learning from one another, and becoming experts together.

I used the Melinda Putz book, *The Teachers Guide to the Multigenre Research Project*. In it, she recommends using FQI (facts, questions, and interpretations) sheets to organize research (Putz, 46). The sheets encourage students to cite their research in MLA format, list facts, develop questions, and decide upon an interpretation for the presentation of their new knowledge. Putz even has handouts that teachers can copy and give to students. I found that students enjoyed creating their own versions of these documents, instead of using the ones from the book. Students created FQI templates in Microsoft Word and were able to customize them to suit their needs. For each resource they found, students needed to develop an FQI sheet. This was met with some resistance at the beginning, but soon became second nature. I asked students about their FQI sheet:

> FQI helps to keep me focus on my topic instead of going outside of the topic.
>
> If you customize for yourself the research makes sense to you. It is more organized.
>
> I customized because it is easier to do it my way.

After a few weeks of accumulating research, and with the help of the FQI sheets, it seemed to me that students were beginning to develop a better understanding of the conflict in Iraq and to drop some of the stereotypes. They went from having little knowledge to asking crucial questions. Some were developing thoughtful opinions about issues associated with the conflict and class discussion became passionate and informed. Even those students who didn't often contribute couldn't resist. Students were asked to talk about their research for the camera:

> Since we've begun our project I've been wondering about the children. If the war is going on, how are they able to attend school? It doesn't seem like it would be safe. I wondered how their parents feel about that. I wouldn't want to attend school where there are bombs going off everywhere. Before America invaded, it seems like it was safer.
>
> I read today that President Obama and Russia want to prevent nuclear weapons from being developed in Iran. Why are our troops in Iraq if there are nuclear weapons in Iran? Isn't the reason that we are there because we wanted to get rid of weapons of mass destruction? Why don't we move the troops to Iran?
>
> I've been, personally, thinking about Iraq's history of warfare. Is the democracy that Bush wanted to establish going to last after we leave or will there be more war and it will just be blown away again?
>
> The women in Iraq are not as disrespected as we think they are. The women have more rights than I thought they did. They have struggled for their rights for a long time. But since America invaded, after the whole 9/11 situation, their rights have been moving backwards.
>
> I learned that a lot of people had the opportunity to leave Iraq when the war started, but they didn't go. And I wondered why they chose to stay. In my book, I read that some older people didn't want to move away, and that a grandmother was telling her grandchildren that the missiles were

coming, but it wasn't going to get any worse. But it did and then they couldn't leave. The Iraqis didn't think that America was going to ruin their cities and separate their families.

I learned that Saddam Hussein had a pretty solid grip on his country. They had good education and a solid infrastructure. He did some horrible things, but he was in no way related to Osama Bin Laden. In fact, Osama had openly stated that Saddam was an infidel, which is a major curse in their tongue. They were just not related to each other. So I wondered why we are in Iraq. It seems like an excuse to finish what Bush's father started.

I noticed students were starting to wonder about aspects of the conflict that they had never considered before. In only a few weeks they had gone from not knowing or even caring about Iraq, to becoming concerned, even angry. It was a small first step, but an important one in their understanding of one of the biggest issues that they, as American citizens, are currently facing. In the official State of Michigan Language Arts Standards and Content Expectations that my class is supposed to be following, English 12 students are asked to "identify and apply their leadership skills and prepare for responsible action as American citizens in the context of a global world" (Michigan). Looking back on the semester, I think my students were, in fact, meeting Michigan expectations, even if my curriculum may be unlike most other English 12 courses across the state. In my view, the task of the teacher is to prepare the next generation so that they can, in a thoughtful and informed way become responsible for the conduct of our nation. Tragically, the conflict in Iraq isn't going to end soon, perhaps not for decades. And others like it may also arise. Some might ask if a semester-long focus on literature of the Iraq War is appropriate. I have come to wonder the opposite. Is it responsible teaching for educators to avoid discussion of our nation's role in Iraq and the decisions that our leaders have made? Is it responsible to allow our students to accept falsehoods and stereotypes about Iraq, the Middle East, and its people?

During the last few weeks of school, I spoke with my English 12 students about our Iraq project. I would like to say that they were still deeply engaged in research and keeping up to date on current events in Iraq. This wasn't the case. For most, the Iraq semester was over and they had moved on to other things. Like yesterday's top story of *CNN*'s news cycle, Iraq was no longer the lead in the students' minds. Frankly, it wasn't in my mind either. Daily life had been keeping my thoughts away from the war and our project. Sadly, Jen and Stacy had both stopped attending school, figuring that the money their husbands were sending home from Iraq was enough to make a high school diploma unnecessary. Our Ning was sitting out there in cyberspace, untouched for some weeks. We had just finished *Frankenstein*. Graduation was days away. I was disheartened.

I called my cousin Amy, a special agent for the government who investigates fraud. She had recently returned from a two-year assignment in Iraq. During our semester of study, she had been a valuable resource. She had told horrific stories about how unsafe it was over there and the corrupt companies who were selling faux bulletproof vests and personnel carriers. Students had been captivated by her stories. I told her how I was feeling a little upset that the students didn't continue to stay up-to-date about the war. Amy told me that she sometimes feels the same way as my students. "You can't stay embedded 24/7, Jeff," she said over the phone, "It can begin to be too much. You need to find a balance."

And maybe that's what the Iraq unit was for the students that semester. We took a break from being distracted by classic novels, plays, and poetry and took a good hard look at something horrible that is actually happening in our world. We found a counterbalance to the distractions from a pop culture and mainstream media that encourages us to believe that everything is fine. And though it is important and relevant, it's hard to stare at something like that for a long time, maybe even harder if you're a teen with enough troubles of your own. I don't know. I want to believe that the students in English 12 left with a file of information from that semester stored in their brains, and when the time comes to make an informed choice or opinion about their world, that they can access those files and use the information stored there. On good days, I do.

Note

1. High school teacher Jeff Patterson describes how his curriculum changed to address the war in Iraq.

7

TEACHING THE ISRAEL–PALESTINE CONFLICT

The Israel–Palestine conflict is not only the most persistent problem in the Middle East, it is at the center in any discussion of terrorism or world peace. No issue creates greater misunderstanding between the Middle East and the "West" – particularly the United States. Remarkably different coverage of the conflict in the Middle Eastern vs. the Western and American media results in widely diverging perspectives. I don't think I can overstate the importance of the Palestinian humanitarian crisis to Arabs and other Middle Easterners. It is a central topic of news reports, documentaries, film, and literature in the region, and the public stances that government leaders take on the issue in many Middle Eastern countries determines the popularity of those leaders. I also don't think I can overstate the distortions, limitations, and confused information that circulate about the conflict. For these reasons I have taught classes on Middle Eastern literature that have begun with, or centered on, Israeli and Palestinian literature and film addressing the conflict. In so doing, I have brought multiple perspectives to bear, including Israeli literature and film as well as speakers who support a Zionist perspective. As you will see, however, my emphasis has been on Palestinian perspectives. I have taken this approach because teaching in the United States I have found my students less informed about and, frankly, less sympathetic to the situation of the Palestinians. Better knowledge of both sides is crucial to developing awareness and to supporting an end to the crisis. There is a great deal of quality, accessible, and engaging literature and film available that can help teachers and students take great strides in their understanding of the Israeli–Palestinian situation from the point of view of the participants.

At the turn of the nineteenth century, the region of the Ottoman Empire that is now Israel–Palestine was almost entirely Arab. Jewish immigration to Palestine grew under British colonial control (1922–1948), especially before, during, and

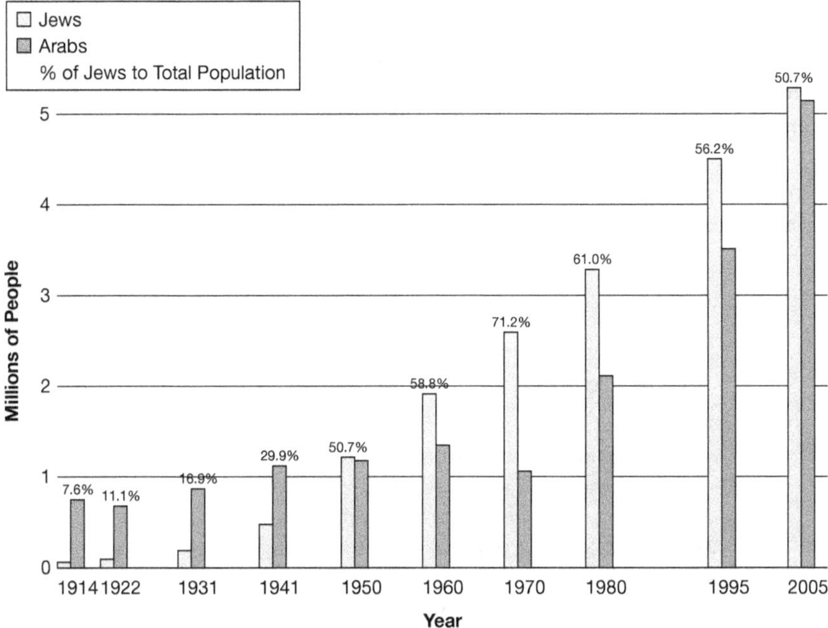

FIGURE 7.1 Population of Arabs and Jews in Palestine/Israel

after the Nazi Holocaust in Europe murdered 6 million Jews and many refugees and survivors fled to Israel. The Zionists fought against the British and, in 1948, David Ben-Gurion and a council of leaders declared the state of Israel. War broke out and the Jews, far better organized and equipped, defeated the Arabs. Over 700,000 Palestinians became refugees. Anti-Semitism, repression, and Zionism soon led to hundreds of thousands – perhaps a million – Jews throughout the Middle East moving to Israel. While many Palestinians were forced to leave their homes and Palestine altogether, high birth rates of those remaining both in Israel and in the occupied territories has led to the current near equivalence of Jewish and Arab populations (see Figure 7.1). This tense situation is constantly evolving through a series of failed unequal wars, attacks, confrontations, negotiations, and growing Israeli occupation and settlement.

America and Israel

Throughout the Middle East, and in much of the rest of the world, the action of Israel and Israeli citizens toward Palestinians is seen as expansionist, oppressive, violent, and contravening human rights. Yet, in Israel and America, Israel is often viewed as a David standing up against a much larger Arab Goliath, a small country surrounded by hostile nations and crazed Palestinians refusing to recognize Israel's right to exist and lobbing rockets at cities or blowing themselves up to kill civilians. Every aspect of the current situation and the history that led to it is contentious and, for good reasons, feelings run high on both sides. At the UN, America is often the only country in the world joining Israel when votes are held condemning Israeli policies.

Indeed, Israel is the largest recipient of American foreign aid, much of it military. Since 1949 conservative estimates of American aid to Israel are over $100 billion, with continuing aid of about $3 billion per year. (McArthur, 10) For these reasons

BOX 7.1 MILESTONES IN AMERICAN SUPPORT FOR ISRAEL

- 1947: The United States supports the UN resolution partitioning Palestine, giving the Zionist authorities control of 54 percent of the land – Jewish settlers are 1/3 of the population.
- 1948: War breaks out between the newly proclaimed state of Israel, and Egypt, Iraq, Jordan, and Syria, who had moved troops into Palestine to oppose the partition of Palestine. Over 700,000 Palestinians – two-thirds of the population – flee into exile in Lebanon, Jordan, Syria, Gaza, and the West Bank. Israel controls 77 percent of historic Palestine. America is the first country in the world to recognize the state of Israel.
- 1966: The United States under President Johnson sells Phantom jet bombers to Israel.
- 1967: Israel wins pre-emptive war against Egypt, Jordan, and Syria and takes control of the remaining 23 percent of historic Palestine (the West Bank, Gaza, Jerusalem, Sinai Peninsula, and Golan Heights).
- 1973: The United States carries out a strategic airlift of arms and supplies to Israel and provides extensive foreign aid.
- 1981: The Strategic Cooperation Agreement is signed between United States and Israel.
- 1982: Israel invades Lebanon and the United States vetoes a UN Arms Embargo on Israel.
- 1985: Creation of U.S.–Israel Joint Economic Development Group (JEDG).
- 2003: United States provides Israel with 9 billion in loan guarantees.
- 2006: United States weapons and jet fuel are used by Israel in an attack on Lebanon. In the UN Security Council the United States is the only country that opposes an immediate cease-fire.
- 2007: United States increases military aid to Israel by 25 percent.
- 2010: Half of all American foreign military financing ($2.8 billion) goes to Israel, along with 3 billion in unconditional loan guarantees.

America is not viewed in the Middle East as a neutral or even a balanced voice in the conflict. It is important for teachers to understand this situation and the attitudes that result.

There are Americans writers who have carefully researched the Israeli–Palestinian crisis and made substantial contributions to helping us understand it. For high school and university teachers who seek to develop a personal and historical sense of the Israel–Palestine conflict the text I most recommend is *The Lemon Tree: An Arab, A Jew, and the Heart of the Middle East* (2006, 340 pages, age 16–college) by the American documentary journalist Sandy Tolan. *The Lemon Tree* evolved from a National Public Radio presentation on "Fresh Air" and won many awards including being 2006 Booklist's "Editor's Choice" for best non-fiction book of the year. The book traces the lives and connections of a Palestinian family that is forced from its home in the town of Ramla in 1948 and the Jewish family from Bulgaria that ends up living in the same house. A readable, carefully balanced and well-documented account (80 pages of end notes and bibliography, 260 pages of text) takes the reader through the history of modern Israel and the Palestinian struggle as seen through the lives of both Jews and Arabs. Tolan has been a fellow at Harvard and Berkeley and is currently a professor at the Annenberg School for Communication and Journalism at the University of Southern California.

Another engaging resource that will provide university or secondary students with historical context are Joe Sacco's graphic novels. Though born in Malta and living his early years in Australia, Sacco is an American journalist and cartoonist from Portland, Oregon. In 1991–92 he made an extensive trip to Israel and the occupied territories from which emerged first as separate comics, but then, in 2001, the intriguing graphic novel *Palestine* (2002, 288, age 14–college) with an introduction by Edward Said. Self-consciously reflecting on his presence as an American in the conflicted area, Sacco, the narrator, talks extensively with Palestinians, learning about their daily lives, and through flashbacks, about the history of the conflict. Sacco's illustrations capture the destitution of the West Bank, Gaza, and refugee camps in a way that is still relevant and provides backdrop for works of Palestinian literature. Sacco understands that he is not a "neutral" observer, and he again uses the approach of serious comic book journalism in his extensive 2009 volume, *Footnotes in Gaza* (2010, 432 pages, age 16–college). I have read, taught, and published about a number of graphic novels, but next to Art Spiegleman's *Maus*, *Footnotes is Gaza* is the most powerful graphic text I have encountered. This graphic novel explores the history of two massacres of Palestinian refugees committed in 1956 by Israeli soldiers in small towns in the southern part of the Gaza strip. In 2002–03 Sacco undertook extensive research including talking to people present at the events, including Israeli soldiers and high-ranking Israeli officers as well as many aging Palestinians. Sacco is determined to find and tell the historical truth. We learn about his difficulties doing so as well as about the current situation (2002–03) of the Palestinians he speaks with.

The illustrations tell rich stories in themselves about the creation and evolution of Palestinian life in Gaza, perhaps the most densely populated place on earth and at the conflictive center of the crisis. This graphic novel is compelling, complex, and extensive, nearly 400 large-format pages. The volume becomes a reflection not just on the Israel–Palestine conflict, but on the nature of the memory of trauma and the challenge of understanding the past.

Teaching Palestinian Literature

My American students know very little about the experience of Palestinians. Perhaps the most important novel in the Palestinian literature unit in my introductory literature class was *Wild Thorns* (1999, 208 pages, age 15–college) by Sahar Khalifeh, an outstanding novelist living in the West Bank. While *Wild Thorns* captures life in the West Bank under Israeli occupation it is not a propaganda piece. It considers complexity on all sides and holds out hope for peace, reconciliation, and coexistence. *Wild Thorns* takes place in the town of Nablus and focuses on the Karmi family whose members have diverse experiences and viewpoints. There is Adil, seeking moderation and commuting across the border to work at a construction site in Israel against his father's wishes, and his beautiful sister Nuwar, secretly in love with a revolutionary. There is also Adil's brother Basil, a teenager who throws stones at Israeli soldiers and ends up in prison, and his cousin Usama, a sensitive boy who left the West Bank to work in the Gulf States but has returned determined to become a resistance fighter. Though set in the 1970s, the book portrays the challenges of everyday life in Palestine for decades, unemployment, military domination, travel through checkpoints, and the exodus of educated people. My students reacted on their blogs:

> I like the contrast between Adil and Usama: the difference in their opinions and ideals and how each thinks the other goes about fighting the occupation by the wrong means. Usama was a poet as a boy, he dies a poet, and in between he seems to have tried to convince himself he was another person, one without dreams and feelings. Adil was, I think, my favorite. He seemed at times to see past the propaganda of both the Jews and the Arabs. He was caught in the middle and trying to accomplish what he could and still maintain some understanding and dignity. And yet he drinks to forget his feelings of anger and injustice. I love the scene where he carries the Israeli child on his back with the weeping widow following him, all cultural taboos and barriers forgotten and broken. They are all just people grieving and struggling in a difficult time.
>
> *(Diane Hall)*

> As each chapter ended, the next one began in a completely new setting with a completely new event. At first, I found it a bit strange, then I realized

> the impact. Eventually I liked the way the novel jumped from story to story, greatly emphasizing the number of issues and hardships these people went through living under such intimidating conditions.
>
> *(Brian Lane)*

> One of the most significant parts of *Wild Thorns*, in my opinion, was the scene where Basil is arrested. There are children flooding the streets, yelling and laughing at the Jewish soldiers. They are screaming in protest to show their disgust at the occupation . . . There is absolutely no innocence left in Palestine, even the children are getting arrested. When Basil is taken off, his father is cold and shows no remorse or sadness that his son is in jail. He merely says, "But what came over the boy? Does he think he can free Palestine all by himself?" (Khalifeh 106).
>
> *(Molly Grube)*

> One thing I found very intriguing as I finished up *Wild Thorns* was the passion and love that several of the characters had for their country. Basil, for instance, illustrates a typical young man who is willing to do anything for his country. He gathers with his friends at the local cafe to discuss the politics and even risks going to prison to stand up for his beliefs. He quickly realizes, though, how much he doesn't understand and how naive he actually is. A lot of parallels can be drawn to American youth, and their response to the 9/11 attacks.
>
> *(Heather Winowiecki)*

Notice how the students explore characters. Developing a personal connection between students and individual characters was a starting point for attempting to cross the large cultural distances between Americans and Palestinians. Teachers can draw on this kind of personal connection fostered by literature to help develop a more comprehensive understanding of the situation. In this regard, Heather's comments turned out to be especially productive of discussion. As I mentioned in the last chapters, many of my students know people fighting in Iraq and Afghanistan, including friends and family members. Reading Sahar Khalifeh's *Wild Thorns*, Heather's blog post connects American young people after 9/11 and rebelling young Palestinians in the West Bank. As we discussed in class these Palestinians may be the very people that, without reading this novel, my students might have thought of as "terrorists." Identifying with characters was developing my students' understanding and building a bridge between American and Palestinian experiences.

While novels and the Internet provide rich resources for cross-cultural studies, shorter works can also be effective, and it may be easier to fit them into the curriculum. In the same class our understanding was enriched by contemporary Palestinian short stories. The evocative four-page story "Stealing

Away, We Returned" by Rasmi Abu Ali captures the experience of Palestinians sneaking back to their homes and olive groves after having been forced to leave (could be used from age 11 to college). My students responded to "Norma and the Snowman" by Yehia Yakhlaf, a story describing a university student who decides to join a group of Palestinian fighters (age 15–college). Both stories are found in Nur and Abdelwahab Elmessiri's *A Land of Stone and Thyme: An Anthology of Palestinian Short Stories* (1996). We also read the collection of short stories *Men in the Sun* (1999, 116 pages, age 14–college) by Ghassan Kanafani – a writer who emerged as the students' favorite. Kanafani's stories often concern the experience of Palestinian refugees and the long (60-page) title story is a disturbing tale of four Palestinian refugees seeking work in Kuwait. I won't give away the powerful ending, but Sara, Frankie, and Dan were compelled to comment:

> I was really surprised with this story. It begins with three different men: Abu Quais, Assad, and Marwan. All of them want to get to Kuwait for the same reason of finding work and getting opportunity so they can survive. Marwan has to support his mother and siblings, Abu Quais has a wife and two small children, and Assad was alone, but needed to find work. All three of them go to this man named Abul who helps smuggle people from Iraq into Kuwait for "the cheapest price" available. And then, they risk their lives crossing the desert with the sun beating down on them like fire, following this oil pipeline called "H4" to the road.
>
> *(Sara Keeler)*

> "Men In The Sun" gave me a whole new perspective on the world. This story's ending has left me in shock, and I feel as though there is this void that the story left empty on purpose. I really liked how the story gave all of its characters life through their memories . . . The characters made you feel their struggle and understand their reasons so well that I really did feel sad for them by the end, even Abul Khaizuran.
>
> *(Frankie Velazquez)*

> I'm sure I wasn't the only person to sit down and read this in an hour because I couldn't stop reading about halfway through it. Though the idea of smuggling workers and being utterly and totally poor in a barren land may be foreign to most of us in this class, the story was quite exciting, and it ended quickly and abruptly, with an echo in the dark desert nighttime sky.
>
> *(Dan Brim)*

Kanafani's other stories are also powerful, and students found the short "Tales of Sad Oranges" and "Letter from Gaza" especially meaningful. John Novak was so intrigued by Kanafani's writing that he went to the library and checked out another collection *Palestine's Children*, a work he strongly recommended. Kanafani was a Palestinian journalist, author, and activist. He and his niece were killed by a car bomb in Lebanon when he was thirty-six years old. Mossad, Israel's intelligence agency, has claimed responsibility for their deaths. Reading Middle Eastern authors will likely lead students to inquire about their lives, to understand a different world through the reader-author connection. Students inspired by Kanafani's writing will want to see Steven Spielberg's 2005 film, *Munich*, which explores the actions of Mossad at the time of the Kanafani killing (Tolan, 181). Nominated for five Academy Awards, including Best Picture, *Munich* offers another background to Kanafani's short stories.

Many Palestinian families are divided, some living in Palestine and others refugees or expatriates in Jordan and Lebanon or scattered throughout the region, with others in America or Europe. For high school or college students an excellent read is *West of Jordan* (2003, 232 pages, age 15–college) by the Palestinian American writer Laila Halaby. Narrated from the point of view of four female cousins: two in Los Angeles, one in the West Bank village of Nawara, and one who travels from Arizona to Nawara. We learn of the difficulties of life under occupation and the challenges facing young women caught between traditional and contemporary culture. For younger students a good choice for learning about Palestinians is Naomi Shihab Nye's young adult novel *Habibi* (1999, 272 pages, age 11–15). Nye is a respected Arab American poet I have met and heard speak at conferences of the National Council of the Teachers of English. *Habibi* is told from the point of view of Liyana, a girl from St. Louis with an American mother and Palestinian father. When she is fourteen, Liyana's family moves to Jerusalem and she learns at first hand about her Palestinian relatives and their relationship with Israel. In a *Romeo and Juliet* twist, Liyana falls in love with Omer, a Jewish boy. This young adult novel is a good pairing for Shakespeare's classic. (The book *Middle Ground* by Sheryl Finkle and Tamara Lilly has materials and ideas for teaching *Habibi*.) Another book for younger readers is *Samir and Yonatan* (2002, 160 pages, age 11–14) by Daniella Carmi. Samir, a Palestinian boy who breaks his leg, finds himself in an Israeli hospital where he discovers surprising friends. His memories give vivid depiction of life in the occupied territories.

Additional Palestinian Resources

Reading Palestinian literature calls for bringing in additional materials. Rather than a background lecture before beginning a novel, I found that the history of the conflict is more interesting to students when they learn about it as part of the context for characters they have come to know through the literature. *Wild Thorns* led my students to want to know more, to be updated on the most recent happenings in the Israel–Palestine situation. At the time President Jimmy Carter's book *Palestine: Peace Not Apartheid* (2006, 288 pages, age 16–college) had been published, it made the *New York Times* bestseller list, and provided valuable background and important updates about the crisis. Carter explained that in Gaza more than half of the population is under fifteen years old, and the per capita income had decreased 40 percent in the preceding three years (176). Teachers could excerpt individual chapters or the chronology in *Palestine: Peace Not Apartheid* to provide context. My student Dan Brim blogged,

> I used to think that it was a matter of "good vs. evil" in the Middle East when I was growing up. After reading Jimmy Carter's book, I see that things are hardly so black and white. The historical chronology in the first ten pages of this book painted a very clear picture for the points being made within the book. The chapter that I got the most out of was most definitely chapter three, Carter's personal recollection and account of the situation during his presidency. His accounts of all the letters and meetings were quite in-depth, and I appreciated the sense of honesty that came along with his writing.

Perhaps the most disturbing thing Carter describes is the separation wall being built by Israel in and around the West Bank and Gaza Strip. As Linda Cross shared,

> The wall constructed around the West Bank area is really unfair to so many. Built right along the border all the way around the West Bank, it divides peoples' homes from their lands. There is even a church where many Palestinian Christians have worshipped for years that is cut off from the people it serves. The church is on one side of the wall and the worshippers are on the other side.

Students who have learned about the situation of Palestinians may be interested in contemporary Palestinian poetry by writers such as Mahmoud Darwish, Fadwa Tuqan, and May Sayigh whose themes are closely tied to the Palestinian struggle. Other resources that were influential to my students' understanding of the wall – and the reaction of Palestinian young people to it – were powerful video clips that I found on YouTube and that we watched and discussed in class. There are so many materials online, the key is to find things that will be meaningful to students; in that endeavor don't neglect YouTube. The first clip we watched "Israeli Apartheid Wall" makes the wall real as a person simply walks along it, observing graffiti, trying to find "a view toward peace," and wondering "Is there anybody out there?" (www.youtube.com/watch?v=rSgkxbHBdII) The second YouTube video we studied was a five-minute trailer about a film called "Slingshot Hip Hop" showed at the 2008 Sundance film festival. In the clip Palestinian teenagers in Gaza, Akka, Tel Aviv, a West Bank refugee camp, and the Israeli town of Lid use rap music to describe their situation. (www.youtube.com/watch?v=1rdS8zNp3ow) Created by the "Palestinian Lyrical Front," the piece shows teenagers excited about rapping on stage for the first time. It depicts Arab

FIGURE 7.2 Boy and Soldier in Front of Israeli Wall

teen girls in tank tops and baseball caps talking about how it was difficult for some Muslims to accept them as rappers but that "they won't stop for anyone." A young man walks along the street and is detained by an Israeli police officer. Two teenagers point to their high school and describe how the library was removed and replaced by a police station inside the school. We watched this short YouTube clip twice and discussed the way the Israeli wall was impacting Palestinian lives, how the young people were responding, and how American rap music, originally expressing oppressed urban life in our country, has become a universal medium. Through YouTube these teenage Palestinian rappers were making an immediate and powerful impression on the students in my class.

Film offers another way for young people to understand the Israeli–Palestinian crisis, and there are many fine films – both drama and documentary – addressing the conflict. A valuable source for films and for learning about films is the website ArabFilm.com. As I mentioned before, I have become aware that many of my students have never seen films with subtitles, so they may need some tips on how to watch and read subtitles at the same time. *Paradise Now* directed by Abu-Assad is one of the best films addressing the Palestinian perspective and, according to Jack Shehaan, author of *Reel Bad Arabs*, one of the best cinematic depictions of Arabs. *Paradise Now* is the winner of many awards including being the first Palestinian film nominated for an Academy Award as Best Foreign Language Film (2006) and a Golden Globe Award in the same category (2005). My student John Ebbing explains, "*Paradise Now* looks into the life of two friends Said and Khaled chosen to carry out a suicide bombing in Tel Aviv. At first excited and honored that they have been chosen, the young men later struggle with actually carrying out the mission." *Paradise Now* gives us images of life in the West Bank and how that world contrasts with Israel – images rarely seen by Americans. It also shows a variety of Palestinian perspectives on suicide bombing, including powerful arguments against it. Making an authentic film shot on location was challenging,

> "One Palestinian group came to us with guns and asked us to stop," Abu-Assad recalls. "Another kidnapped the location manager, forcing the team to appeal to Yasser Arafat to intervene for his release. Filming took place amid a maelstrom of gunfire, tanks, landmines and helicopters. Worst were the missiles, one of which hit a car yards from where they were working. Eventually six crew members and an actor fled the set, fearing for their lives."
>
> *(Johnston)*

My student Megan Carson says of the film,

> With my own system of values and beliefs about suicide bombing already firmly set in place, I found it interesting to view the subject through a different lens and point of view. I have always thought of suicide bombers as being unreasonable and radical, stupid for being so careless with their own lives. I guess I never looked at the bigger picture. My judgment was clouded by the obvious hate suicide bombers have for those they are attacking. My first instinct has always been to side with the victim, without necessarily ever learning the back story. This film rocks my world.

Another student, Owen Horton, says,

> I think a film like this can do a lot to drum up moderate support on both sides. Sure, there will be those who are horrified by the "humanizing" of a suicide bomber; but, the problem is, they *are* humans, and we need to understand that. In fact, peace depends on understanding that one crucial fact.

For our students to understand the anger that drives characters in *Paradise Now*, it is important to have additional background on life in the Palestinian territories. There are many resources for this. One that I recommend is *Ripples Cross* (2005) a ninety-minute documentary about the peace-making journey of American college student Mark Turner. The film opens with Mark speaking to a class of high school students at a Model UN event and explaining that it is hard to trust media sources unless you gain information at first hand. A student at Colorado College, Mark decides to sell his car, buy a video camera, and go to the Israeli-occupied territories in Palestine. Participating with an international group of peace activists, Mark begins to learn about the realities of oppression as faced daily by Palestinian people. High school and college students will be strongly drawn into the conflict by this simple, low-budget, yet powerful documentary about young people making a difference. This is a good starting point for study of the conflict; other reading and films about Palestine will make much more sense to students after they have seen the documentary footage in this film.

The film *The Iron Wall* (2006) directed by Mohammed Alatar (available online at Google Videos) describes the history of the development of Israeli settlements in Palestinian territories in the West Bank. Alatar is a Palestinian peace activist born in Jordan and living in the United States. The film extensively interviews both Palestinians and Israelis. According to the film, only 20 percent of the Israeli settlers who live in the West Bank are "ideological" meaning that they have decided to settle in the West Bank because they are part of a conservative, orthodox religion that advocates that Jewish people have a God-given right to areas inhabited by Palestinians. Most Israeli settlers are actually living in the West Bank for economic reasons: it is less expensive for Israelis to live in the settlements within the Palestinian territories than housing options inside of Israel because the Israeli government subsidizes the settlements.

Palestinians do not only live in the West Bank, the Gaza strip, or as refugees in other countries but also 20 percent of the population within Israel is Muslim Arab. The novel *The Attack* (2006, 257 pages, age 16–college) written originally in French by the Algerian Yasmina Khadra but available in English translation since 2006, is a gripping exploration of the lives of Palestinian citizens of Israel and one of best books I know for thinking about terrorism. The story centers around an Arab-Israeli citizen, Dr. Amin Jaafari, assimilated and integrated into Israeli society as a respected surgeon at a hospital in Tel Aviv. One night after working tirelessly to help the victims of a terrorist attack in a local restaurant, he learns his beautiful and loving wife has been found dead among the victims. Indeed, according to the police, it seems that *she* was the suicide bomber. The novel is explicit about the suffering caused by the suicide attack, yet the course of the book is the effort of Dr. Jaafari to understand how and why the intelligent, modern woman he was married to gave up her life in the Palestinian cause. In essence the novel becomes a detective story about the conditions of Palestinians and a revelation of the seemingly endless cycles of violence.

Israel bombarded and invaded Lebanon in 2006, killing over 1,000 and displacing more than 1 million Lebanese. An important conflict for students to learn about, there is a film that would interest them: *Under the Bombs* made by the Lebanese director Philippe Aractingi. The film describes the journey of a mother looking for her son sent to spend the summer in Lebanon just before the Israeli attack, and the unlikely friendship she develops with the taxi driver who risks his life to help her. The film was actually shot on location during and immediately after the invasion, so much of the footage has a documentary quality.

BOX 7.2 ARAB–ISRAELI LOSS OF LIFE

Box 5.3 in chapter 5 discussed the loss of life in the Iraq War. Statistics don't capture human suffering or the pain of the loss of even one life. They also don't address those injured, made homeless, or turned into refugees. Below is similar information about the wars, conflicts, and ongoing struggle between Israeli, Palestinians, and Arab states in the region. The numbers are approximate and do not distinguish military and civilian deaths.

Conflict	*Arab Losses*	*Israeli Losses*
1948	15,000	6,000
1956	2,500	180
1967	18,000	900
1967–70	5,000	370
1973	12,000	3,000
1982	22,000	368
1987–92	900	475
2000–06	5,500	1,100
2006	1,670	160
2008–09	1,400	13
Total	83,970	12,566

Source: White, Mathew. "Mid-Range Wars and Atrocities of the Twentieth Century." Web. 15 Nov 2010. http://users.erols.com/mwhite28/warstat4.htm#Israel.

Israeli Literature and Perspectives

Israeli and Modern Hebrew literature is a large and rich field with many outstanding, award-winning authors including S.Y. Agnon (Nobel Prizewinner), A.B. Yehoshua, Amos Oz, David Grossman, and many others. My students and I have read a wide variety of texts and authors in translation seeking works about life in contemporary Israel that would be appealing to English-speaking secondary and college students, particularly works that address the Palestinian conflict. Many of Israel's most celebrated writers focus on Jewish history and Diaspora, rather than on Israel *per se*. Others, such as Yehoshua, write thoughtful works for adult audiences that are, either by theme or historical context, often too mature or too difficult for introductory study by younger readers. We have come across a number of works that perfectly fit the bill, especially the novel *The Panther in the Basement* by Amos Oz, the short stories of Etgar Keret, and several recent Israeli films. Fortunately our efforts were supplemented by Linda Silver – a librarian and specialist in Jewish books for children and teens – who, in an article in the *English Journal* responding to a previous article of mine (including portions of this chapter), put forward an excellent list of young adult literature written from an Israeli perspective.

The Panther in the Basement (1998, 160 pages, age 13–college) is a gorgeously written novel told from the point of view of a twelve-year-old boy living in Jerusalem in 1947 near the end of the British occupation and just before the declaration of the state of Israel. The novel captures the growing sense of solidarity among Israelis, while, at the same time exploring questions of reaching across cultural lines. Capturing the perspective of the young narrator, the bookish Proffy, the reader moves between childhood role-play and a make-believe underground resistance movement, and the actual independence struggle. Even though the British are the recognized enemy, Proffy is able to befriend a British soldier and see across the rhetoric of hatred and violence. Students will see the excitement of the creation of the Jewish state from an inside perspective, and at the same time recognize that ideas of enemy and warfare are put into question. This is a sophisticated coming of age novel appealing to readers of all ages.

As Silver points out, there are a number of outstanding young adult novels written in Israel and translated into English. A work that will help high school students understand the Israel–Palestine conflict is *A Bottle in the Gaza Sea* (2005, 149 pages, age 12–17) by Valerie Zenatti, written in 2005 and translated from Hebrew to English in 2008. While the narrative device of this book is a bit contrived – a seventeen-year-old Israeli girl asks her brother on military duty in the Gaza Strip to put a bottle into the sea with her name and email address hoping she can find a Palestinian to converse with – the book provides a realistic look at the difference in the lives of Israelis and Palestinians in a way that will appeal to readers at the secondary level. The bottle is found and a communication ensues that allows each side to better understand the other. Students will learn about barriers that keep Israelis and Palestinians apart, the constrained life and choices for Palestinians, the diversity of perspectives within Israel, and the trauma suicide bombings inflict in Israel. This trauma and loss is also powerfully evidenced by the *Bat-Chen Diaries* (2008, 110 pages, age 12–adult) a collection of writings and illustrations by Bat-Chen Shahak, an Israeli girl killed on her 15th birthday on a bus by a suicide bombing in Tel Aviv. Another Israeli book appropriate for middle school readers that more optimistically explores relations with Palestinians is *Running on Eggs* (1999, 128 pages, age 12–14) by Anna Levine.

A remarkable collection of short stories *The Bus Driver Who Wanted to be God* (2004, 130 pages, age 14–college) by Etgar Keret includes a disturbing four-page story written from the perspective of an Israeli Special Forces soldier apparently guarding a Palestinian checkpoint. Keret is an astonishing writer and in his brief piece "Cocked and Locked" he explores the everyday violence and anger between the antagonists, and how that anger is tied to militarism and codes of manliness. The adult language of this piece makes it unsuitable for most high school classrooms, yet there are many stories in the collection that, with heavy irony, address life in Israel and that would be excellent in high school, particularly the title story, "Breaking the Pig," and "Shoes." I didn't think of the longest story in the book, "Kneller's Happy Campers" (40 pages – subsequently made into a film, *Wristcutters: A Love Story*) about the afterlife of people who commit suicide as relating to political questions, until I read the comments of my student Katie Burpo. She wrote:

> The casting of the afterlife as a senseless, bureaucratic wasteland speaks to the absurdity of any governing principle which simply perpetuates the illusion that there is some theoretical way of uniting people [thus] "Kneller's Happy Campers" allegorically interrogates the legitimacy of a religious state.

While the focus of this chapter is on literature addressing the Israel–Palestine conflict there are a number of excellent Israeli literary works about other dimensions of life in Israel – several are recommended at the end of the chapter by my graduate student Sarah Davis, including titles by Yehoshua and Grossman.

My students have watched films made by Israelis that raise powerful questions about extremism and militarism. The Israeli film *Time of Favor* (2000) swept the Israeli Academy Awards winning Best Film, Best Actor, Best Actress, Best Cinematography, and Best Screenplay. It is a highly religious film that explores the impact on a team of soldiers of the preaching of an extremist rabbi. His daughter, Michal, is an attractive, independent young woman. Compelling characters, a love triangle, and a suicide-bombing plot held my students' interest. They found the film fascinating to compare with *Paradise Now*. In *Time of Favor* the suicide bombing is tied to Jewish religious extremism and a love rejection. While the topic in both films is suicide bombing, there is no glimmer in the Israeli film that would connect suicide bombing with the real life conditions of a community; rather it is portrayed as a personal and ideological act. Even though much of the action takes place in a Jewish settlement in the West Bank, the idea that the settlement might cause difficulty for Palestinians or encroach on their territory doesn't arise in the film. In this sense, while the films address closely related themes, they do not really talk to each other. Nonetheless, each offers insights into their respective societies.

Beaufort (2007) is an Israeli war film set in Southern Lebanon in 2000. Nominated for an American Academy Oscar for best foreign film and for many awards in Israel, it depicts the experience of a unit of the Israeli army stationed in a hilltop fortress in Southern Lebanon in 2000. Katie Burpo summarizes the film well,

> Lofty ideals, religious extremism, heroic glorification, all of this seems beside the point in this gritty examination of the mundane terror that is war. The characters are mostly concerned with their proximity to discharge. They long for home. This desire comes as no shock, for who, in their right mind, feels comfortable on the battlefield? However, the conceptual reasons for the soldiers' disenchantment are more complex and speak not only to the

> contemporary conflict in Palestine/Israel, but also to the U.S. presence in the Middle East. Early in the film, we get a sense that none of the characters have a vested interest in any sort of cause. They are jaded, cynical, and unsentimental regarding their allegiance to the state of Israel . . . The parallel between such conditions and our current conflict in Iraq are evident. Weren't we supposed to be in and out like Desert Storm? Have we, too, learned to accept "at war" as our nation's natural and indefinite state?

Another powerful Israeli film addressing the conflicts that I recommend for teaching students aged sixteen and up is *Waltz with Bashir* (2008). This film also swept the Israeli Academy awards and was nominated for best foreign film in the United States. Several students identified it as their favorite work of the semester. In a unique and fascinating animated format, the film explores the troubled memory of an Israeli soldier who was a witness to the famous 1982 Sabra and Shatilla massacre of Palestinian and Lebanese civilians. The history of this event is well known in the region, but our students may need some background. Since the 1948 war, and still today, there have been many Palestinian refugees in Lebanon. Another group in Lebanon is the Maronite Christians, sometimes politically close to Israel. Days before the massacre the Maronite leader, Bachir Gemayel, was assassinated by an agent of the government of Syria – not connected to the Palestinians who were in the camps, although Syria supported the Palestinians. Nevertheless Maronite soldiers eager for revenge were sent into the camps by the Israelis and provided with support at night from flares shot over the camps by the Israeli army. (The flares are a focus in the film.) According to one witness the camp was as bright as "a sports stadium during a football game." The Israeli army has been accused of guarding the exits from the camps and not allowing anyone to leave while the massacre took place. The number of casualties is disputed: some say as low as 350, others ten times higher, 3,500. An investigation by the Israeli government found Ariel Sharon personally responsible and he was forced to resign as head of the defense ministry (though he later became prime minister). Moreover, an independent commission found that Israel's invasion of Lebanon in 1982 violated international law and the invasion was condemned by the UN Security Council. The U.S. had apparently told Israel not to occupy the area of Lebanon where these camps were located, and assured the Muslims of West Beirut, including Palestinian refugees in the camps, that they would be safe. My student Victor Jimenez explains that the film records:

> a journey made by the film's protagonist Ari Folman . . . [who] participated in the 1982 Israel invasion of Palestine, but somehow he does not remember any detail of it. He is haunted by a dream and tries to find meaning behind this hallucination. Throughout the movie we see him interview many of his friends that went to the same war, and piece-by-piece he attempts to remember.

Kristin Felts points out that the film is portrayed

> through the eyes of a soldier. Soldiers are not supposed to form judgments about what they are doing, they are supposed to obey orders and do their job. Obviously what happened was very traumatic for him, or else he wouldn't have lost his memories of it. Also, I am sure the soldiers fighting beside him were his friends, why would they be betrayed as terrible people? Like him they were there because it was required of them. I thought it took courage to make a movie about his own life, and to not portray anyone as perfect.

For Bailey Waterhouse particular scenes were memorable:

> Something that I thought was key in the movie was when one of the characters was in the tank and the other officer in the tank with him asked him what they were supposed to do, what they were supposed to shoot at. The main character said he did not know. "Just keep shooting," he was ordered. These soldiers were in the war but had no idea what they were supposed to do, what they were fighting for! They killed innocent civilians because they were scared.

The ending of the film is powerful as the animated format suddenly switches to actual documentary footage of the aftermath of the massacre. Like *Footnotes in Gaza*, *Waltz with Bashir* is a study of trauma, responsibility, morality, and historical memory. As Katie suggested, these Israeli films about invasions and occupations of Lebanon may have special resonance for Americans returning from or reflecting on military duty in the invasion and occupation of Afghanistan or Iraq.

Many Israeli writers, and many Jews and Israelis, are dedicated to peace, to seeking a meaningful two-state solution with a homeland for the Palestinians. Sometimes they find themselves at odds with the official polices of their government, or the extreme behavior of Israeli settlers or defense forces. It is important for our students to learn about these courageous Jews and Israelis, who offer, I believe, some of the most hopeful possibilities for peace in the region. The American–Jewish intellectual Judith Butler argues:

> There is no one Jewish voice, and in recent years, there are increasing differences among us, as is evident by the multiplication of Jewish groups that oppose the occupation and which actively criticize and oppose Israeli military policy and aggression. In the United States and Israel alone these groups include: Jewish Voice for Peace, American Jews for a Just Peace, Jews Against the Occupation, Boycott from Within, New Profile, Anarchists Against the Wall, Women in Black, Who Profits? Btselem, Zochrot, Black Laundry, Jews for a Free Palestine (Bay Area), No Time to Celebrate, and more.
>
> *("You")*

Additional Israeli groups dedicated to peace include Peace Now, Gush Shalom, Peace Team, the National Census, Courage to Refuse, E Women, and a number of the left-wing political parties. Some of Israel's most famous literary artists are active in these groups including A.B. Yehoshua, Amos Oz, and David Grossman. There are also important organizations of Israelis and Palestinians working together for peace, such as Givat Haviva, A Different Future, Crossing Borders, Combatants for Peace, Encounter, One Voice, Peace Child Israel, Nemashim, Sadaka Reut, Seeds of Peace, Windows, Brit Shalom, Interfaith Encounter, etc. These groups have done outstanding work, received international awards and recognition, yet are rarely visible in the mainstream media, which reports disagreement and conflict rather than efforts to promote peace and understanding. The accomplishments of the groups bringing together Israelis and Palestinians are especially impressive given that they are kept separate, not only by walls and checkpoints, but also by regulation: under Israeli law it is illegal for Israeli citizens to visit the occupied territories and illegal for Palestinians to enter Israel – with a two-year imprisonment for Israelis who help them do so (Mackey).

Researching groups working to bring peace to the region is an excellent way for students to learn more about the conflict and approaches to ending it. With this kind of research students learn not to demonize Israelis or Palestinians, and to begin to see hope for peace resolutions. Ashley Hillyard drew our attention to a series of National Public Radio programs about Jewish and Muslim dialogues in Los Angeles. Their efforts were reported on the NPR program *Speaking of Faith* and now available for free online. Ashley writes,

> This morning, Michigan Public Radio's *Speaking of Faith* covered the story of a group of people living in LA, called New Ground, who are working to build understanding in the heart of political conflict. Two girls participating in the program, Malka and Aziza, were chosen for a radio interview. Malka, a Jew and Aziza, a Palestinian discuss their persistence in attempting to understand one another and develop a friendship. They claim that the key is realizing your similarities and constantly trying to tackle the "elephant in the room." For them the word "Zionism" is one of the hardest to overcome. To Malka the word means salvation and community and to Aziza it means oppression and exclusion. By continuing to ask questions, the two girls say they have been able to reach a deeper understanding of conflict and resolution.
>
> *("Four Pairs of Interfaith Fellows")*

An excellent resource addressing Israelis and Palestinians working together for peace is the award-winning 2006 documentary film *Encounter Point*, available online. The film traces efforts of people on both sides who have lost precious family members to the violence but are determined, nonetheless, to work together to know each other and find a peaceful solution. Among those people are the parents of Bat-Chen Shahak, the fifteen-year-old girl killed in a suicide bombing mentioned above.

Teaching about the Israel–Palestine conflict, as in all teaching about the Middle East, it is valuable to draw current events and new resources into the curriculum. Historical materials provide context for developing awareness of contemporary controversies and issues. Literature and film personalize the conflict, and invite students to learn from the perspective of others. This kind of critically informed, yet empathetic learning is sorely needed in the polarized context of the Israel–Palestine conflict.

Further Reading

Mornings in Jenin (2010, 350 pages, by Susan Abulhawa, age 16–college) is a powerful and disturbing epic of one Palestinian family over four generations addressing the experience of occupation and refugees.

Women of the Wall is a documentary film chronicling the struggle for women's rights in the state of Israel, particularly women's rights to pray in public at the famous Kotel, or Western Wall. The women in the film go against tradition by wearing the prayer rug and other religious articles that only men traditionally wear, and by carrying and reading from the Torah st The women in the film meet once a month to pray as a group at the wall, even though that area of the wall is reserved by law for men (Ashley Auberman).

David Grossman's *Smile of the Lamb* (1983 translated from Hebrew in 2003, 336 pages, college) is a difficult book to get into but, once you internalize its rhythms, it becomes difficult to put it down. Each chapter is a stream-of-consciousness glimpse into the mind of one of four main characters: Uri, his wife Sosh, his friend Katzman, and the outcast storyteller Khilmi. The first three are non-practicing Israeli Jews, but Khilmi is an Arab storyteller. Uri and Katzman are soldiers in the occupation force in Khilmi's Palestine (Sarah Davis).

Yahya Yakhlif's novel, *A Lake Beyond the Wind* (1991, translated to English 1999, 160 pages, age 16–college) depicts Palestinian life in 1948 during the rise of Israeli power within Palestine. The Palestinian townspeople that this novel focuses on still believe that the Arab Liberation Army will succeed in defeating the Israelis, whose new settlements begin to neighbor their villages (Ashley Hillyard).

A Woman in Jerusalem (1989, translated to English from Hebrew 2006, age 16–college, 256 pages) by A. B. Yehoshua, one of the best known Israeli writers, author of nine novels and many shorter works, this novel is the tale of one man's attempt to find the identity of a woman killed in a terrorist bombing in Jerusalem and then his quest to return her body to her homeland. It doesn't address the Israel–Palestine conflict. Topics for class discussion include the lack of character names (the only character named in the book is the dead woman), the sensationalism of the press, the varying concepts of what it means to be humane, and moral duty (Sarah Davis).

8

TEACHING MOROCCAN LITERATURE OF MIGRATION

David Alvarez[1]

> Fourteen kilometers. Murad had pondered that number hundreds of times in the last year, trying to decide whether the risk was worth it. Some days he told himself that the distance was nothing, a brief inconvenience, that the crossing would take as little as thirty minutes if the weather was good. He spent hours thinking about what he would do once he was on the other side, imagining the job, the car, the house. Other days he could only think about the coast guards, the ice-cold water, the money he'd have to borrow, and he wondered how fourteen kilometers could separate not just two countries but two universes.
>
> *Leila Lalami,* Hope and Other Dangerous Pursuits, *p. 1*

Clandestine Immigration: A Global Story

For the past 20 years ongoing clandestine and illegal immigration from Africa into Europe has been a frequent news topic in many European and African countries. In a variety of craft, most of them overcrowded and unseaworthy, migrants follow several different sea-routes between the southern and northern shores of the Mediterranean, routes that stretch between Morocco and mainland Spain, between Tunisia and Sicily, and, to a lesser degree, between Libya and Egypt on the one hand and Greece on the other. In addition to these routes across the Mediterranean Sea there are also Atlantic routes between Africa and the European Union, specifically between Senegal and Mauretania on the one hand, and Spain's Canary Islands on the other. By far the busiest of these routes are those that straddle the Strait of Gibraltar, which is where Spain–Europe and Morocco–Africa are physically closest, parts of the Strait being only eight miles wide. However, the ramifications of the clandestine passage of people across the Strait are felt as far away as Nigeria to the south and Norway to the north.

Furthermore, and as my students at a comprehensive university in West Michigan are quick to notice, this migration is a chapter in a global story that includes another ongoing stream of clandestine migration from one country to another, one with which they are more familiar: that between Mexico and the U.S. What motivates migrants to leave their homes? How do they remake their lives if they make it over to the other side? What happens to them if they are forced to return to their places of origin? These are some of the questions that students are curious about and that the literature of migration can help answer. In this essay I describe and assess the ways in which one young U.S.-based Moroccan writer, Laila Lalami, has portrayed clandestine migration between Morocco and Spain in a book of inter-related stories and I indicate why the strand of contemporary world literature that her text represents is worth teaching in U.S. and English-speaking classrooms in the age of globalization.

Breaching Europe's "New Berlin Wall"

As is the case with the U.S.–Mexico border, in public discussions of migrants and of migration the Strait of Gibraltar is rarely represented merely as a neutral feature of the landscape or as a technical line of demarcation between two countries. Rather, in much of the discourse surrounding the issue of clandestine migration the Strait also connotes a perceived gulf between two ostensibly irreconcilable religions (Christianity and Islam), between "civilization" and "barbarism," and more reductively and crudely still, between an undifferentiated "us" and a monolithic and menacing "them." And as is also the case in the United States, Spain and the EU have responded to the numerous covert crossings that take place across the Strait with a panoply of harsh immigration laws and with increased surveillance along the length of the Strait and its neighboring coastlines. Despite these measures, numerous migrants keep attempting to breach what the Spanish novelist Juan Goytisolo has dubbed "the new Berlin Wall" in an attempt to achieve a better life inside what critics of the EU's immigration laws dub "Fortress Europe."

Attitudes Towards Clandestine Immigrants

Legal and open emigration from Morocco and other African countries into Europe on a significant scale began in the 1950s, when Europe's post-World War II labor shortage prompted European governments to encourage migration from their former colonies. As a result, there are now large populations of African and other Third World immigrants and their local-born descendents in several European countries, most notably Britain, Germany, Spain, and France. In contrast, large-scale clandestine immigration from Morocco and other parts of Africa into Europe has taken place continuously only since 1995, when several European countries implemented the Schengen Agreement. This accord created a borderless zone within

Europe while making access to the signatory countries much more stringent than before for third-country nationals, especially those from the global South.

Statistics for how many people have undertaken the crossing since the mid-90s and for how many do so per year are obviously hard to come by, but it is widely accepted that many tens of thousands of migrants have done so. How many migrants end up staying in Spain or elsewhere in the EU is also unknown but estimates range to up to a million undocumented African migrants (chiefly from Morocco but also from as far south as Nigeria) in Spain alone. At the same time, however, although many migrants manage to make it into Europe and create new lives for themselves, many others are caught either during the crossing or once ashore and deported back to their countries of origin. Those whose countries of origin cannot be determined (often such migrants are minors) are detained in “immigration reception centers” and can eventually apply for naturalization. An unknown number die in the passage when the overloaded small craft onto which they are packed capsize and they drown. Yet despite the fact that the dangers attendant upon clandestine migration are well known in the migrants' communities of origin, and despite the fact that unemployment is high in Spain, even in the midst of the post-2008 recession, Spanish and Moroccan dailies frequently carry reports of drownings and deportations involving clandestine immigrants, evidence that the crossings continue to take place on a significant scale.

FIGURE 8.1 Straights of Gibraltar

In the countries from which the migrants hail, there are mixed opinions as to the wisdom of undertaking such a perilous journey, one that can easily end in tragedy or shame. While occasionally a family may readily encourage the north-bound emigration of one of its own, typically the decision to migrate occasions much anxiety for those close to the migrant. Such anxiety may be palliated if the migrant makes good in Europe and becomes a source of remittances and other forms of economic support. Nevertheless, even in the best of cases, clandestine migration tends to cause strains within families and communities and in recent years non-governmental organizations from Tunisia to Senegal have campaigned for the need to improve conditions at home so that clandestine migration may cease to exert such a pull on the impoverished and desperate. At the same time, however, the EU has in recent years begun to apply pressure on African countries to stem the flow of migrants, if need be through repressive measures. Since many of these countries continue to be plagued by poverty, under-development, and lack of employment opportunities for large numbers of their citizens, the motivation to migrate remains a potent one, even as the circumstances that migrants face in making their journeys are becoming increasingly adverse.

As for Europe, public opinion is sharply divided over the question of the status and character of undocumented migrants, in ways that echo similar disagreements in the U.S. In the case of Spain, for instance, there are those who recall their own experiences as migrants to more prosperous Western nations during the period when their country was unevenly developed and who regard African migrants with sympathy as a result. In contrast, some politicians and the more sensationalist media outlets tend to associate clandestine immigrants with criminal behavior or with a perceived (or manufactured) threat to Spanish ways of life. There are also racist elements in Spanish society whose hostility to African immigrants can sometimes find violent physical expression, as in the notorious attacks on Nigerians and others in the Andalusian province of Almeria. This historically hardscrabble region, which once exported Spanish laborers to the developed economies of northern Europe, has in recent years become prosperous thanks to the labor of undocumented African workers who tend the greenhouses and heavily irrigated fields that provide European supermarkets with fresh produce all year round. At any rate, whatever the response to the presence of migrants among individual Spaniards or amid discrete sectors of Spanish society, it tends to be the case that immigrants in Spanish and European public discourse remain largely anonymous and faceless. On the whole, they are portrayed as a problem to be solved, whether from a sympathetic or unsympathetic standpoint.

Moroccan Writers and the Literature of Clandestine Immigration

For a more penetrating and nuanced understanding of the human realities of clandestine immigration between North Africa and Southern Europe than is usually available in political and media discourse, reliable guides are needed and in this situation writers are among the best guides we have. Four of Morocco's most notable living authors – Youssouf Amine Elalamy, Mahi Binebine, Tahar Ben Jelloun, and Leila Lalami – have devoted full-length works of fiction to the topic at hand, all of which are available in English translation.[2] The first of these books to appear, Binebine's *Cannibales: Traversee dans l'enfer de Gibraltar* [*Cannibals: Passage through the Hell of Gibraltar*] came out in French in 1999 and was published in English in 2003 as *Welcome to Paradise*. Next to appear was Elalamy's *Les clandestins* [*The Clandestine Immigrants*] first published in French in 2000 and appeared in English in 2008 as *Seadrinkers*. Lalami's *Hope and Other Dangerous Pursuits* was published in a hardcover edition in English in 2005 and has since been published in paperback editions and has been translated into seven other languages. The last of the four texts, Tahar Ben Jelloun's *Partir* (*To Leave*), appeared in French in 2006 and was published in English translation as *Leaving Tangier* in 2009. Although the four texts are in some respects markedly different from each other in tone and in literary mode (their modes range from fantasy through melodrama to the grotesque, although all four books are laced with realism), all of them are motivated by the same basic plot element – Moroccan characters make or seek to make a clandestine journey across the Strait of Gibraltar and into Europe – and all four are animated by a humanistic concern for the lives of such characters. In what follows I focus on Lalami's *Hope and Other Dangerous Pursuits*, a collection of interlinked stories about four Moroccan migrants to Spain that I have regularly taught in English department survey courses on World Literature as well as in an Honors Program course on contemporary African literature.

Laili Lalami

Born in 1968, Lalami is the youngest of the four writers and the only one of them to write in English, the writerly language of the other three being French. Raised and educated in Rabat, Morocco, Lalami undertook post-graduate studies in the United Kingdom and in the U.S., to which she moved in 1992, and where she now works as an assistant professor of creative writing at the University of California, Riverside. (She is thus herself a migrant, albeit a more privileged one than the migrants she writes about, and has written an essay on being a Moroccan immigrant to the U.S.) Since publishing *Hope and Other Dangerous Pursuits*, Lalami has published another work of fiction, *Secret Son* (2009). In addition, Lalami has published numerous essays on Morocco, the Middle East, and Islam – as well as reviews of books by Moroccan, Middle Eastern, and sub-Saharan African authors – in such national periodicals as *The Los Angeles Times* and *The Boston Globe*. Moreover, she maintains an active presence on the Internet through her well maintained website (http://lailalalami.com), which includes her blog, podcast interviews, texts of her articles, video recordings of her readings, and other teachable materials.

Hope and Other Dangerous Pursuits

Lalami first published her debut book in the U.S. where it received favorable reviews from sources as varied as *The Nation* and *People Magazine*. The book has since been translated into seven other languages, including Spanish. Formally and conceptually, *Hope and Other Dangerous Pursuits* is perhaps the least formidable of the four major works of fiction on the topic of clandestine immigration. By the same token, however, it is the most accessible of the four, since it is written in spare, idiomatic prose and structured around a readily assimilable format. In an introductory section entitled "The Trip," the story starts off *in medias res*, in this case, the clandestine passage across the Strait of Gibraltar under cover of darkness. This section evokes the fear and tension that permeates an overloaded boat on which several migrants hope to reach the shores of Spain before their launch capsizes within a hundred yards of the Spanish coast. It also introduces us to the four characters into whose lives the two remaining parts of the narrative will delve. In the four discrete sections that make up "Part I: Before" we learn about the circumstances that led the four characters to undertake the crossing, and in the four chapters that make up "Part II: After" we discover what transpires after they attempt to reach the other side.

One of these characters, Murad, is the focalizing center of "The Trip" and it is with his story that the book begins and ends. Murad, who lives in Tangiers, from which the Spanish coast is clearly visible on most days and nights, has a degree in English but his studies have not enabled him to secure stable and gainful employment. Instead, he barely ekes out a living by working as an unofficial guide for tourists. Eventually, after his mother neglects to consult him over his younger sister's dowry, he tires of the haphazard nature of his work and of the shame he feels at not being regarded as the man of the house and finally succumbs to a trafficker's repeated attempts to entice him into making the crossing into Spain.

In reading the lives of the other three main characters, we discover that, as is the case with Murad, while economic reasons loom large in their decision to leave Morocco for Europe, in no case is the prospect of being able to earn sufficient money to make ends meet the only reason for their departure. Other motives include the physical and psychological need of a mother of three to get away from a drunken and physically abusive husband; the shame a husband associates with not being able to provide for his wife and her family; and a young female student's fear of being persecuted by the security forces for having spoken out against the King and against corruption.

While the book's first main section focuses on the characters' departures from their homes and lives in Morocco, the second section explores the upshot of their initial journeys. In the case of two of the characters, we discover that their planned migration has failed and that they have been forced to return to Morocco. There, they have first had to confront the dishonor that attaches to being an unsuccessful returnee. Moreover, they have simultaneously had to face once again some of the very problems that prompted their decision to leave. Nonetheless, in both cases the characters eventually manage to secure modest improvements in their station, Murad by putting his knowledge of English to good use in a shop that sells curios for tourists and Halima by selling her home-made pastries at the local market. The stories of both of these characters conclude on an open-ended note of tentative hopefulness. By the end, their future no longer seems prescribed and radically circumscribed. In contrast, for the two characters who manage to remain in Spain, the outcome of their clandestine passage to Europe seems more mixed. Faten – an ardent Islamist during her college days – is reduced to prostituting herself on the streets of Madrid. Aziz, who is unable to save up enough money to return to Morocco flush with cash as he had unrealistically hoped, discovers on a long-awaited visit home that his wife is reluctant to leave behind her daily routines and familial attachments in Casablanca to start a new and unpredictable life in a foreign city. He also realizes that he no longer loves Zohra and that he feels out of place among his co-nationals. Yet despite the seemingly bleak conclusion of their decision to migrate, both characters have attained at least a measure of self-determination. At the end of Faten's story, for instance, we find her confidently rejecting the self-serving and patronizing advances of a young Spanish client who foists his fantasies about submissive Muslim women onto her. We also find her relishing a recipe she cooks for herself and for the hard-up Moroccan roommate who has hitherto looked down upon her because of how she earns a living. And while Aziz is alienated from his city and from his wife, at the same time he has found a new sense of himself in the foreign land that has imperceptibly but definitively become his home.

In narrating for us the lives of these four ordinary Moroccans, the stories provide us with much sociological information on everyday life in contemporary urban Morocco. Furthermore, the realist register and contemporary North American English in which the tales are couched convey a sense of actuality that serves to counter the kind of exoticism to which Morocco has often been subjected in literature and film, e.g., in the fiction of American novelist and long-time Tangier resident, Paul Bowles, one of whose novels Murad gives up on reading when he decides to take a stab at representing his own reality through literary writing, and specifically, through a retelling of folktales his father used to tell him. At the same time, however, the stories neither romanticize the characters nor portray them as abject victims of circumstances. Aziz, for instance, is in his attitude to his wife a rather unsympathetic character and Halima's judgment in undertaking the trip across the Strait with her little children can be found wanting. In a later section of this essay, I will comment on the significance of this honest portrayal of the characters. First, however, I want to provide a note on some of the ways in which as teachers we can usefully contextualize the stories for our students.

The Multiple Contexts of Hope and Other Dangerous Pursuits

Since the majority of the students who take my undergraduate courses at Grand Valley State University tend to know little about the historical, cultural, political, and economic realities of the world outside the borders of the United States, and since the stories both assume a basic knowledge of Morocco and make reference to a variety of extra-textual facts (e.g., the names of Moroccan and Spanish cities) I find it useful to devote a considerable amount of time to contextualizing *Hope* (at least one class period). Since contextualization cannot be exhaustive, I choose to emphasize the following points:

- Morocco's situation directly across the Strait of Gibraltar from the south-western-most country in Europe and its role as a gateway between the Atlantic and Mediterranean worlds on the one hand, and between Africa and Europe on the other. This position has among other things led to Morocco's being settled and sometimes conquered by a wide array of peoples in the course of its 3,000-year-long history: Phoenicians, Romans, Carthaginians, Vandals, Arabs, sub-Saharan Africans, Portuguese, Spaniards, and the French. The diversity of physiognomies among Moroccans is one consequence of this multiple immigration from different places over many centuries. Another is the complex, multilayered nature of contemporary Moroccan culture.
- Morocco's location at the westernmost extremity of an arc of predominantly Muslim societies that stretch from Southeast Asia to the Atlantic Ocean. The westward expansion of Islam from the Arabian Peninsula led first to the Islamization and Arabization of Morocco's indigenous Amazigh (Berber) communities, and a century later, to the joint Arabo-Berber invasion and conquest of the Iberian Peninsula, events that led to the creation of a Moroccan-Iberian civilization ("Al-Andalus") and to an 800-year presence of Muslim Arabs and Amazigh on Iberian soil, the legacies of which can still be admired or appreciated today in the impressive monuments of southern Spanish cities (e.g., the Alhambra Palace complex in Granada) and in the music, cuisines, and physiognomies of the peoples of both Morocco and Spain. Some Spanish politicians, historians, and journalists speak in alarmist tones of current immigration into Morocco as being a latter-day repetition of the invasion led by Tariq Ibn-Ziyad (whose name endures in the toponym Gibraltar, from the Arabic "Djebel Tarik" ("Mountain of Tariq") in 711 CE. In "The Trip," Murad reflects ironically on this history and on Islamophobia and fear of re-conquest in contemporary Spain:

> Murad can make out the town where they're headed. Tarifa. The mainland point of the Moorish invasion in 711. Murad used to regale tourists with anecdotes about how Tariq Ibn Ziyad had led a powerful Moor army across the Straits and, upon landing in Gibraltar, ordered all the boats burned. He'd told his soldiers that they could march forth and defeat the enemy or turn back and die a coward's death. The men

> had followed their general, toppled the Visigoths, and established an empire that ruled over Spain for more than seven hundred years. Little did they know that we'd be back, Murad thinks. Only instead of a fleet, here we are in an inflatable boat – not just Moors, but a motley mix of people from the ex-colonies, without guns or armor, without a charismatic leader.
>
> *(2–3)*

- Morocco's geographic, topographic, demographic, and cultural diversity. With regards to the latter two points I emphasize the fact the while outside of Morocco the country tends to be thought of as an Arab and Arabic-speaking country the reality is much more complex. While a majority of Moroccans take pride in being Arab and in speaking Arabic, a significant minority (up to 40 percent) identify themselves as Amazigh (i.e., Berber), and an indeterminate number of Moroccans (e.g., the current king) are of mixed Arabo-Berber descent. Furthermore, there are small but socially significant Jewish, European, and sub-Saharan African minorities. The long presence of Jews in Morocco and their largely harmonious relations with their Muslim co-nationals can help broaden students' understanding of the historical relationship between Jews and Arabs. In Lalami's book, after he gets deported from Spain, Murad ends up working for a Jewish shop-owner in Tangiers.
- The reasons for large-scale emigration in Morocco's modern history. There are over a million Moroccans living across Europe as well as in Canada and the U.S. With its focus on four individuals, Lalami's book does not paint a broad picture of the scale of Moroccan emigration to the West. Nor does it delve into the systemic reasons for the mass migratory flows of which the characters are a part. In order for students to gain a wider and deeper understanding of the phenomenon than the stories on their own can provide, it is useful to briefly explain the economic reasons for mass migration, namely, entrenched poverty, and lack of gainful employment and opportunities in both rural areas and in urban slums. While Morocco has undergone considerable socio-economic development in recent years, especially since the 1998 accession to the throne of King Mohammed VI, and while at the micro-level resilient grassroots entrepreneurship partially makes up for the structural deficiencies of the economy's state and corporate sectors, development is keenly uneven, unemployment remains chronically high, and hopes of achieving a better life in Europe continue to pull at the imagination of many unemployed or underemployed Moroccans.

Tools and Materials for Contextualization

In order to elucidate these and other points, I avail myself of maps of Morocco itself, of Morocco in relation to the Mediterranean Basin, north and south, of

Morocco in relation to the Arab World stretching eastwards, and of Morocco in relation to the rest of the African Continent. We also look closely at satellite photographs of the Strait of Gibraltar (numerous examples are available on the Internet) that can dramatically illustrate both the relatively short distance that separates Morocco from Spain and more broadly, Africa from Europe, and the treacherousness of journeys that must take place on unseaworthy craft under cover of darkness across a busy waterway that is under constant surveillance and that is plagued by powerful currents and strong winds that sometimes attain gale-force strength. In addition to scrutinizing maps and photos, we listen to samples of Morocco's diverse musical traditions and styles, from the classical Iberian music kept alive in those Moroccan cities to which refugees from Al-Andalus fled, to 1970s protest folk-rock, to contemporary hip-hop. (Much of this music is available on YouTube and I have amassed my personal collection on visits to Morocco.) Finally, since all the stories in *Hope* mention a variety of Moroccan dishes, I pass around cookbooks that illustrate the diversity and richness of Moroccan cuisine.

Moroccan Literature of Clandestine Migration as Counter-Discourse

In addition to illuminating the immediate contexts of the stories, the geographical, historical, and anthropological contextualization that I outline above can help students situate the tales in the larger framework of significance of world history and of contemporary global realities. For instance, it comes as a surprise for many students to learn that a Muslim civilization of Moroccan provenance once flourished on European soil, and that for long periods it was characterized chiefly by peaceful co-existence and by high cultural and social achievements. The history of Al-Andalus, which is alluded to in Lalami's book and which contemporary Moroccans and Spaniards are both heirs to, can serve to illustrate the idea that history is contingent and that current conflicts are not fated to occur. This contextualization is a particularly important move at a time when relations between the West and the Muslim world are characterized by a variety of severe strains and stresses and when mass media in Western countries rarely situate the international events on which they report in frameworks of meaning that are attentive to local nuances and to historical developments. In other words, in addition to providing readers with a literary and aesthetic experience, the study of literature and of its contexts can in this instance serve an important and dual social function: that of humanizing for us the lives of people who are often represented as our cultural "Others" and that of re-imagining our current global circumstances in the light of a deeper and against-the-grain awareness of history.

By a variety of literary means, *Hope and Other Dangerous Pursuits* and the other Moroccan literary texts about clandestine migration portray migrants in ways that contrast notably with the manner in which they tend to be represented in the Western mass media. Although these texts portray the migrants as people who are burdened with very serious problems, they do not represent the migrants *as problems*. Rather than focus on the problems that they might pose for Spanish society – even as problems that call for sympathetic solutions – they are portrayed as individual human beings whose lives are marked but not defined by the imperative to migrate.

In other words, the literary texts under discussion can help us see the contemporary world in a way that runs counter to conventional understanding. Thus, in these texts migrants are represented neither as "illegal" nor as "aliens," but as human beings who may run afoul of the law of the countries into which they clandestinely enter, who may be frequently regarded as alien presences by many citizens of the host countries, but who in these texts are portrayed as individual human beings first and foremost, individuals with names, families, identities, personal histories, hopes, fears, aspirations, and flaws. All of them are depicted as people who have been born into an untenable situation, one that deprives them of a decent livelihood and of their dignity, and who decide to undertake a journey that may rob them of their very lives but which holds out the promise of a better chance at living a decent life.

Eschewing any explicit judgment on the choices, realities, or legal status of the characters whose lives they evoke, the four texts bring to the fore the complex circumstances in which migrants are embedded, both at home and in the countries they seek to enter. Along with other similarly focused texts of Moroccan or Spanish provenance, they all have this feature in common: in telling the story of a character like Aziz Ammor or of Halima Bouhamsa they all seek to restore to the actual human beings on whose lives these fictional characters' lives are ultimately based a measure of their humanity, as I can attest from having heard and read numerous positive student responses to Lalami's fiction. Not all responses have been positive, however. One student wrote in her self-evaluation that she is so strongly opposed to illegal immigration into the U.S. that she found it very hard to read stories in which illegal immigrants are portrayed in a seemingly sympathetic way. Nonetheless, having taught Lalami's book to over 200 students over the course of five years, I can safely say that such views are not commonly held. Instead, most of my students coincide in pointing out that the stories have made them see that people are people, whether their nationality be American or Moroccan. One measure of the impact that *Hope and Other Dangerous Pursuits* has on my students is that many of them choose to write a creative option in response to the stories instead of a regular literary-critical paper. Whatever specific creative response they pursue – whether it be to rewrite some aspect of the story from the point of view of a minor character (e.g., Aziz's wife) or to imagine a different outcome for a major character – students who choose this option tend to report two notable facts: that they were driven to write creatively in response to the stories because the latter moved them, and that in delving into the characters' lives in a more personal way than objective literary criticism typically allows, they felt even more deeply for the characters and for their circumstances.

Conclusion: Beyond the So-called "Clash of Civilizations"

I want to end this essay with a comment on a film with which I typically begin the section of my courses that I devote to *Hope and Dangerous Pursuits*. The film – by the France-based Algerian-Romani director Tony Gatlif – is entitled *Vengo* ("I Come") and it tells the story of a blood feud between two Spanish Romani families. But before it delves into that rather hackneyed theme, the film opens with a fresh and startling sequence that brings together people from both the northern and southern shores of the Mediterranean in a way that contemporary political realities don't often allow for and that we hardly ever see depicted in our mass media, that is, as equals. In the sequence, flamenco musicians from Spain and Sufi musicians from Egypt face each other in the interior of a Spanish castle and perform a haunting improvised piece in which their respective instruments and melodies play off each other and blend to create a hybrid form of music that is greater than the sum of its notable parts. Roving among the musicians and the members of the audience who stand around them, the camera's eye accords all of them equal importance. Like Gatlif's film, Lalami's book reaches across the geo-political divides that characterize our world and in its own modest way calls in question the dangerous notions that we inhabit self-contained and implacably opposed civilizations. Instead of promoting alarm and mistrust, the book breaches walls of ignorance and borders of prejudice and serves instead as a bridge of understanding between peoples.

Notes

1. The literature of migration addresses the contemporary economic, cultural, and human exchange between the Middle East and the West. David Alvarez, born in Gibraltar and currently professor of literature at Grand Valley State University, shares his experience teaching this literature.
2. Elalamy and Binebine live in Morocco – although each of them has spent long periods in the United States – while Ben Jelloun and Lalami have spent most of their adult lives in France and in the United States respectively. Lalami's book is readily available in the United States, where it is published in paperback format by a major trade publisher, Harcourt Books. Ben Jelloun's novel is similarly accessible in the United States, where it is also published in paperback by a major press, Penguin. In contrast, the novels by Morocco-based Binebine and Elalamy were published in English translation by small commercial publishing houses (Granta Books and Lexington Books respectively). Elalamy's text is available in paperback but is considerably more expensive than Lalami's or Ben Jelloun's. The English-language edition of Binebine's novel is no longer in print, although copies of it are available through second-hand booksellers on the Internet. Other Moroccan authors have written works of fiction on this topic in both French and Arabic but to the best of my knowledge none of these works has been translated into English. The same is true of the sizeable list of works on this subject written by Spanish authors.

9

LITERATURE BY AND ABOUT MUSLIM AND MIDDLE EASTERN IMMIGRANTS IN THE WEST

This chapter is something of a departure from the rest of the book, in that rather than focusing on how teachers in English-speaking countries can incorporate literature and information about the contemporary Middle East into their curriculum, here we will look at the rapidly growing groups of Middle Eastern and Islamic peoples now citizens in the West – and how to address misinformation about them and tell their stories to our students. A rich tradition of multicultural teaching and scholarship has emerged in English-speaking countries focused on people of African, Native, Hispanic, Jewish, and even Asian origin, whereas Muslim people of Middle Eastern background, regardless of their country of origin, have fallen through the curricular cracks. Despite increasing numbers in the English-speaking world, despite – especially since 9/11 – growing and well-documented cases of discrimination, and despite public disputes over veiling, mosques, and religious practices, the life and experiences of Middle Eastern and Islamic people living in the English-speaking West remain nearly invisible to the vast majority of students and teachers.

How timely then that there is now a high-quality new literature in English about the experience of Middle Eastern and/or Islamic people living in America, Australia, Canada, United Kingdom, and Europe. This literature is an essential part of any contemporary multicultural curriculum. Moreover, there are almost certain to be in your area Muslims and/or people with Middle Eastern origins willing to be a resource for your students, both so that they can learn about minority communities, but also to develop, as illustrated elsewhere in this book, more informed perspectives on the Middle East and Islam.

Of course, immigrants and Islamic people living in English-speaking countries and the West are an enormously diverse group, and no one text, individual, or immigrant group is or can be representative. Interestingly, the distribution of

Middle Eastern people in America, Canada, United Kingdom, or Australia does not match the distribution of Middle Eastern or Islamic people in the rest of the world. Certain social classes, ethnic, and religious groups and subgroups are over or underrepresented because individuals and groups immigrated at specific times, and for different reasons. While the statistics I use are all approximate, they help us begin to understand the significant presence of Middle Eastern and Islamic people in the English-speaking world.

There are large and growing numbers of people of Arabic background in all English-speaking countries. In America there are at least 3.5 million Arab Americans found in all 50 states, roughly half in California, Michigan, New York, Florida, and New Jersey. Most Arab Americans are Christian (63 percent), a mix of Catholics, Eastern Orthodox, and Protestants. The rest are either Muslims (24 percent), or Jews or do not have a religious affiliation (13 percent). In contrast to Europe and Canada, in America "Arabs" are considered by the official government census to be "white." As in many English-speaking countries, the largest group of people with an Arab background is from Lebanon. Well-known Arab-Americans include Ralph Nader, Frank Zappa, Salma Hayek, Steve Jobs, Diane Rehm, Christa McAuliffe, John Sununu, Spenser Abraham, Edward Said, and many others.

Arabic people are also one of the largest and fastest growing non-European ethnic groups in Canada and Australia, with about 350,000 people of Arabic background in each country. More than half of Arab Canadians are foreign born and, overall, the population is young, with 96 percent able to speak Canadian national languages (English or French). In Canada as many Arab Canadians are Christian as Muslim. In the 2002 Canadian census, 88 percent of those who reported an Arabic origin indicated that they had strong sense of belonging to Canada, while at the same time, 52 percent said that they had a strong sense of belonging to their ethnic or cultural group ("The Arab Community").

Iranian–Persian Americans have lived in the United States in small numbers since the 1930s, but after the 1979 revolution in Iran there were many immigrants, as well as students studying in the United States, who decided to stay, so that the United States now has the largest number of Iranians outside of Iran – over 400,000. There are another 100,000 in Canada. These numbers include a significant number of Iranian–Armenian Christians. Many of the Iranians in America and Canada come from the educated elite in Iran and are skilled professionals. Approximately 40 percent are Muslims, 40 percent are non-religious, and 20 percent Jewish, Christian, Baha'is or Zoroastrian. Teachers may find interesting a website about Iranian American writers, IranianAmericanWriters.org.

There are about 450,000 Armenian Americans, arriving from the end of the nineteenth century up to 1920 during a period of oppression and genocide in their homeland and relative openness in American immigration policy. Well-known Armenian Americans include Andre Agassi, Cher, Michael Vartan, William

Saroyan, and Eric Bogosian. Religious Armenian Americans belong to several different Christian groups.

There are something like 200,000 Turkish Americans, Turks having been in the United States since the seventeenth century. Many emigrated from the Ottoman Empire between 1900 and 1914. There is a growing population of people of Turkish background in Canada and Australia, and there are also people of Kurdish background in all three countries.

Muslim Americans are diverse, multiethnic, and multiracial. Though no precise count of Muslims Americans has been made, estimates vary from 3–8 million; within the Muslim American community 7 million is a widely accepted figure. There are likely over 2 million British Muslims, over 800,000 Muslim Canadians, 350,000 Muslim Australians and Muslim South Africans, and 40,000 Muslim New Zealanders. As of 2010 there are 1,200 mosques in the United States and 1,500 mosques in the United Kingdom. American Muslims are about 35 percent South Asian (Pakistani, Indian, and Bangladeshi), 25 percent African American, 25 percent Arab, and 15 percent other (including Turks, Iranians, Bosnians, Malays, Indonesians, and Kenyans.) About half of American Muslims are Sunni, a quarter not affiliated, the rest have other affiliations.

Islamic people came to the United States as early as the eighteenth century as African American slaves. Perhaps as many as 20 percent of the slaves brought to the U.S. had some knowledge of Islam or were Muslim. In 1796, the then President John Adams signed a treaty with Morocco – the first country in the world to

FIGURE 9.1 Islamic Center of America, Warrendale, Michigan

formally recognize the United States – declaring the United States had no "character of enmity against the laws, religion, or tranquility, of Mussulmen." In the nineteenth century, Arabs from the Ottoman Empire came to the U.S. and some settled, particularly in the areas of Dearborn Michigan, Quincy Massachusetts, and Ross, North Dakota. By 1950 there were twenty mosques in America. Muslims increased in number in the twentieth century; recent immigrants are the largest part of the Muslim population.

The majority of native-born American Muslims are in different African American Muslim groups, including the Nation of Islam – all together these groups comprise about a quarter of American Muslims. The Nation of Islam was started in the 1930s by Wallace Fard Muhammad, led by Elijah Muhammad, and had as its most famous member, Malcolm X. Malcolm X joined the movement in prison, and, when released in 1952, became a leader until his break with Elijah Muhammad in 1964. Subsequently Malcolm X made a trip to Mecca and became a Sunni Muslim. He was assassinated soon thereafter, in 1965. In 1963, the group had 23,000 members. After the death of Elijah Muhammad in 1975 his son, Warith Deen Muhammad, led the group and more closely aligned it with Sunni Islam – membership significantly increased to, perhaps, 200,000. Some rejected these reforms and re-established the Nation of Islam under Louis Farrakhan, with about 20,000 members.

According to surveys, Muslim Americans have statistically more years of education and slightly higher income levels than the overall American average, and are somewhat more religious. According to a 2007 religious survey, 72 percent of Muslims believe religion is "very important," compared to 59 percent holding that view in the overall population. ("Islam in the United States"). There are many Muslim groups including the American Society of Muslims, the Islamic Society of North America, Islamic Circle of North America, Islamic Assembly of North America, and The Muslim Students' Association (active on university campuses). American Muslims tend to be socially conservative, but only 12 percent of Muslims believed that American military action in Iraq was justified.

Given Islamophobia, as I have also discussed in Chapter 1, it is important that we teach secondary and college students about Islam. In this chapter I want to talk about some of the ways I have tried to address Islam directly and build bridges between my non-Muslim students and Islamic people. Even in Michigan, a state with a large number of Muslims, many of my students have never knowingly met an Islamic person, spoken with them about their religion, or visited a mosque. Yet, in any part of the United States or Canada it is remarkably easy to find speakers who might come to your class, and mosques, Islamic centers, and Islamic schools that your students might visit; simply go to www.IslamicFinder.org and put in your zip code! I have been able to arrange for a number of my classes to visit a mosque in our town. We removed our shoes, spoke with the Imam, learned about Islamic rituals of prayer, and were invited to ask questions. We experienced a warm hospitality and were treated with Middle Eastern desserts of honey, nuts, and filo pastry. The mosque's Imam is a young man called "Hafez" (in Arabic "Hafez" means "guardian") because he had the entire Quran completely committed to memory in Arabic (his native language is Urdu). He recited some of it for us. Here are some of my students' responses:

> Last Thursday my classmates and I went to the Kalamazoo Islamic Center st It was an amazing learning experience. First, we were given a tour of the center by the Imam himself. After that, he told us some stories about his religious background explaining how he got to where he is today. You could tell by just talking with the Imam how passionate he was about his religion, for it is his life. While I found how important it is to not always believe everything you hear – many of my misconceptions and stereotypes about Islam were broken. At the end of our visit, we were able to sit down with the Imam and ask him any questions we had. I learned that all kinds of people pray at a mosque, black, white, Indian, it doesn't matter because there, they are all the same. In the mosque people become family, and I thought that was really cool.
>
> *(Mary Hitt)*

> Our class trip to the Islamic Center was by far the most rewarding and informative experience I have had so far in our class study of Middle Eastern Literature. The Imam was so friendly and knowledgeable it was hard not to like him. Having been raised Catholic and taught to fear Muslims it was reassuring to feel safe and at home in a frequently visited place of worship by Muslims. I found it extremely interesting to find out that the Imam held Jesus Christ with the utmost respect – some Christians I know poke fun at the Islamic figure of Muhammad. After our trip I came to the conclusion that there is no need to fear Islam or Muslims, they are pretty much following a religion similar to my own, but through the interpretation of a different man.
>
> *(John Ebbing)*

> I had taken a religion class last year that taught me a little bit about Islam, but nothing could compare to being able to hear about the history and meaning behind the religion from the Imam himself, and being able to see the religion in action. I wish I could have stayed longer than I did. I was very appreciative that the Imam was able to explain different traditions in Islam and that he took the time to correct some of the misconceptions that we might have had about the religion. For example, the ladies' prayer room being separate was not because women are considered inferior but because they want to protect their pride as they kneel and bend over during prayer. I was also appreciative that the Imam was able to make so many connections between Christianity and Islam, which helped me understand that Islam

> does not reject Christianity, but rather does not take all of the same views. This conversation gave me the feeling that all were welcome in the mosque.
>
> *(Jennifer Wiley)*

> Going to a mosque is something I never would have done if not for this class. It was a cultural experience that I really enjoyed – everyone should go at least once.
>
> *(Saralynn Bush)*

Literature is an important starting point for understanding the experience of Muslims living in the West. A wonderful young adult novel that my college students read – and ideal for middle school and high school students as well – is *Does My Head Look Big In This?* (2008, 368 pages, age 12–17). Set in Australia and tracing the experience of a middle-class Palestinian girl who decides to wear the hijab, this is Randa Abdel-Fattah's first novel; her other novels, *Ten Hate Me* (2010, 304 pages, age 12–17) and *Where the Streets Had a Name* (2010, 320 pages, age 12–17) are also excellent possibilities for teaching. Watching *Sex in the City* and having crushes on teenage boys, Amal, the main character of *Does My Head Look Big In This?* will appeal to young readers likely to identify with her struggle for social acceptance. They will learn about a variety of experiences of Muslims living in the West from both Amal and her Muslim friends who come from families with widely different social practices. My students were strongly positive:

> The author did a great job of showing the multitude of challenges that an average teenage girl goes through. Each character had numerous difficulties to face, and developed solutions through out the whole novel. What was great for our class, was that this book showed the added stress that the main character Amal had to deal with due to her [Palestinian] ethnicity. She was a very strong female character (for a 16-year-old) and her thoughts were well developed. I loved that this novel did not just address the challenge of racism, but also other stereotypes which cause constant negativity to developing teens. Whether or not you are from a different culture, made no difference in this book, because it was easy to relate to each character's struggles and triumphs. I also loved that the story emphasized the difference between religious and cultural dictates. One of my favorite moments in the novel is when at the class forum the class president asks Amal to "discuss terrorism and how Islam condones it" and Amal then asks her if she would be happy to discuss the KKK and Christianity. Zzingg.
>
> *(Katie)*

Jennifer Wiley tells an interesting story that she relates to her reading of *Does My Head Look Big in This?*

> During my freshman orientation st as we were walking the campus we passed a Muslim woman. This woman was completely covered up in a pale pink scarf, with matching long sleeved shirt and pants made of this flowing material. All you could see of her were her eyes. I remember thinking that she was beautiful . . .
>
> And then one of the boys in my group yelled out to her "What the hell?! It's summer, what are you wearing?" Our group leader told him to be quiet, and he proceeded to whisper to all of us, "she looks like a clown."
>
> Just telling this story still makes my blood boil. It shows the horrible lack of respect and understanding that many American teens and adults have for Muslim women. Reading *Does My Head look Big In This?* we got our first good inside look at a woman (or girl) under the veil while living in western society, and at the ignorance of many Westernized people toward women who choose to wear the veil. I loved seeing the normalcy and humanity of Amal, the way that she felt so passionate about wearing the veil and the pride she held in knowing that it was more than a fashion statement; it was a symbol of devotion to her God. This novel makes me wonder what the woman we saw on campus that summer was thinking. At the time I assumed she would be embarrassed and sad, and who could blame her? But now I wonder if, on top of that, she might have experienced a moment of pride for representing her faith and enduring the torment of those who do not understand it.

My students also enjoyed reading short stories by the feminist and magical realist writer Ghada Samman from her collection *The Square Moon* (1999). Samman was born in Syria, lived for many years in Lebanon, and, since the 1980s, has resided in Paris. The stories in this collection tell of the complexities and cultural conflicts of Lebanese people living in France. "Beheading the Cat" tells the story of Abdul, a young French Lebanese man considering proposing to Nadine, a free spirited, bungee-jumping, independent college student who "grew up in Paris and was a brilliant mixture of the magic of East and West" (4). Nadine asserts, "Yes, I am Lebanese. But I am not another copy of my mother" (8). In the midst of his contemplations arrives the apparent ghost of his long dead aunt Badriyya offering to marry him to a young, subservient and traditional Lebanese bride.

> I actually liked this story a lot . . . I really liked Nadine's character, she knows what she wants and knows how to get it. If Abdul can't handle her, then it is his loss. She doesn't need a man to define who she is as a person. Abdul struggles with the traditional arranged marriage and values his aunt lays out for him, and wanting someone like Nadine to have a connection with, but at the same time also tame. I thought it was interesting that Nadine referred to him as her Lebanese Hamlet focusing on the key line "To Be or Not To Be" as a allusion to his wishy-washiness. This story showed the

> struggle between traditional Lebanese values (the aunt) and modern Lebanese values (Nadine).
>
> *(Saralynn Bush)*

High school and college students will find this story an interesting take on cultural change of immigrant communities.

We also watched a fascinating independent film, *Arranged* (2007) directed by Diane Crespo and Stefan Schaefer. It tells the story of two young women, Rochel (Zoe Lister-Jones) an Orthodox Jew and Nasira (Francis Benhamou), a Syrian-born Muslim, who are both first-year teachers at a public school in Brooklyn. Over the course of the year they become friends and discover many similarities, especially that both of their families are arranging marriages for them. The film points to common cultural practices from the Middle East for both traditional Jews and Muslims, and we learn how, even though the marriages are arranged, the young women still have an important voice in the process. An interesting counterpoint is the school principal, a feminist from the 1960s, who is concerned that the young women are oppressed.

> I really enjoyed this film, *Arranged*, probably the most so far. I liked how the two women allowed themselves to have the best of both cultures. The modern, American culture where Muslims and Jews both get along and can be good friends. And their traditional religious cultures by upholding modesty as well as their families' standards of arranging marriage. They were not pushed over by anyone, not the children, the principal, or their families. I thought it was great that the movie emphasized how both women's parents wanted the best for their daughters. I think there is a misconception that the women in arranged marriages have no choice, but this film breaks down the stereotype to show these women do have choices.
>
> *(Saralynn Bush)*

> I think that the principal was my favorite character because she added so much humor and tension. She also showed that Americans can be so ignorant . . . In general I felt like the acting was very real and believable, especially the children and the parents. The children showed that at a young age we are very curious and have a strong thirst for knowledge and unity. The parents of Raquel showed that all ages and generations have prejudices.
>
> *(Molly White)*

> It was interesting to see how the whole process worked for both religions, and to see what parts of it the girls liked and what parts they did not agree with. It was wonderful to see both of them so happily married in the end, with such bright futures ahead of them.
>
> *(Ashley Aubermann)*

FIGURE 9.2 "Arranged"

Humor is an important element to undoing stereotypes and a number of writers of Middle Eastern origin draw extensively on humor. Firoozeh Dumas, born in Abadan, Iran moved to Whittier, California at the age of seven; she has written two hysterically funny chronicles of growing up and living in America: *Funny in Farsi: A Memoir of Growing Up Iranian in America* (2003, 208 pages, age 12–college) and *Laughing Without an Accent: Adventures of an Iranian American, at Home and Abroad* (2009, 256 pages, age 15–college). *Funny in Farsi* was a finalist for the PEN award; ABC considered creating a sitcom based on it; and the translation has been a best-seller in Iran. While these books inspire laughter at language barriers, American ignorance of the Middle East, consumerist culture, religious difference, and the Iranian hostage crisis, they bring to the reader an important immigrant perspective. Although I have heard and spoken with Dumas, I have read but not yet taught her books. I came across some comments relevant to teachers in Amazon.com reviews:

> Recently we had our middle school and high school students read *Funny in Farsi*. What a hit. The kids loved the stories. They could really relate to stories of her childhood. It also helped them understand the immigrant experience from another perspective. Ms. Dumas helps students understand the universality of family life.
>
> *(Rad)*

> *Funny in Farsi* is a special gem for anyone teaching Middle Eastern culture or immigration experiences. Spoken with a clear non-judgmental voice, Firoozeh Dumas portrays the trials and tribulations of moving to America and her family's attempt to be a part of the American culture. Filled with laugh-out-loud tales from her childhood, this book is sure to please while presenting an entirely different perspective on American life.
>
> *(High School Librarian)*

> A community college teacher in Sacramento, I'm a big fan of *Funny in Farsi* – for its generous humor, compassionate spirit, and accessibility for a wide range of students. The author appeared at my campus in March of 2006 and was a big hit at a classroom visit of ESL students (students from around the globe) who related to Firoozeh's stories of her Iranian family assimilating into our culture. At a talk to the campus community, she won new fans who appreciated her hilarious anecdotes from *Funny in Farsi* and her rich humanity of spirit. Especially at this time in our lives when we might attend more than ever to our shared experiences, Firoozeh Dumas' book makes a significant contribution.
>
> *(H. Schneider)*

Another humorous film that can be shown to students in whole or part to undo stereotypes is *Allah Made Me Funny: Live in Concert* (2008). This film captures the routines of three American Muslim standup comedians, Muhammad Amer, Preacher Moss, and Azhar Usman as they tell jokes about racial profiling, how they are treated boarding airlines, and the reaction of friends, family, and strangers to Muslim Americans.

In addition to meeting Muslims and reading about Islam, given the intensity of stereotypes and the fanning of hatreds by attacks on mosques, threats to burn the Quran, and so on, I think it important for students to research Islamophobia, the prejudice against or irrational fears of Islam or Muslims. Giving these fears a name is a starting point for challenging ignorance, and the news and Internet are full of disturbing stories and images that students can examine.

Literature by Muslim Middle Eastern people living in the West is a rapidly growing field, with individual works, edited collections, films, and engaging studies increasing available.

Further Reading

Living Islam Out Loud: American Muslim Women Speak, edited by Saleemah Abdul-Ghafur (2005), is a collection of short essays about their lives by younger (under 40) American women Muslims from a diversity of backgrounds. Topics addressed include dating, marriage and sexuality, hijab, variations of faith and belief, and the contemporary evolution of Islam in America.

An Apartment Called Freedom by Ghazi Algosaibi (1996) tells the story of Saudi Arabian young men living as students in England.

Only in London by Hanan Al-Shaykh (2001) follows four airplane passengers from Lebanon, Morocco, Iraq, and England as their lives interweave in London.

How Does it Feel to be a Problem? Being Young and Arab in America by Moustafa Bayoumi (2008) tells the story of seven young Arab Americans in post 9/11 America.

Inclined to Speak: An Anthology of Contemporary Arab American Poetry edited by Hayan Charara (2008) includes 160 poems by 39 different Arab American poets.

Once in a Promised Land by Laila Halaby (2003). Jassim and Salwa own a beautiful house in Albuquerque, New Mexico. Jassim drives a Mercedes, and Salwa makes enough money to send large sums to help her Palestinian family in Jordan. Unfulfilled in spite of the comforts and luxuries of their American life, they lie to each other and so worsen their alienation from one another. The September 11th attacks only make matters worse in terms of Jassim's and Salwa's relationship. (Chelsea Leatherman)

Dinarzad's Children: An Anthology of Arab American Fiction 2nd Edition edited by Pauline Kaldas and Khaled Mattawa (2009) includes 19 stories from a diversity of Arab American perspectives.

Season of Migration to the North by Taleb Salih (1989) is a classic postcolonial novel from the Sudan (1966), originally in Arabic, about a man who studies in England, the contrast of cultures, and a series of unhappy relations with women.

10

TEACHING MUSLIM STUDENTS

While learning how to teach students of diverse cultural backgrounds is recognized as an important consideration in teacher preparation and ongoing professional development, there is precious little work done to support teachers, school districts, and universities in working effectively with Muslim students and families. Especially given the stereotypes and hostilities toward Islam that exist in many Western countries, it is critical for teachers to be thoughtful about how to support their Muslim students. Of course, the overwhelming majority of the teaching staff in English-speaking countries has a Christian background. At the same time the numbers of Muslim youth in schools and colleges is rapidly growing; as discussed in the previous chapter there are over 10 million Muslims in America, Canada, Britain, and Australia. The failure to adequately prepare and support teachers working with Muslim students continues to lead to significant misunderstanding, conflicts, and controversies that only occasionally make the news.

As we have seen, Muslims in the West are an extremely diverse group, whether native citizens or immigrants. Most are not from the Middle East – Muslims come from all parts of the world and all racial groups. Indeed, the majority of people with Middle Eastern origins living in the United States and Canada are Christian, not Muslim.

Muslim students may be brand new to the country and in cultural shock – or they may be native-born and as culturally "with it" as any student. The experience of Muslim children and young people in English-speaking schools is most significantly influenced by their knowledge of the English language and local culture, and whether they are natives, first, second, or later generation immigrants. Muslim families may be more traditional, more close-knit, with strong "family values," but this is not always the case. Just because a female might wear a headscarf (hijab) to class does not imply that she or her family is liberal or conservative, or that the decision to wear hijab was made for her by her parents, rather than a decision she has made on her own.

Education and teachers are highly valued in Islam. Even Muslim parents who are recent immigrants, especially mothers, may be eager to talk to teachers, but they may be uncertain about making the first move. Teachers who develop rapport with families are likely to quickly gain trust and will be all the more able to support student success. Setting a tone of respect is the starting point. Including Middle Eastern literature in the curriculum and helping students learn about Islam, as this book indicates, can demonstrate that respect. Inviting in speakers from the community can help develop trust. Even small efforts to connect to the local Muslim community may make a significant difference. Reading this book, talking to people, or visiting a mosque are good starts for teachers wanting to support their Muslim students. Learning about Islam is another step. Teaching about Islam and inviting parents or local leaders to the classroom is another (see Chapter 1). As you become more familiar with Islam, take note of similarities between Islam, Christianity, and Judaism and share with students. Teachers who read this book are in a position to become not only a resource to their students, but also to their colleagues, administrators, and communities. Regardless of the teacher's level of knowledge, I think it wise to approach a practitioner of any faith with openness to learning. At the same time, be thoughtful about the use of language. The term "Muslim" refers to people who profess the religion; the word "Islamic" is more abstract – in English it is better talk about "what Muslims believe" rather than "Islamic belief or practices" because "Islamic" refers to the whole religion and may be too generalizing.

FIGURE 10.1 Muslim Student

Just as with Christians or any other faith, there is a wide range of degree of devotion between different families and practitioners. A person who is less devout does not necessarily see themselves as any less Christian or less Muslim. For Muslim students religion may be a regular feature of daily life, not simply for worship one morning a week. (Friday is the holy day of the week for Muslims, and for the devout, prayer takes place every day.) In this sense, their religion is something Muslim students bring to school with them, and, in the U.S., their right to do so is protected by the constitution. Five prayers a day are expected of pious Muslims, including at midday and in the afternoon. The times for these prayers vary depending on the length of daylight hours, and there is flexibility in the time of prayers so that they can usually take place before or after classes or at lunch. Schools with Muslim students have set aside quiet rooms where they can pray. If Muslim students are attending a public school they know they will mix genders in the classroom, but in the lunchroom, recess, or after school traditional Muslim students may avoid such mixing. Teachers of secondary and college students might ask students about their comfort in mixing genders in collaborative or team group projects. Traditional students may feel more comfortable talking with adults of the same gender, and may want to avoid physical contact, including dating, dancing, shaking hands, or directly looking in the eyes of a person of the opposite sex. Teachers need to help all of their students learn to recognize, for example, that wearing a hijab is normal, and that it is disrespectful to tease Muslim students, comment behind their back, or ask a Muslim girl to remove her headscarf. Some differences in cultural practice can become issues in schools. As modesty is a high value, Muslim students will likely not be comfortable in physical education classes when changing clothes is required for participation. Some Muslim students may be "halal," just as some Jewish students are "kosher," and are restricted from eating pork and other foods, even chicken, depending on how it has been prepared. Teachers and school personnel can ask parents and students if the way the food is prepared is OK for them.

Ramadan is an important month-long observance for Muslims that teaches patience, modesty, and spirituality and that involves fasting from early in the morning till sunset. During Ramadan, Muslims ask forgiveness for past sins, pray for guidance and help in refraining from everyday evils, and try to purify themselves through self-restraint and good deeds. Although Ramadan is always on the same day of the Islamic calendar, the date on the Gregorian calendar varies, since the Gregorian calendar is a solar calendar and the Islamic calendar is a lunar calendar. This difference means Ramadan moves in the Gregorian calendar approximately eleven days every year. Fasting Muslim students may ask to leave the lunchroom during Ramadan so they can avoid smelling food and watching other students eat. Such requests should be respected. Teachers should be aware that everyone reacts to fasting differently and some fasting students may be tired, dizzy or drowsy. They may have been up late at evening prayers (Taraweeh) especially during the last ten days of Ramadan. Being supportive of fasting will likely be appreciated by the student and family. Teachers should also not assume that all Muslim students will fast, or that they will pray five times per day, and they certainly can feel free to ask students if they are fasting and talk to them about the holiday. Just as Christians wish people well on Christmas, teachers and students can wish Muslims well during Ramadan. Eidul Fitr (Eid) is the Islamic holiday that marks the end of the fasting period of Ramadan and is a special celebration involving wearing one's holiday best, communal prayer, feasting and dispersing of food.

Another important holiday is Eid Al Adha, the "Festival of Sacrifice" which commemorates the willingness of Abraham (Ibrahim) to sacrifice his son as an act of obedience to God. Instead, God allowed him to sacrifice a ram. Traditionally families sacrifice a domestic animal, such as a sheep, goat, or cow, giving a third each to themselves, their neighbors and the poor. Eid Al Adha is a time to be thankful for food and housing, and to spend time with family and friends. The date is approximately 70 days after Ramadan, and at the end of the time of the traditional pilgrimage. It is appropriate to say "Happy Eid" for either holiday, and Eid greeting cards are available online.

In addition to respecting Muslim students' religious differences, it is important to learn about the ethnicity and educational background of Islamic or Middle Eastern students including more recent immigrants. Some may be highly educated in their own language or some, from poorer countries, for instance Yemen, Somalia, or refugees from Iraq, may not have had schooling or missed schooling even in their own language. Those students who do have significant education prior to being in an English language school may have had quite different schooling experiences and expectations. In some Muslim societies education is more fact-based and less focused on either collaboration or competitive individualism. Group discussion, team work, questioning authority, taking your own or individual stands, innovating or independent thinking, may take time to develop. (And one has to also ask how well those methods and values, much proclaimed, are, in fact, promoted in Western schools increasingly under regimes of standardized testing.)

Immigrant students may especially appreciate information about how they will be graded and expectations for their work, and it is important to encourage what they have done right or well. Like all students, Muslim students are likely to take supportive or critical comments from teachers seriously. They may feel tremendous shame in a bad grade or failing or in others finding out about their "failure." More traditional or newer arrivals might attempt to "bargain with the teacher" to try to "fix it" somehow. They need to be encouraged to keep things in perspective, and to be open to trying again. As with many immigrant groups, second generation students may be having quite different experiences growing up than their parents, which can be difficult on both sides. Parents who don't speak English may be dependent on children who are able to learn the language more quickly. Some Muslim students may be more likely to bring gifts to teachers.

If there is a group in your class of recent immigrants from the same country it might be culturally consistent to identify one student, perhaps the oldest, to be a class or group "leader." More recent arrivals logically turn to those with more experience for guidance. Exchange students may be concerned about speaking out in public, and (sometimes justified) fears of losing their visa. For college students in America and Canada there is a national Muslim organization, the Muslim Students Association: www.MSANational.org, "a non-profit organization that strives to facilitate networking, educating, and empowering the students of today to be citizens of tomorrow's community." On my campus this group not only supports Muslim students, but also frequently hosts events and speakers where the whole campus is invited.

Teachers should not assume that all Middle Eastern or Muslim students automatically bond with each other. Within the Middle East and Islam there are animosities and different points of view, some of which are historical, deep-seated, and may have more to do with other factors than differences in religious belief. A familiar example: while conflicts in Northern Ireland between Protestants and Catholics are sometimes portrayed as "religious," these conflicts have more to do with economic and political discrimination and oppressions – the same is true of differences between Sunni and Shiite. Depending on the region and on individuals, there may be tensions between Sunni and Shiites, between Turks and Armenians, Greeks and others who were long ago under Ottoman Rule, between Arabs and Iranians, between Northern Arabs and Southern Arabs, etc. Creating assignments where teachers can learn about their students' background may have many advantages, including being helpful when pairing or grouping students.

The variety of Muslims in the West also creates opportunities to learn about the diversity of Islamic practice. In an email to me (8-14-10) Monica Eraqi writes,

> Akbar Ahmed has recently completed *Journey Into America: The Challenge of Islam*, and it focuses solely on the similarities and differences between 100 mosques in America, from the most conservative to the most liberal, African American mosques, Bosnian, Albanian, Arab and Asian mosques. I really could relate to the book just because of where I live [in Southeastern Michigan]. I regularly attend several mosques depending on where I am during the time of prayer. Sometimes a Lebanese Shia mosque in Dearborn, or an Albanian one in St. Clair Shores, which is also not far from an Egyptian one, or the Pakistani/Indian mosque in Rochester Hills. It's a great mix that I felt was exemplified in the book and might shed some light onto the different Muslim communities in the U.S. That's what makes this nation great. When I am in Egypt I am attending mosques that have relatively the same ideologies and are predominantly Sunni. There aren't many places on earth where I could attend so many mosques, so close to home, meet different cultures, and really understand the diversity of my religion.

> That helped so much as I traveled through Bosnia and Turkey. It helped me know what to expect.

This diversity of Muslim religious practice creates opportunities for teachers and students as well.

While respecting their differences, teachers should not assume that Muslim or Middle Eastern students have not been exposed to diverse or "new" cultural ideas. New technologies including the Internet, satellite, cable television, DVDs and the accessibility of downloading films is rapidly changing things even in conservative societies such as Saudi Arabia. Many people from the Middle East are well informed about America and the West, and indeed look up to Western culture in many ways, while having reservations about other aspects. At the same time certain topics may be uncomfortable for traditional Muslim students, such as books that show disrespect for parents or elders, have sexual or homosexual themes – sensitive teachers can support their Muslim students by making available optional or alternative reading.

Above all, never underestimate what Muslim students are capable of.

Further Reading

Muslims in America: A Short History by Edward Curtis (2009) is a short, accessible history telling the diverse story of Muslims in America. The book includes photographs, chronology, and information on immigrant and African American Muslims.

Educating the Muslims of America is a wide-ranging collection of essays edited by Yvonne Haddad, Farid Senzai, and Jane Smith (2009) that addresses Islamic schooling, resources for Muslim children, homeschooling, the experience of Muslim women on university campuses, and teaching about Islam in public and private schools.

All American Yemeni Girls: Being Muslim in a Public School by Loukia Sarroub (2005) focuses on the Yemeni community in Michigan, the complexities of ethnic and religious identity and conflicting pressures between home and school.

Muslim American Youth: Understanding Hyphenated Identities Through Multiple Methods by Selcuk Sirin and Michelle Fine (2008) is a rich study of the experience of Muslim youth – each chapter contains a fascinating interview of a young person representing different experiences.

11

READING AND TEACHING LITERATURE IN TRANSLATION

Vivan Steemers[1]

For most English speakers the only access we have to an authentic Middle Eastern literature – be it Arabic, Turkish, Persian, Kurdish or Hebrew – is via translation. It is therefore essential to ask ourselves the following question: what are the implications of being completely dependent on a translation for the understanding of a foreign work of literature, written in a language – and sometimes in an alphabet – totally unfamiliar to the reader and deeply embedded in a foreign culture?

Although Webster's dictionary informs us that "to translate" means "to put into the words of a different language," the act of translating does not simply consist of the substitution of a string of words in one language by their "equivalents" in another language, due in the first place to vocabulary as well as grammatical differences between languages. "Traduttore, traditore," a well-known Italian adage meaning "translator, traitor," reveals the challenges that translators face when they attempt to fully render the experiential other world in a translation. Of course, literary translations provide more challenges for the translator than non-literary ones. How, for instance, does one deal with translations of metaphors, puns, proverbs, irony, proper names with a meaning, connotations, cultural artefacts, historical references, language registers – colloquial, informal, and formal – regional dialects or accents in dialogue, to name just a few of the hurdles to be overcome by the translator? To draw an example from the perhaps more familiar French language: in the case of the proverb "Les chiens ne font pas des chats" the translator has the choice between a literal rendering – "Dogs don't make cats" – or the English equivalent "The apple doesn't fall far from the tree." The first choice would attract attention to the translation, coax a smile or raise an eyebrow; the second one would virtually go "unnoticed" by the reader, whose processing of the words would take place "smoothly:" the translator would have 'domesticated' the proverb.

Lynn Visson illustrates the inadequacy of the equivalence theory with the Russian translation of the English word 'friend.' The Russian language has three different words for this notion: one for a casual acquaintance ("znakomyi"), a second that refers to a closer acquaintance or friend ("priatel") and a third for a real friend ("drug") (60). Visson argues that Americans take minutes to make friends, while Russians take months or years. So while the translator is addressing a choice of words, there exist, at a deeper level, cultural issues as well. Even the translation of a simple everyday cultural 'artefact' such as bread reveals often unforeseen cultural differences. Although the equivalent of the word 'bread' in French is 'pain,' in German 'Brot' and in Punjabi 'naan,' the mental picture of the reader in the various languages will generally vary considerably: from an elongated, white, crusty "baguette" to the French reader, to a dark, firm whole wheat for the German reader and a soft, flat version for the Punjabi. (The example draws partly on Walter Benjamin, 78–79.) Notwithstanding their nuclear meaning of 'breadness,' the reality these terms refer to differs, each possessing a local meaning that is culturally determined. Indeed, the Spanish philosopher José Ortega Y Gasset maintains that the act of (literary) translation is at best an aspiration: "it is utopian to believe that two words belonging to different languages, and which the dictionary gives us as translations of each other, refer to exactly the same objects" (96). Different languages are generated by diverging mental pictures, disparate intellectual systems and philosophies. How can we possibly ever render adequately these nuances in a translation and create the correct mental picture in the mind of the reader?

Confronted with these issues, translators have various options. They can maintain the foreign term of the source text and supplement it with a brief explanation in a footnote, a glossary, or comment in the preface, thus adding a sense of 'foreignness' to the translation. The drawback of this solution is that the translated literary text may read more like an instructional, didactic, or even ethnological text and forfeit part of its literary quality if the translator resorts too frequently to this approach. The translator may also provide a translation that comes as close as possible to the original word, but that is part of the culture of the target text, thus "domesticating" it. For example, on New Year's Eve the Dutch eat "oliebollen," a literal translation – "oily balls" – would not sound very appetizing, yet the choice of "doughnuts" – although somewhat similar in substance but quite different in taste – would create the impression that the Dutch eat a typical American delicacy, which is far from the truth! The translator might also opt for a description or explanation of the problematic term within the text, and consequently lose again part of the literary quality present in the original text. In the case of "oliebollen," one would virtually have to provide a recipe! Finally, the translator may simply insert the untranslated word in the target text, leaving it up the reader to find out the exact meaning if s/he so wishes, yet adding an exotic touch to the text. An example would be the word "khamasin" winds in one of Mahfouz' novels (2000): "This year spring is pleasant:

BOX 11.1 THE WORD "HONOR"

A relevant example of the cultural complexity that can attend translation from Middle Eastern literature is the word "honor," as in people defending their honor, or losing their honor. The word "honor" encountered by readers of Middle Eastern literature translated to English may be a translation of the term "*namus*," a word known throughout the region including in Arabic, Turkish, and Farsi. *Namus*' origin in Arabic is "the one you confide in" and is also tied to the Greek word meaning "law or custom." In Islam *namus* is the law or enlightenment given to Muhammad during the first revelation. Translating "*namus*" as "law" as it might be from Arabic, or "honor" as it might be from Turkish doesn't capture the range of obligation, mutual responsibility, and structure of authority in traditional Middle Eastern families and communities. Traditionally, the older male figure of the family or community has an obligation to protect the *namus* of the family, to defend the family and household from gossip and physical threats. Subordinate members of the family have an obligation to maintain the *namus* of the family and should do so by behaving ethically, honestly, and with respect for private property, women, and male and female appropriateness. (Interestingly, if the word "honor" in English now tends to be thought of as the quality or recognition of an individual, in its origins it was more strongly a collective term of relationships, having to do with reciprocal responsibilities of social rank.) To maintain the *namus* of the family unmarried women especially must be modest, not flirt with men, or engage in sex before marriage. Although strictly forbidden by civic law, among certain rural groups likely closer to pastoral traditions, such as the Kurds or Bedouins, restoration of *namus* may be considered to entail the suicide or killing of the offending person or a relative, usually female. In this context maintaining the honor of a family may be not only about pride or a reputation for up rightness, but also safety as a family without honor is vulnerable to attacks from others. (For more on honor killing see Chapter 3.)

Source: Allen Webb

the *khamasin* winds are rare" (48). The reader may or may not want to discover that these winds are fifty-day-long spring sand storms. A second definition of "to translate" presented by Webster's dictionary is "to move from one place or condition to another, to transfer." An important question in this context is to what extent the translator intends to 'transfer' the reader to another culture, the culture of the original text.

Until a few decades ago, approaches to translation tended to be restrictive: theorists essentially discussed the rendering of words from one language into another. One of these earliest linguistic-oriented commentators on translation was Jerome who in the fourth century translated the Bible into Latin. His primary question was: should the translator translate word-for-word or sense-for-sense? Jerome opts for the sense-for-sense, following the example of the Roman orators Cicero and Horace, transferring thus the 'meaning' – the 'truth' – of the original

BOX 11.2 TERMS FOR RESPECTED LEADERS

In Middle Eastern works translated to English many terms are left untranslated because of the lack of a similar word in English. Such words typically call for additional work for students to more fully understand meaning. For example, there are a number of terms with religious and political origins describing respected leaders but with important distinctions of meaning:

Sheikh – An honorific term in Arabic that means "elder," and can refer to an older wise man or religious leader trained in Islamic studies. Though rare, there have been some women *sheikhs*. Arab Christians use the term for respected men, and its origin is similar to the Latin word from which the English word "senator" derives. *Sheikh* connotes a person of means and refined habits.

Mullah – A term of respect for a local cleric or mosque leader, similar to a pastor. *Mullahs* may be sent by the central government to villages that they don't come from, thus they may be seen even in the communities of the mosques they serve, as outsiders, even suspect, or, just as some pastors, as beholding to the authorities or wealthy members of the mosque. The term *mullah* is used for religious leader in some Jewish communities.

Imam – In Sunni Islam means "prayer leader" or recognized religious leader or teacher. In Shia Islam an Imam is a leader of the community; for some sects they are considered to be chosen by God and free from sin.

Bey – "Lord" or aristocrat, a Turkish term used throughout the Middle East. The first three rulers of the Ottoman Empire were called "*bey*," the title later became "*sultan*." The title "Bey" came to be applied to district administrator and lower-level minor military governors. Later it became a form of formal address, such as "sir," perhaps similiar to the Cockney English use of the word "guv'nor." The term is used after a person's name.

Agha – Also a title from Turkish and the Ottoman period, used, like *bey* after a person's name to indicate a civilian or military officer, but lacks the sense of gentility or aristocracy associated with *bey*.

Source: Allen Webb

text. Beginning in the seventeenth century, whether the translated texts are regarded as translations, imitations, or adaptations, foremost in the commentators' minds are questions concerning the fidelity of the translator to the original text. To what degree should the translator remain faithful to the source text – by producing a literal rendering – or claim liberty in creating a readable interpretation? Most commentators hold the opinion that a translation should not attract attention to itself, should, in fact, create an illusion of transparency, of not being a translation. Even today, if one were to ask most critics or readers – who seldom master the original language – what they would qualify as a good translation, their answer would most probably be: a "readable" or "smooth" translation, in other words: a text that does not *feel* or *sound* like a translation. Often no mention is made of the accuracy of the translation, possibly due to the reviewers' lack of knowledge of the foreign language. In contemporary Anglo-American culture, "transparent" texts correspond with "invisible" translators, according to Lawrence Venuti. Apart from the fact that the work of translators remains often unacknowledged, their role as an interpreter is grossly underestimated. Every careful translation is not only an interpretation of an original text, but also is informed by political and cultural belief systems.

One theorist who rejected the transparency or the "domestication" of the translation – its assimilation into the domestic culture – was the nineteenth-century German theologian and philosopher Schleiermacher who introduced the concept of "foreignization" or "foreignness." He wanted the German reader to "encounter the foreign" (Schleiermacher, 53) and grasp "the author's characteristic spirit" (Schleiermacher, 56) as well as the exoticism of the original text. This was a nationalistic, ideological decision: Schleiermacher's ulterior goal was to fertilize the national literary soil and enrich the German language with foreign words for a cultural elite, thus empowering the nation via its language.

Since the 1970s, translation theory has increasingly focused on the role of ideology, "the collective control or shaping of cultural knowledge" (Robinson, 185). The key question is not only: How is a text translated? But also, and even more importantly: Which literary texts are translated and why? Into and from what languages, and across which world regions ("first" or "third" world

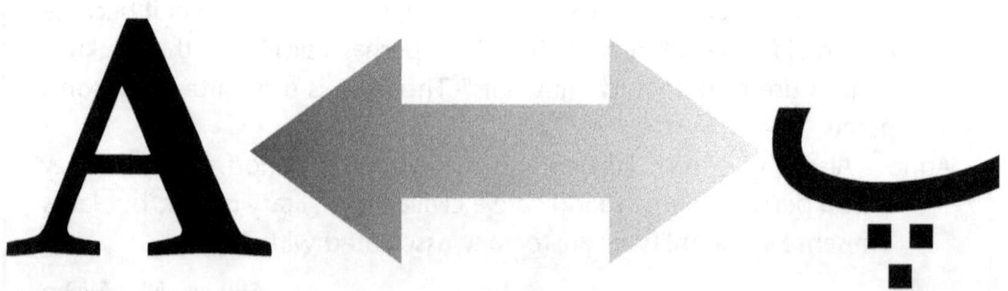

FIGURE 11.1 Translation Arrow English/Persian

countries)? According to Venuti, the business of translation is "fundamentally ethnocentric" (Scandals, 11). Texts for translation are mainly selected for the ease with which they are integrated into the receiving culture and the degree to which they correspond to prevalent images – cultural clichés – of the foreign culture and thus fix rather than question stereotypes of foreign cultures. For instance, the average Anglo-American reader is likely to be intrigued by the story of an urban Iranian woman fighting for democracy in her country, thus reinforcing the image Americans receive via their mass media of the Iranians' supposed need for American notions of democracy. The typical Anglo-American reader might be less intrigued by a novel from an Iranian author narrating the saga of her family living in a remote village, far away from the political turmoil (a story that may resemble to a certain extent the life of an American in an agrarian setting). Of course, publishers must profit from the translation and sale of books, so translating and publishing books that will appeal to ideas, even stereotypes readers already have about the Middle East may be the norm rather than the exception.

Translation theorists emphasize rightly the economics of literature in translation: "Patrons – once wealthy aristocrats – now take the form of presses and publishing houses, universities and granting agencies, which are in turn dependent on such groups as a readership, a critical establishment or government officials" (Tymoczko, 31). The publishing industry – including university presses and granting agencies – is one of the "realities of power and authority" (Said, 1983, 5) that makes texts possible. Often publishers select for translation foreign writers simply because they are "established" authors, laureates of literary prizes, whose translations are likely to warrant sales. Undoubtedly, the most effective "canonizaton" for any author is being awarded the Nobel Prize for Literature. Among the plethora of illustrative examples, the prolific Egyptian writer Naguib Mahfouz, winner of the Nobel Prize for Literature in 1988, whose work has been widely translated, is an interesting case in point. Most of his writing, according to Jacquemond, consists of well-constructed realistic novels that conform to the Western idea of a classic novel, presenting simultaneously the ideal mix of the exotic and the familiar or domestic (152). However, when Mahfouz was awarded this eminent international literary prize important members of the Arab literary establishment contended that the Arab novelist Abdul Rahman Munif was a more "meritorious candidate" (Hatim, 133). Basil Hatim notes that by the mid-1980s one or two minor works by Munif had been translated into major European languages in a far from "fluent" style (i.e. the translator had not domesticated the original text). Basil also suggests that Munif's work is "strongly referential" and "politically morbid" (133), qualities much appreciated by the Arabic critical establishment, but deemed inappropriate by Western publishers and translators for their readership. Hence, "consecration" by a national literary establishment of a literary work does not guarantee its success when transferred to another culture, even when it involves two Western cultures. For example, in 2006 the American author Jonathan Littell received the prestigious French literary prize, the Prix

Goncourt, as well as the Grand Prix du Roman de l'Académie Française, for his French novel *Les Bienveillantes*. Acclaimed by the French literary establishment, the novel, originally written in French by an American and translated into English (though not by the author himself), subsequently received mixed reviews in the United States and sold poorly. (In English this fictitious autobiography of a German Nazi officer received the title *The Kindly Ones*.) Literary tastes evidently differ between cultures.

The quantity of texts translated between one culture and another may be highly asymmetrical, often as a result of the imbalance of political or cultural power. For example, merely 1–2 percent of works that are translated between European languages and languages of the "third world" and Asia, involve "third world"/ Asian texts being translated, whereas 98–99 percent of the translations involve the European language text (English, French, German etc.) being translated to the "third world"/Asian languages (Jacquemond, 139). Perhaps this is not surprising, since the profit in this exchange for the Anglo-American publisher – who is part of the politically and culturally dominant power – comes from selling English language texts abroad. Striking imbalances also exist between the European languages, such that between 2–4 percent of total book production in U.S. and UK comprises translation, whereas in France this figure ranges between 8 and 12 percent, in Germany it amounts to 14 percent, and in Italy 25 percent (Venuti, *The Translator's Invisibility*, 12–14) "[C]ultural hegemony confirms, to a great extent, economic hegemony," states Jacquemond (139), who studied trends in French-Arabic translation. He observes that translators who translate from the powerful, hegemonic culture/language into a dominated or subservient culture/language typically work to serve the hegemonic culture, while the translators from a dominated to a hegemonic culture act as "authoritative mediator[s]" (155), adapting the works to fit preconceived notions of the dominant cultures. Moreover, authors in a dominated culture who dream of reaching a large audience will themselves tend to write for translation into a hegemonic language, and this will require conforming to some extent to stereotypes already held in the dominant culture. These problematics are clearly at work in the translation and publication of works from the Middle East in English, as is addressed in many points in this volume.

Of course, there are important exceptions. Texts are translated and made available that do not simply cater to the stereotypes of the English-speaking or "first world" reader, and those texts become especially important for teachers. There is an intellectual minority – within the hegemonic as well as the dominated culture – that attempts to resist these influences (Jacquemond, 155). Since the 1980s, scholars, writers, and translators, inspired by postcolonial theorists, have in particular attended to the influence of economics and power relations on cultural exchanges between the "first" and the "third" world in general, including the dynamics of translation and publication.

What are the implications for the teaching of literature in translation? Teachers and students should be aware when reading any translated text that a translation and a translator are involved. Both should be made "visible." A translator can be recognized and acknowledged in the same way as an author, and students may consider that the translation they are reading is, in some measure only, one of many possible interpretations of the source text. There are many ways to make the question of translation evident in the classroom. Teachers might have students compare different sample translations of the same text. Illustrative of the creative role of the translator is the volume *One Hundred Frogs: From Renga to Haiku in English* by Hiroaki Sato, where the author has collected one hundred "translations" – versions, parodies, re-creations – of the same Japanese haiku. Furthermore, attention can be drawn to the "situatedness of the texts and interpretations" (Venuti, Scandals, 93). Each translation – like each literary text – is produced within a certain cultural context at a specific historical moment as well as for a particular constituency. It is for instance not uncommon that a British as well an American translation exist for the same foreign novel; classic works of literature, be it *Arabian Nights* or Homer's *The Odyssey* have been translated into English by many different translators, each one adapting the foreign work to the prevalent views on language and culture of their time period, inscribed with their specific cultural values. The target language is constantly changing, and so is the reader.

We need to be thoughtful about the inscription of domestic/stereotyped values in texts that are translated to English and aware of the power dynamics involved in the publishing industry in our globalized world. At the same time, such concerns must not prevent us and our students from the vital learning that takes place from translated works. During discussions on the implications of reading in translation, invariably the "loss" of translation will be brought up. As we have seen, this is understandable in view of the obstacles the translator faces. Nevertheless, according to Steiner, the very act of translation compensates this loss, "enlarges the stature of the original" (196); the original work is thus "enhanced" and in terms of the public it reaches it is "left more prestigious" (196). Benjamin refers to this phenomenon as the "afterlife" (76): translations provide an afterlife to the literary work for generations to come. Each translation will be a transformation of the original – this is inherent to the notion of 'afterlife' – adapting to a renewed language and transformed culture, providing a fresh interpretation. Therefore, translations are part of the immortalization process of the original work of literature; however imperfect, they are often the only means for readers who do not master the original language to glimpse into the minds of foreign authors and to appreciate their physical and psychological world.

Note

1. Most teachers are trained to teach texts originally written in English, yet teaching texts in translation, as recommended throughout this book, calls for careful thinking about the dynamics of both translation and publication. Vivan Steemers helps us with these issues.

12
CONNECTING BRITISH AND AMERICAN LITERATURE TO THE MIDDLE EAST

Teachers of survey courses in British and American literature, or more general courses in the humanities, literature, history, or culture, may be eager to think about how they can explore representations of the Middle East and its peoples in their courses, and, when appropriate, connect those representations to more complete depictions in modern works from the region. Such teachers will be interested to learn that many of the authors they teach in their classes have written about the Middle East, including Dante, Boccaccio, Chaucer, Shakespeare, Coleridge, Shelly, Irving, Hawthorne, Poe, Alcott, Melville, Twain, and more. Scholarship by Edward Said, Daniel Vitkus, Hilton Obenzinger, Jack D'Amico, David Bergeron, Nabil Matar, Luther Luedtke, Michael Stevens, and others drawing on new interest in multiculturalism and Orientalism provides us with important insights and comparative possibilities for teaching. In a brief way, this chapter points to opportunities to examine representations of the Middle East in survey courses where these topics have not been often examined but yet hold great potential for better understanding Western literature, and its long relationship with the Middle East. As we shall see, even characters as familiar as Tom Sawyer and Huckleberry Finn have surprising and interesting Middle Eastern connections! Drawing on this kind of investigation – and by using whole class, literature circle, or independent reading of contemporary texts – teachers of traditional courses can draw on historic and thematic connections to segue from authors they are currently teaching to many of the Middle Eastern works addressed throughout this volume.

As discussed in Chapter 1 and throughout this book, there is a long history of relations between Europe and the Middle East, between Christians and Muslims, that dates from before the Crusades and up to the present. Often, as we have seen, that relationship has been marked by fear, suspicion, and hostility. At other times, and sometimes in surprising and contradictory ways, that relationship has involved fascination, friendship, respect, and intellectual, cultural, scientific, and religious exchange. Examining British, American, and European literature can illustrate and allow students to examine the stereotypes and complexities of Christian–Muslim relations.

Recently, I taught an introductory college literature course addressing literature of the Middle East, but I began the class by focusing on the representations of the Middle East in works by canonical authors. Preparing the for class, I was intrigued by the diversity and richness of the texts that I discovered already in the canon, some of it well known and commonly taught, though not usually from a "Middle Eastern perspective," works such as Dante's *Divine Comedy*, Shakespeare's *Othello*, and Shelly's "Ozymandias." Other works also by well-known authors were relevant but taught less often. Once the focus is shifted to examining representations of the Middle East, previously less canonical pieces emerge as important and interesting. All of the texts I used in my class, as well as those I haven't yet used but recommend in this chapter, were published before 1921, and thus these original literary works are in the public domain, free of copyright issues, and available to students, teachers, and scholars in free, easy-to-find and use, online archives. Many are also, of course, in libraries or available in thrift or scholarly editions.

Before delving into the specifics of my teaching experiments, some historical context is necessary. Of course in Chapters 1 and 5 we have looked at the inequities in the relationship of European and Middle Eastern countries and the simultaneous development of Orientalist thought. Part of the fascination of historically earlier materials is not simply the presence of myths and stereotypes, though they are certainly to be found, but also the ways in which perceptions of "the Other" are in flux, complicated, contradictory, and, at times, even complimentary.

Given the power of the Christian church both as an economic and cultural force in medieval Europe, it is not surprising that religious differences have long been an important aspect of identifying non-Christians. Karen Armstrong talks about the darker side of early Christian images of Muslim people:

> At about the same time that the myths of Charlemagne, King Arthur, and Robin Hood were being evolved in the West, the myth of Mahound, the enemy and shadow-self of Christendom, was firmly established in the Western imagination. To explain Muhammad's success, the legends claimed that he had been a magician who had concocted false "miracles" to take in credulous Arabs and destroy the Church in Africa and the Middle East . . . His mystical experiences were explained away by the claim that he was an epileptic, which at that time was tantamount to saying that he was possessed by demons. His sexual life was dwelt on in prurient detail: he was credited with every perversion known to men.
>
> *(Armstrong,* Islam, *26)*

As mentioned in Chapter 1, depictions of Muslims were also connected to Jewish and anti-Semitic myths and legends, one of the most powerful and disturbing captured in Chaucer's "Prioress Tale" about the murder of an innocent Christian boy by a community of Jews. Discrimination against Jews and Muslims was common:

> Christians were forbidden on pain of excommunication and the consequent confiscation of their property to take service in the houses of Muslims and Jews, to look after their children, to trade with Muslims and Jews or even to eat with them. In 1227 Pope Gregory IX added the following decrees: Muslims and Jews must wear distinctive clothing; they must not appear on the streets during Christian festivals or hold public office in Christian countries; and the muezzin [call to prayer] was forbidden to offend Christian ears by summoning the Muslims to prayer in the traditional way. Pope Clement V (1305–14) declared that the Islamic presence on Christian soil was an insult to God.
>
> *(Armstrong, 28)*

The Spanish conquered the Iberian Peninsula in 1492, and soon thereafter both Jews and Muslims were expelled or forced to convert at the point of a sword. Of course, in European history there have been scholars, religious and political leaders who sometimes demonstrated more openness to learning about Islam, translating the Quran into Latin and so on, especially during the Renaissance, but they were the exception. In Dante's *Inferno* Muhammad is found in the next-to-deepest circle of Hell, the place for frauds. He is viewed as a "schismatic," and Islam as an evil offshoot of Christianity. He is found there with Ali ibn Abi Talib, cousin and son-in-law to Muhammad, who Dante credits with the division between Sunni and Shiite:

> Between his legs were hanging down his entrails;
> His heart was visible, and the dismal sack
> That maketh excrement of what is eaten.
>
> While I was all absorbed in seeing him,
> He looked at me, and opened with his hands
> His bosom, saying: "See now how I rend me;
>
> How mutilated, see, is Mahomet;
> In front of me doth Ali weeping go,
> Cleft in the face from forelock unto chin;
>
> And all the others whom thou here beholdest,
> Disseminators of scandal and of schism
> While living were, and therefore are cleft thus.

> A devil is behind here, who doth cleave us
> Thus cruelly, unto the falchion's edge
> Putting again each one of all this ream,
>
> When we have gone around the doleful road;
> By reason that our wounds are closed again
> Ere any one in front of him repass."
>
> (The Inferno, *Canto 28)*

This horrifying description of Ali ibn Abi Talib is not the only violent portrait in Dante's *Inferno*; many once-revered Christians, including former Popes, also suffer remarkable tortures. Yet it is clear that Islam is viewed as a reprehensible religious sect.

I didn't begin with Dante in my class but instead with the interesting positive depiction of Saladin in Boccaccio's *Decameron* (2003). Saladin (in Arabic Salah ad-Din, 1138–1193) was one of the great leaders of the Muslims of Egypt and Syria against the European crusaders and yet celebrated in Europe as a chivalrous knight. (Students may know him from the action epic film *Kingdom of Heaven* (2005) where he is portrayed by Ghassan Massoud.) Boccaccio's story is the ninth story of the tenth day, and we used the online version in English translation from Brown University's *Decameron Web* (www.stg.brown.edu/projects/decameron/engDecShowText.php). In Boccaccio's story Saladin comes to Italy in disguise and is offered generous hospitality by an Italian lord, Torello, who, later, during a crusade, finds himself Saladin's prisoner. When Saladin discovers the prisoner is his former host, he treats him royally, and has his magicians fly him home overnight so he can be with his wife. I was charmed by the story's vivid scenes of banquets, night torch parades, and hawking. My students also enjoyed the tale. Brian Lane commented,

> Saladin seems to share the same heroic qualities as any other "good" guy in a classic saga. As was said in class, a knight in shining armor. Torello returning to his wife is similar to almost every love story of a war movie that's hit the box office . . . with a touch of *The Notebook*. [a 2004 romantic movie about a young couple who fall in love in the 1940s]

In contrast to this positive, ethical, and romantic portrayal of Saladin in Boccaccio, my students read Chaucer's "Man of Laws Tale" (ll. 1–380) and encountered a strikingly different characterization of Muslims. The tale is the story of Constance, a European girl who marries the sultan of Syria, converts him to Christianity and then escapes his death and a massacre of his court led by her mother-in-law (found online in both Middle English and Modern English translation at the Electronic Literature Foundation, www.canterburytales.org/canterbury_tales.html). Sarah Keeler was struck by the deceptions in the story and made connections to the present:

> Plans were sabotaged by the mother-in-law, who deceived everyone in her "willingness" to change her religion. In the end, Christianity is glorified and Jesus saves Constance from being defeated and guides her to Italy where her arrival is seen as a miracle and the Muslims are evil anti-Christs. As in modern times, most people influenced by Christian beliefs [consider] the Middle East evil and Muslims as deceiving terrorists. Erroneous as that statement is, longstanding perceptions cloud the truth about their culture, as well as how closely tied the two religions actually are.

Molly Grube was intrigued by an apparent reversal in the representation of women. Instead of seeing the Western woman as liberated and the Muslim woman as oppressed, she saw something quite different in Chaucer's story:

> Given my preconceptions dealing with how women are treated today, I was surprised to see the roles switched in *Canterbury Tales*. Constance, a Christian woman, was actually the one being persecuted and submissive. The Sultan's mother had the full attention of the male council and her orders were followed by them.

Perhaps the powerful and usurping mother-in-law figure in this tale provided evidence to pious members of Chaucer's late medieval readership of the perversion of Islam. If so, the reverse of the stereotype today may have the same effect. As we examined in Chapter 3, constant representation of women as oppressed under Islam may lead to distortions about Islam for contemporary Christian readers.

While Dante's depiction of "Mahomet," and Chaucer's depiction of Jews and the Sultan's mother participates in anti-Semitic discourse, Dante, Chaucer, and Boccaccio are great literary artists and final judgments should be measured. While Chaucer repeats a well-known, frequently sermonized anti-Semitic tale, he puts it in the mouth of the shallow Prioress, revealing a dark and frightful side to her superficial piety. Not all Muslim characters in *The Inferno* are in the inner circles of hell. Like Boccaccio, Dante also holds Saladin in high esteem and places him on the outside margin of hell among the virtuous pagans he so admires. Interestingly, some scholars attribute the organization of the *Divine Comedy* itself to Dante's knowledge of the famous story of the Isra and Miraj, the night journey of Muhammad to Heaven via Jerusalem described in Sura Al-Isra in the Quran and Hadiths where he meets many prophets including Adam, Abraham, Moses, Jesus, and John the Baptist.

Thinking about the portrait of Others is an important and complex undertaking in literary studies. A leading thinker about the ways in which "Others" are examined, Tzvetan Todorov, set forward in *The Conquest of America: The Question of the Other* three crucial dimensions that come into play: 1) value judgment: is the Other "good" or "bad," an "equal" or an "inferior"? 2) distance: is the Other like us or different, are his values admirable or despicable, do we impose our values on the Other or do we respect his values? and, 3) knowledge: are we ignorant or informed about the Other? (185) A classroom considering the portrait of Muslims or Middle Easterners in canonical writers can consider each of the these dimensions in any one representation. And those representations can also be considered in the broader context of the literary work or author. For instance, a variety of questions could be explored about *The Inferno* and the representations we have seen. When Dante includes multiple Muslim characters portrayed differently, some tortured in an inner circle and another admired but still on the margin of Hell, does this: show Dante's judgment of Muslims to be balanced? (level 1) Domesticate differences and impose values? (level 2) Demonstrate knowledge or ignorance of Islam? (level 3).

The complexity of representation of the Other is a topic scholars and students have considered in Shakespeare's portraits of Shylock and Othello. Having already encountered representations of Middle Eastern people as heroic and mysterious, honorable and violent, gracious and lustful, and upstanding and deceptive, my class turned to consideration of *Othello*. The Renaissance was a time of warfare, as well as economic and ideological competition between Europe and the Islamic world. In England plays and pageants depicting the Turks were common; "between 1579 and 1624 over sixty dramatic works featured Islamic themes, characters, or settings" (Bergeron, 265). In his essay "Turning Turk in *Othello*" the scholar Daniel Vitkus explains that some of the same ignorance that leads to stereotyping today was present at the time of Shakespeare – the English frequently confused and conflated terms as different as Turks, black Africans, Muslims, and Moors, even linking Muhammad and the Pope as devilish enemies to good Protestant Christians. In post-Reformation England fears of religious conversion were of serious concern. Not only did Englishmen dread Roman Catholic enemies and threats of forceful conversion, but there was also the growing imperial power of the enormous Ottoman Turkish Empire and its extensive colonization of Christian territories across Europe. Vitkus argues that the Turks regularly captured British vessels and even directly raided the English coastline, in part to capture Englishmen to enslave, make them work on their ships, and so on. Apparently, these captured Christians would sometimes convert, either to save their lives or to enter into commerce with the Muslims. Sermons were regularly preached in English churches against this type of "conversion." During this period, not all contacts with Islamic people were negative – there was a group of Moorish ambassadors who visited and were well received in London only a couple of years before *Othello* was written.

Given that the Turks were seen as a threatening empire, the English audience for Shakespeare's *Othello* would understand the urgency that the Duke of Venice and the other Venetian characters express to defeat the Turkish threat and, thus, their turning to Othello to protect them. The intrigue of the play is how such a noble man turns savage. As my student Linda Cross put it: "My first impression of him [Othello] was a man of great honor and strong mind. He had earned the

FIGURE 12.1 Desdemona Asleep (John Graham, 1803)

respect of many by his earlier actions in battle, so I expected him to have a much stronger character. One not so easily led astray by ideas that were suggested and then manifested."

Of course, *Othello* is the tragedy of the "Noble Moor" cursed with eternal damnation for killing his wife and himself. Vitkus argues that Othello can best be understood in the context of the historical and cultural relations between the English and the Turks. He believes that Othello himself, in a sense like the captured Englishmen, "turns Turk," that is, he takes on the aspects of the English stereotypes of Ottoman Turks and becomes an enemy to the Venetians in the play.

Although Vitkus's careful historical argument is challenging for college freshman, I had our whole class read Vitkus's essay. Dan Brim wrote,

> The Vitkus piece, as promised, was difficult and tough to read, but I felt it provided an extensive amount of background information on the time period we're dealing with. Prior to reading this, I thought race and religion were but small points in William Shakespeare's *Othello*, but now, I realize it is much more emphasized than I would have ever realized.

Diane Hall wrote a paper arguing that by the end of the play, "Othello possesses characteristics that were [stereotypically] attributed to Muhammad. He is lustful, violent, angry, and delusional." Drawing on Vitkus, Diane claimed that,

> The play *Othello* does in some sense portray Islamic culture; however, it functions on a larger level to warn the audience about the dangers of conversion . . . These conversions are the result of subtle actions and words that eventually so envelop the victims that they cannot see clearly and cannot perceive the consequences of their actions.

From the Vitkus essay and their careful reading of *Othello*, students made important connections between the Renaissance and the present day. Heather Winowiecki wrote,

> I thought it was intriguing that many European Christians believed that Moors were looked upon as having skin "demonic black, burnt by hellfire and cursed by god." It seems that seventeenth century Christians were very uninformed about the Islamic religion and there were quite a few misunderstandings . . . Although there was cause for alarm because of the barbaric attacks [on Europe by Ottomans], I believe that there was an excess of worry by much of the English community. One could possibly compare this to the present outlook on people of Middle Eastern descent, given the past six years of tension, terrorist attacks and war. I even catch myself sometimes judging a person based merely on their skin or what they are wearing . . . Islam used to be "defined as a licentious religion of sensuality

> and sexuality." I find it interesting that today we think of it as almost completely opposite, representing a repressive outlook towards women and an overall lack of love, sex, and sensuality.

The connections, similarities, and differences Heather finds between prejudices in Shakespeare's day and in our own is facilitated by the effort we were making to read Shakespeare and the other writers not only as literary artists, but also as writers in history and participants in a broader cultural discourse.

We continued our study of representations of the Middle East in British fiction by looking at the *Rubaiyat of Omar Khayyam*, Coleridge's "Kubla Khan," and Shelly's sonnet "Ozymandius." All of these works contain Orientalist ideas and imagery, and portraits of the "Other," interesting for students to dissect. Because the work was so enormously popular in Europe and contributed to the development of stereotypes about Middle Easterners I also had my students read a variety of tales from the *Arabian* or *1001 Nights*. The online late-nineteenth-century (1885–1888) translation we read by the explorer and intellectual Sir Richard Burton is fascinating, though also full of coarse sexuality and troubling racism and sexism. Another work we looked at was *Rubaiyat of Omar Khayyam*. I admit that I find the *Rubaiyat* beautiful poetry, though I know it partakes of stereotypes and repetitions about the Middle East, magnified by Edward Fitzgerald who was more a creator of the work than a translator. The idea of a paradise of ease, sensuality, wine, and carelessness is just so alluring . . . In class we not only looked at the poetry but also images from several publications. It wasn't hard for students to identify troubling and even racist depictions in some of these, such as the illustration I have included here by Arthur Szyk from the 1946 Heritage Press edition of the *Rubaiyat* (see Illustration 12.2).

Describing an Other is not just about the Other, it is also about the Self. By projecting negative traits onto an Other – for instance violence, lust, indolence, or ignorance – the Self is not only elevated, it is purified. These traits are found among them, not us. Othering protects not only from knowledge of one's own character but also from awareness of one's own actions. They are barbaric; we are civilized. Survey courses in British or American literature often return to questions of national character. Thus, in these courses, examining representations of the Middle East opens to exploring how self-definition or self-fashioning works and important questions about the course's underlying assumptions.

After looking at the representation of the Middle East in medieval, renaissance, and later British texts, it also makes thematic sense to have students deepen understanding by reading or viewing more modern works. My introductory literature class turned to contemporary literature from the Middle East, and much of our experience is recounted elsewhere in this volume. Throughout the class we referred back to the representations of Muslims we had examined in early European and British texts, thus enriching our thinking about the more recent literature we were reading.

FIGURE 12.2 The *Rubaiyat*

The Middle East in American Literature

American literature courses often begin with a study of the Puritans, and the specially recognized position they saw themselves developing as a new, God-inspired settlement in the New World. Sailing to the Massachusetts Bay Colony in 1630, John Winthrop, drawing on the Sermon on the Mount, described the new settlement as a "City upon a Hill." The idea was that America was to be the new Promised Land, the New Canaan, the New Israel. John Rolf of the Jamestown colony identified the new settlers as "a peculiar people, marked and chosen by the finger of God." Franklin and Jefferson wanted the nation's new seal to include images of the Promised Land. The theme of America as the new Israel threads itself through Manifest Destiny, the appropriation and settlement of the continent, all the way to the self-conceived role of America's millennialist mission as leading military power in the world today. This fundamental association of American self-identity with a specific way of understanding the history of the Middle East locates this region of the world surprising close to the center of American literary history. It also raises questions about connections between American self-identity and a particular Judeo–Christian historical narrative of the Holy Land. There is a range of canonical writers and texts in the American tradition that can serve as jumping-off points for the investigation of representations of the Middle East – and for critiques of American self-perception as divinely inspired.

A number of the earliest American texts explicitly addressing the Middle East are the captivity narratives of Americans captured by Barbary pirates. An extensive and fascinating examination of the Islamic world by an early American writer is *The Algerine Captive* by Royall Tyler in 1797. Available both online and in a 2002 Modern Library edition, *The Algerine Captive* is divided into two volumes. As we have seen in our discussion of English writing at the time of Shakespeare, concern about the capture of Christians by Moroccan pirates was a popular theme even hundreds of years earlier. The second volume of *The Algerine Captive* relates a fictionalized account of an American doctor taken as a slave in Algiers. The text combines adventure and captivity narrative (not unlike the narratives of Native American captivity) with an almost anthropological examination of Muslim religion, history, cities, government, clothing, food, marriage customs and daily life. There is a fascinating dialogue between the author and a "mollah" on the topic of Islam vs. Christianity, redounding most positively to Islam. As a slave, the doctor makes a voyage to Egypt and crosses the Arabian Desert where he visits Medina and Mecca. The author is cheated by Jews in Algiers and Alexandria and these passages draw on stereotypical anti-Semitic portraits. Volume II is just over 100 pages and certainly readable by high school or college students.

Another interesting captivity narrative from the same period is Susanna Haswell Rowson's 1794 play *Slaves in Algiers, or, A Struggle for Freedom*, Rowson was the author of *Charlotte Temple*, the best-selling novel in America until *Uncle Tom's Cabin*. Anne Miles describes teaching *Slaves in Algiers, or, A Struggle for Freedom* to university students in Northern Iowa, where she and her students find important parallels between the eighteenth-century captivity narrative and present day events in Iraq.

> Reading *Slaves in Algiers* was not the first time in the captivity class we had had occasion to consider recent events in Iraq. From the opening day, a touch-point for our discussions was the story of the captivity and rescue of Jessica Lynch, taken captive in an ambush in Nasiriyah in March 2003 (two major versions of the narrative, the TV movie *Saving Jessica Lynch* and the book by journalist Rick Bragg, *I Am a Soldier, Too: The Jessica Lynch Story*, appeared during the course of the semester). The intense public fascination with Lynch's captivity and rescue and the less-than-subtle spin the events received in the hands of the military and the media made it abundantly clear that, though we might dwell in class on texts written in the seventeenth and eighteenth centuries, the genre cannot be consigned to a dry past full of impossible religious beliefs and short on alternative narrative thrills.

Anne Miles' approach of combining early American texts with thematically related contemporary ones is interesting and opens up discussion relevant to current events in the Middle East. The idea that the Middle East is a place where Americans are captured and reduced to slavery by North African Muslims certainly presents an exotic and dangerous setting for American citizens – perhaps it is not surprising to learn that the United States from 1801–1805 under president Jefferson formed the American navy in order to wage war against Morocco, Algiers, Tunis, and Tripoli (the "Barbary States", a quasi-independent part of the Ottoman Empire). In 1805 the war was ended by the first U.S. Marine expedition and a much larger number of Greek, Arab, and Berber mercenaries who marched across the desert from Alexandria to assault and capture the Tripolitan city of Derna, marking the first time in history that the United States flag was raised in victory on foreign soil, and memorialized in the line from the "Marines' Hymn" about "the shores of Tripoli."

Many nineteenth-century American writers draw on Middle East images and themes in their writing. Washington Irving was fascinated with Arab empires and arranged to live in a former Arabic palace, the Alhambra in Granada. This led to his publication in 1832 of *Tales of the Alhambra*, an engaging collection of his contemporary travels including histories, folk legends, and myths of the Moorish period in Spain. Lazaro Lima writes,

> Irving's fascination with Islamic Spain brought us one of the first popular accounts of Islam to the United States. In the tale, "Legend of the Arabian Astrologer" from *The Alhambra*, for example, we see the depiction of "a Moorish king named Aben Habuz" who was spellbound by a young and beautiful Christian princess whose "dark eyes were like sparks of fire on

> the old yet combustible Aben Habuz" (15). The young Christian princess' beauty and wiles ultimately destroy Aben Habuz's kingdom as foretold by the king's astrologer, leaving only the Alhambra as a symbol of Islamic greatness; a greatness subjugated by Christianity. (2)

In his 2007 dissertation in history *Spanish Orientalism: Washington Irving and the Romance of the Moors*, Michael Stevens argues that Irving, who also wrote a history of the New York colony and of Christopher Columbus, was part of a discourse about the inadequacy of Spain in governing its New World colonies and the appropriateness of American authority in the hemisphere (189).

The Middle East is a surprisingly persistent literary theme in American literature, though often for the sort of exotic, sensual, or even spiritual othering that we saw in British literature. Nathanial Hawthorne's heroines often have Middle Eastern characteristics. In *Nathanial Hawthorne and the Romance of the Orient* Luther Luedtke points out:

> Hester Prynne's "rich, voluptuous Oriental characteristic – a taste for the gorgeously beautiful" – bewilders and invigorates the Puritan Rev. Arthur Dimmesdale in *The Scarlet Letter*. Zenobia in the *Blithedale Romance* bears the name and tragic majesty of an "Oriental Princess," specifically of the proud Syrian queen whom Aruelian vanquished at Palmyra in A.D. 272.

FIGURE 12.3 Court and Lion Fountain [in the Alhambra], 1816

> Like her dark sisters, Miram in *The Marble Faun* displays "a certain rich Oriental character in her face."
>
> *(xvi)*

Luedtke believes that Hawthorne had a life-long fascination with the Orient, stemming from the logbooks of his father's journey to East India that he read as a young man. Edgar Allen Poe was also intrigued by Middle Eastern narratives. As a youth he wrote his longest poem "Al Aaraaf" drawing on the Quran to create a sense of dreamscape and otherworldliness. His poem "Tamerlane" treats a Turkish-Mogul emperor who ignores his love for a peasant in order to achieve power. "Israfel" is another poem that draws on the Quran to celebrate the power of love and poetry. Poe's strange short story "The Thousand-and-Second Tale of Scheherazade" is a satire of the *Arabian Nights*. Many of Poe's best-known stories were published in 1840 in a collection titled *Tales of the Grotesque and the Arabesque* (Poe, 1984) – though it is not clear what he meant by "arabesque." Ralph Waldo Emerson was an admirer of Middle Eastern literature and put together a collection of Persian Poetry translated from German, comparing its language favorably with the bible. Emerson and Thoreau both read literary and spiritual texts first from the Middle East, and then from India, reading which had an influence in the development of Transcendentalism.

In the study *American Hieroglyphics* John Irwin traces an attraction to Egypt, the Middle East, and new understandings about language emerging from the decoding of hieroglyphics in the writing of Emerson, Thoreau, Whitman, Hawthorne, Melville, and, especially, Poe.

American women writers of the nineteenth century shared this interest in the Middle East. In 1860 the novelist Maria Susanna Cummins, one of the most popular novelists of her day, published *El Fureidis* set in Lebanon. A romance about an American who falls in love with a beautiful Syrian girl, and about his deceitful native guide Abdoul, the scholar Steven Hammelman maintains that the work repeats Orientalist stereotypes and also supports the extension of American empire (2). Louisa May Alcott wrote a short story in 1869 called "Lost in a Pyramid: The Mummy's Curse" influenced by a children's book by Sarah Atkins and Giovanni Belzoni entitled *The Fruits of Enterprise*, where explorers use mummies as human torches to find their way through the winding corridors of Egyptian pyramids. John Warrren writes,

> Of course, the mummies were portrayed as looking particularly vengeful . . . He [the explorer] discovers some seeds in the pyramid, and carries them back to America. His fiancée decides to plant the seeds, which then grow into grotesque flowers. Upon their wedding, she wares [sic] one of the flowers and inhales their scent, sending her into a coma as she becomes a living mummy.
>
> *(1)*

Clearly Alcott is part of a tradition that has included exotic and frightening Middle Eastern tales, from *The Mummy* to the Indiana Jones movies.

Two of America's greatest novelists, Herman Melville and Mark Twain visited the Holy Land (Melville in 1857 and Twain ten years later) and wrote substantial works set there – works that are not typically taught, or perhaps even familiar to teachers, but which could be drawn on, especially those by Twain, to facilitate study of representations of the Middle East in American literature. Hilton Obenzinger locates Melville and Twain's writing and the Middle East in a particular tradition:

> Both books are part of a "subgenre" or field of American Holy Land literature based on direct travel to Palestine, a literature in which representations, controversies, and anxieties involving the certainties of religious and national identities contend upon a heightened field of mythic meanings, with all Holy Land books seeking in one way or another to appropriate Palestine for the American imagination. With American conceived as the New Jerusalem . . . the old Holy Land was encountered as a terrain of crucial cultural dynamics both challenging and reaffirming America's narrative of settlement as divine errand.
>
> *(x)*

While part of this tradition Melville and Twain are also critical of it. Rather than any simple exoticization of the Orient, they use representations of the Holy Land and encounters there to question American religious revivalism as well as imperialist and nationalist myths. Traveling in a time before significant Jewish settlement of Palestine, Obenzinger explains that Melville and Twain describe meeting "millenialist" Christians arguing for the "necessity of Jewish repatriation to Palestine as a prelude to the return of Jesus." Melville calls this a "preposterous Jew mania" (xi) and describes why, in the 1850s, it seems to him highly unlikely that there would ever be a Jewish state in Israel:

> The idea of making farmers of the Jews is vain. In the first place, Judea is a desert with few exceptions. In the second place, the Jews hate farming. All who cultivate the soil in Palestine are Arabs. The Jews dare not live outside walled towns or villages for fear of the malicious persecution of the Arabs & Turks. Besides, the number of Jews in Palestine is comparatively small. And how are the hosts of them scattered in other lands to be brought here? Only by a miracle.
>
> *(Obenzinger, 82)*

While Melville's observation may have been understandable in its historical context, he certainly was wrong about the capacity of many Jewish people to establish themselves in Israel. As a traveler to the Holy Land, Mark Twain also made interesting observations about the zealotry of Christian travelers. He clearly recognized the ways in which the views of American tourists in Palestine were shaped more by their previous beliefs than by whatever reality they were to find there. As he writes in *The Innocents Abroad*,

> I am sure, from the tenor of books I have read, that many who have visited this land in years gone by, were Presbyterians, and came seeking evidences in support of their particular creed; they found a Presbyterian Palestine, and they had already made up their minds to find no other, though possibly they did not know it, being blinded by their zeal. Others were Baptists, seeking Baptist evidences and a Baptist Palestine. Others were Catholics, Methodists, Episcopalians, seeking evidences indorsing their several creeds, and a Catholic, a Methodist, an Episcopalian Palestine. Honest as these men's intentions may have been, they were full of partialities and prejudices, they entered the country with their verdicts already prepared, and they could no more write dispassionately and impartially about it than they could about their own wives and children. Our pilgrims have brought *their* verdicts with them. They have shown it in their conversation ever since we left Beirout [sic]. I can almost tell, in set phrase, what they will say when they see Tabor, Nazareth, Jericho and Jerusalem—*because I have the books they will "smouch" their ideas from.*
>
> *(511)*

Twain's insightful 1869 comments about the partialities and prejudices of nineteenth-century pilgrims describe an activity of appropriation familiar from our discussion of Said's analysis of Orientalism. Clearly this American travel writing about the Holy Land, and the critiques of that writing by Melville and Twain, can be connected to contemporary attitudes toward the Middle East.

The major work of Herman Meville's later years is the two-volume iambic tetrameter epic *Clarel*, presumed the longest poem in American literature. *Clarel* draws on Melville's visit to the Holy Land in the 1850s and seems to be universally acknowledged by students, critics, and even Melville himself as a popular failure. Obenzinger says,

> Years after its publication Melville would describe Clarel – the dark, philosophical satire, part Hellenistic symposium, part Hebraic jeremiad and lamentation that was shaped from his Holy Land sojourn – as "a metrical affair, a pilgrimage or what not, of several thousand lines, eminently adapted for unpopularity."
>
> *(66)*

If *Clarel* further illustrates the importance of the Middle East for the canonical writers of American literature, contemporary college and secondary students are likely to be more engaged by more approachable works.

Some of the most approachable nineteenth-century American writing about the Middle East is, indeed, by Mark Twain. As we have already seen, Twain's insights about the region and especially about American understanding and approaches to the Middle East are startlingly modern. *The Innocents Abroad,* published in 1869 about a trip to Europe and the Holy Land made two years earlier, was, during his lifetime, Twain's best-selling work. While writing *Huckleberry Finn* Twain was also working on his own burlesque of the *Arabian Nights* (never published). As is evident from the quotation above, *The Innocents Abroad* mocks the sentimental and romantic travel books of its day, as well as the smug and self-righteous attitudes of Americans toward the rest of the world. Twain's ironic narration pokes fun at Americans who are bored with aspects of Egypt that might be more familiar and instead seek a stereotyped "Orient" that will fulfill what they have heard about in the tales of the exotic East that fill popular travel narratives.

> Alexandria was too much like a European city to be novel, and we soon tired of it. We took the cars and came up here to ancient Cairo, which is an Oriental city and of the completest pattern. There is little about it to disabuse one's mind of the error if he should take it into his head that he was in the heart of Arabia. Stately camels and dromedaries, swarthy Egyptians, and likewise Turks and black Ethiopians, turbaned, sashed, and blazing in a rich variety of Oriental costumes of all shades of flashy colors, are what one sees on every hand crowding the narrow streets and the honeycombed bazaars.
>
> *(615)*

FIGURE 12.4 "Pyramids and Sphynx" Illustration from *Innocents Abroad*

Twain satirizes the tourist commodification of all things supposedly ancient from Christian religious sites to the pyramids. After having been carried to the top of a pyramid by an Egyptian, Twain mocks the thinking of sanctimonious Christians of his day,

> But in the midst of sorrow, joy blooms. Even in this dark hour I had a sweet consolation. For I knew that except these Mohammedans repented they would go straight to perdition some day. And they never repent – they never forsake their paganism. This thought calmed me, cheered me, and I sank down, limp and exhausted, upon the summit, but happy, so happy and serene within.
>
> *(623)*

Twain's critique of Americans in the Holy Land not only includes their "innocence," simplicity, cultural and religious stereotyping, willingness to impose beliefs and ideas but also hints at a more disturbing threat of violence. There is a fascinating scene in Chapter 55 where Twain describes the cowardly, idiotic boasting of American tourists in Egypt, willing to commit violence when encountering Bedouins, which they view as if they were Native Americans "on the war path,"

> Some of us will be shot before we finish this pilgrimage. The pilgrims read "Nomadic Life" and keep themselves in a constant state of Quixotic heroism. They have their hands on their pistols all the time, and every now and then, when you least expect it, they snatch them out and take aim at Bedouins who are not visible, and draw their knives and make savage passes at other Bedouins who do not exist. I am in deadly peril always, for these spasms are sudden and irregular, and of course I cannot tell when to be getting out of the way. If I am accidentally murdered, some time, during one of these romantic frenzies of the pilgrims, Mr. Grimes must be rigidly held to answer as an accessory before the fact. If the pilgrims would take deliberate aim and shoot at a man, it would be all right and proper – because that man would not be in any danger; but these random assaults are what I object to.
>
> *(540)*

The Innocents Abroad offers a number of fascinating scenes and observations teachers can draw on to bring the Middle East into American literature courses.

One text addressing the Middle East that students, from high school to college, will enjoy is *Tom Sawyer Abroad*. Even though *The Adventures of Huckleberry Finn* (1884) is the most taught novel in American high schools, and *The Adventures of Tom Sawyer* (1876) is well-known and popular, many teachers may not be aware that Twain wrote two sequels also featuring the characters

Tom, Huck, and Jim: *Tom Sawyer Abroad* (1894) and *Tom Sawyer, Detective* (1896). Set in North Africa and Egypt, *Tom Sawyer Abroad* shows by title alone Twain attempting to capitalize on his previously popular works. Like the *Adventures of Huckleberry Finn, Tom Sawyer Abroad* is also told from Huck's point of view. The novel opens as Tom suggests that the three of them go on a crusade. I quote at length from their fascinating conversation:

> "What's a crusade?" I [Huck] says.
>
> He looked scornful, the way he's always done when he was ashamed of a person, and says:
>
> "Huck Finn, do you mean to tell me you don't know what a crusade is? . . . Why, a crusade is a kind of war."
>
> I thought he must be losing his mind. But no, he was in real earnest, and went right on, perfectly ca'm.
>
> "A crusade is a war to recover the Holy Land from the paynim [pagans]."
>
> "Which Holy Land?"
>
> "Why, the Holy Land – there ain't but one."
>
> "What do we want of it?"
>
> "Why, can't you understand? It's in the hands of the paynim, and it's our duty to take it away from them."
>
> "How did we come to let them git hold of it?"
>
> "We didn't come to let them git hold of it. They always had it."
>
> "Why, Tom, then it must belong to them, don't it?"
>
> "Why of course it does. Who said it didn't?"
>
> I studied over it, but couldn't seem to git at the right of it, no way. I says:
>
> "It's too many for me, Tom Sawyer. If I had a farm and it was mine, and another person wanted it, would it be right for him to—"
>
> "Oh, shucks! you don't know enough to come in when it rains, Huck Finn. It ain't a farm, it's entirely different. You see, it's like this. They own the land, just the mere land, and that's all they DO own; but it was our folks, our Jews and Christians, that made it holy, and so they haven't any business to be there defiling it. It's a shame, and we ought not to stand it a minute. We ought to march against them and take it away from them."
>
> "Why, it does seem to me it's the most mixed-up thing I ever see! Now, if I had a farm and another person—"
>
> "Don't I tell you it hasn't got anything to do with farming? Farming is business, just common low-down business: that's all it is, it's all you can say for it; but this is higher, this is religious, and totally different."
>
> "Religious to go and take the land away from people that owns it?"
>
> "Certainly; it's always been considered so."

Jim he shook his head, and says:

"Mars Tom, I reckon dey's a mistake about it somers – dey mos' sholy is. I's religious myself, en I knows plenty religious people, but I hain't run across none dat acts like dat."

It made Tom hot, and he says: "Well, it's enough to make a body sick, such mullet-headed ignorance! If either of you'd read anything about history, you'd know that Richard Cur de Loon, and the Pope, and Godfrey de Bulleyn, and lots more of the most noble-hearted and pious people in the world, hacked and hammered at the paynims for more than two hundred years trying to take their land away from them, and swum neck-deep in blood the whole time – and yet here's a couple of sap-headed country yahoos out in the backwoods of Missouri setting themselves up to know more about the rights and wrongs of it than they did! Talk about cheek!"

. . . I couldn't say nothing, and Jim he couldn't for a while; then he says:

. . . De hard part gwine to be to kill folks dat a body hain't been 'quainted wid and dat hain't done him no harm. Dat's it, you see. Ef we wuz to go 'mongst 'em, jist we three, en say we's hungry, en ast 'em for a bite to eat, why, maybe dey's jist like yuther people. Don't you reckon dey is? Why, DEY'D give it, I know dey would, en den—

(13)

Here Twain critiques not only the historical crusades but also contemporary imperialism; Tom, Huck, and Jim's visit ("mini-invasion" Obenzinger calls it) to North Africa and Egypt in a balloon can be read as a spoof of American foreign interventions. Twain became increasingly a critic of imperialism. His 1905 pamphlet *King Leopold's Soliloquy* satirizes the legitimating of Belgian rule of the Congo and, even soon after *Tom Sawyer Abroad*, in 1900 he was an outspoken critic of America's invasion of the Philippines. Twain was quoted in the New York *Herald*, October 15, 1900:

> It should, it seems to me, be our pleasure and duty to make those people [Filipinos] free, and let them deal with their own domestic questions in their own way. And so I am an anti-imperialist. I am opposed to having the eagle put its talons on any other land.

In *Tom Sawyer Abroad* the trio go from the Sahara to Egypt and the Pyramids where, for a time they leave Jim standing on the head of the Sphinx waving an American flag. When they discover that the natives had crowded around:

> Tom was very indignant, and asked him why he didn't show the flag and command them to GIT, in the name of the United States. Jim said he done it, but they never paid no attention. Tom said he would have this thing

> looked into at Washington, and says: "You'll see that they'll have to apologize for insulting the flag, and pay an indemnity, too, on top of it even if they git off THAT easy."
>
> *(85)*

Twain's criticism of the American "eagle putting its talons on other lands" couldn't be more plain, or more prescient.

In this chapter I have focused on the most canonical and frequently taught writers of the British and American tradition to show that they have, with perhaps surprising frequency, written about the Middle East. Their writing opens up many opportunities for teachers of American and British literature to address the Middle East in their classes, to raise questions about distorted or stereotyped representations, to look thoughtfully at connections between past and present, to think about British and American self-perceptions and role in the world, and to draw on canonical writers to investigate pressing issues in the present day. Pairing these writers and works with contemporary Middle Eastern literature described elsewhere in this book creates possibilities for dialogue, for richer, and more complex understanding.

Further Reading

American Palestine: Melville, Twain, and the Holy Land Mania by Stanford professor Hilton Obenzinger (1999) is another model of scholarship that keeps in mind contemporary realities in the Middle East while examining the importance of the region to self-perception in nineteenth-century American literature. Many authors are discussed in addition to Twain and Melville.

Turks, Moors, and Englishmen in the Age of Discovery by Nabil Matar (1999) is an approachable historical examination of the life of Turks and Moors in England, captivity narratives of Englishmen held by Muslims, how ideas about American Indians, homosexuality, and religion and holy war were tied to relations with the Muslim world.

Turning Turk: English Theater and the Multicultural Mediterranean 1570–1630 by Daniel Vitkus (2008) is an outstanding example of careful historical research in contemporary literary scholarship. Addressing the English Renaissance theater and the contact between England and Mediterranean cultures including the Muslim world, Vitkus' discussion includes Christopher Marlowe as well as Shakespeare (esp. *Othello, Merchant of Venice*, and *The Tempest*).

CONCLUSION

At a time of polarizing political tensions and profound misunderstanding of contemporary Middle Eastern peoples, cultures, religions, and histories, teaching literature of today's Middle East takes on singular importance. The knowledge generated in classrooms examining literature from today's Middle East needs to be shared beyond the classroom walls. Knowledge creates responsibility, and an important component of reading and studying this literature is teachers and students thinking together about how students can communicate with others about what they are learning. Doing so can include activities and projects in their own school and community, developing online resources, creating connections to people in the Middle East and related organizations, and becoming active citizens.

I have had students select topics, themes, or texts that they are especially interested in and, individually or in teams, create poster displays that we have presented both at "science fair" type events and posted on classroom and hallway walls. This kind of presentation involves bringing together images and text – an increasingly important skill and one that I directly teach. These events work nicely when several classes can establish poster displays together. I have had students do poster displays at public evening events at the university, at high school parents' nights, and at professional teacher conferences. I teach them how to talk about their posters, create handouts, and share what they have learned. Teachers have arranged for secondary students to speak with and share work and texts with students in younger grades. Inviting the school and the community to be part of the learning is one way teachers can help create the freedom they need.

In the age of the Internet it has become remarkably easy to share student work with audiences beyond the teacher. I have had my students develop a range of academic websites, wikis, and blogs where they share the content they are learning with broader audiences. We talk about how to present yourself and your work online, how to write for a public audience, and I integrate learning about online writing tools and resources into my literature courses. I consider developing these skills an essential part of learning to write in the twenty-first century, and I consider the teaching of writing as one of the objectives of every class I teach. Throughout this book you have seen many examples of online student writing and you can explore the original sources from my website at allenwebb.net. My student's online writing frequently engages readers beyond our classroom and myself. Students typically inform friends and family members about their online publications and share links with them. I sometimes rely on published work from previous classes both as models for online presentation and for developing content knowledge for current students. Moreover, student online writing commonly generates responses from readers my students and I will never know personally. Readers comment on their blogs, join and continue to develop our wikis, and create links to student-created webpages, some of which have had thousands of hits.

The Internet also facilitates more complex forms of presentation. I have had students create short videos using I-Movie about specific texts and themes that they have uploaded to YouTube. My students have created podcasts about what we are learning in class, and used sites combining visual and audio tracks such as Voice Thread. My students have used presentation tools such as Prezi and Glogster to make highly engaging slideshows and poster presentations. My former doctoral student, Robert Rozema, and I share many of these and other online teaching and publishing experiments in our book *Literature and the Web: Reading and Responding with New Technologies* (2008).

BOX C.1 CREATING TEACHER FREEDOM

I have come to believe that the freedom we need, to do the teaching we believe in, is often something we have to create, rather than something handed to us. Of course there are fundamental principles of free speech and academic freedom that should give teachers a great deal of freedom and safety to teach texts, topics, and ideas that they believe are important for their students. We need to know these freedoms and stand up for them. Unfortunately such freedom and safety is not always available or is challenged by administrators, parents, or even colleagues. While the need for teachers to create their own freedom may be greatest from pre-school to high school, that need can also exist at the university level.

Teachers too often consider themselves limited by narrow interpretations of course catalogues, curriculum guides, state or national standards, or school policies. While, of course, these documents and policies are important and need to be respected, they nearly always require interpretation. Careful reading and examination of policies often reveals far more flexibility

continued . . .

than teachers typically take advantage of. Knowing policies, developing flexible or liberal interpretations, and finding diplomatic ways to share those interpretations is one of the first steps in developing teacher freedom.

Clear communication reduces the vulnerability of teachers and facilitates more adventurous curriculums. Teachers addressing Middle Eastern literature may want to remind students, probably on the syllabus or the first day of class, that controversial issues are part of the learning process and inform them that diverse points of view and different religious beliefs will be explored. Discussions are more open and students become more authentically involved when a true diversity of perspectives is available in the reading. Many high school teachers have written letters explaining their course and approach to parents. As a high school teacher I found it useful to invite administrators, colleagues, and parents to my classroom to participate in the discussions my students and I were engaged in. Even though these invitations were only infrequently taken up, issuing them helped create trust and freedom. Alternative assignments for students whose parents believe particular reading is not appropriate can also defuse concerns. In Chapter 1 I have addressed the topic of teaching religious texts in schools, another area where there is a great deal more freedom than many teachers realize.

I have presented about my teaching at professional conferences and published articles in professional journals at state and national levels. These actions lend credibility and authority to the teaching I am doing and bolster my professional confidence. Sometimes when interesting or unusual activities go especially well, or students make meritorious accomplishments, teachers invite coverage in the local newspaper. This kind of positive reporting can help teachers gain respect in their communities, and increased freedom in their curriculum.

Teachers are aware that censorship and removal of texts from libraries and courses has a long history. It is also important to know that professional organizations have a long history too, of supporting teachers when censorship issues arise. For example, the National Council of the Teachers of English has an Anti-Censorship Center, and has published position statements addressing "The Students Right to Read," "Guidelines for Selections of Materials," "Rationales for Teaching Challenged Books," etc. The National Council of the Teachers of Social Studies has a position statement on "Academic Freedom and the Social Studies Teacher" that strongly advocates for the importance of teaching controversial issues. The National Library Association – as well as librarians and media specialists – is also an important resource. Teacher unions, including the National Education Association, the American Federation of Teachers, and the American Association of University Professors, have resources. And teachers

continued . . .

working under negotiated contracts typically have additional rights and protections. Many institutions have specific censorship policies and procedures for curricular complaints. Schools that don't have such policies should develop them, as the existence of a policy and a form to fill out can do a great deal to protect teachers and defuse potentially adversarial situations.

The censorship we probably fear the most is direct challenges against curricular materials, assigned reading, or library holdings made by students, parents, administrators, community members, or church or political groups. Other forms of censorship are subtler. Sometimes schools or departments have particular policies – or budget restrictions – that limit the selection of books or reading. Yet, curricular policies often involve folklore. I once had a series of conversations with three English teachers who had worked in the same high school for many years. Teacher X told me, "Our curriculum in this district is set. We have a list of books and we have to teach every book on the list. Nothing can be added or taken away." Teacher Y told me, "The district has a long list of approved books and we have a wide variety of choice about which books we choose from the list." Teacher Z, working just down the hall, told me, "I teach what I want to teach; in this district we have complete freedom." Perhaps the example is extreme, but I am intrigued by the way that certain teachers seem to find creative ways to interpret policies, obtain materials, and create leeway, while their colleagues in the same institution consider themselves constrained or limited.

The most pervasive form of censorship is self-censorship. It takes place when teachers choose to stay away from texts, issues, or discussions that might be best for their students because they fear materials or ideas might be challenged or disapproved of by someone else. In the case of self-censorship we "play it safe" rather than engage students in important issues. Ironically, self-censorship is probably more damaging to students than open censorship because it specifically avoids public discussion of the constitutional freedoms on which democracy is based. Fear of risk taking, reluctance to stand up for what one believes in, or even a lack of interest in new and challenging ideas is destructive to the teaching process and to the teacher as a person and professional. While there are many resources and organizations ready to help teachers create intellectual freedom in the classroom, the courage teachers most need must come from within.

As I have mentioned at several points, there are many opportunities for students studying contemporary Middle Eastern literature to connect to people and organizations from the region. One resource teachers may be curious about is epals.com. This website organizes email exchanges between individuals and classes of students from different countries and parts of the world. Many Middle Eastern countries are represented. When I checked the site in October of 2010 there were over 600 invitations from Turkey and over 800 from Egypt – most of the ones I saw were from teachers looking to connect their students studying English as pen pals to classes of students who are native speakers. What a terrific resource for a teacher using Turkish or Egyptian literature! Establishing that kind of pen pal relationship would be a nice topic for a local newspaper to cover, and possibly provide positive press, and increased freedom, for a teacher including Middle Eastern literature in their courses.

On the Internet, teachers and students can find any number of organizations focused on supporting peace or economic development in the Middle East, reducing militarism, resisting Islamophobia, and/or educating people about the Middle East and related issues. Students can research organizations and learn more about how people are developing positive and proactive responses to the issues they are reading about and researching through their literary study. In some cases it may be appropriate to contact such organizations and develop educational and supportive connections. Preparing informed students who know how to think critically, understand the perspective of others, and act on their beliefs is at the heart of the mission of schooling in a democratic society.

When I was a child, I heard it said that it was bad manners to discuss religion, politics, or controversial topics at dinner. Stendhal once remarked, "Politics in a work of literature is a pistol-shot in the middle of a concert, something unseemly to which we nevertheless cannot fail to give our attention." Yet, *Teaching the Literature of Today's Middle East* makes that case that we do need to be talking about religion, politics, and timely and controversial questions when we teach literature, whether in classes in English, humanities, or the social sciences.

In this sense *Teaching the Literature of Today's Middle East* participates in an evolution in the teaching of literature that has developing since at least the 1970s. As the literary canon has expanded to include works written by women, racial and ethnic minorities, and postcolonial writers from around the world, new texts have brought multiple perspectives and called for new pedagogical approaches. The skills of close reading and attention to literary genre, language, and form – especially fostered by previous generations under the name "New Criticism"– are now supplemented by increased attention to social, cultural, historical, and political contexts drawing on feminism and gender studies, ethnic and multicultural studies, Marxism and post-Marxism, New Historicism, postmodernism, deconstruction, film studies, and so on. (New Criticism itself was a deliberate move away from the political and historical approaches that guided literary study in the 1930s.) Literary and cultural scholarship and theory have significantly developed in recent years, deepening the range of questions under consideration. Issues of Self and Other, inclusion and exclusion, dominant and subordinate points of view, and high vs. popular culture have appropriately become important questions in literature and humanities courses. Multicultural teaching has come to be the norm rather than the exception. Cultural studies approaches have brought together a wide range of texts including visual, informational, and mass media along with literary. Literature facilitates difficult and controversial questions – questions that are likely more relevant to important questions of the day and the real lives of students.

Teachers who embark on the interesting and engaging study of teaching literature from the contemporary Middle East will be leading their students, communities, and profession on an important and pressing journey. The Middle East is a region undergoing tremendous change, and continued evolution and development in teaching about the Middle East will, of course, be needed. *Teaching the Literature of Today's Middle East* provides essential background and extensive resources to help teachers address one of the most critical regions of the world, bridge misunderstanding, and facilitate vital connections between the Middle East and Europe, America, and the English-speaking world. At the time of this writing, continued warfare in Iraq and Afghanistan, misunderstandings of the aspirations of Middle Eastern people, tensions between Israel, Palestine, and Iran, Quran burning, and attacks on mosques are the daily norm. Perhaps the teaching you do will help make these events and others like them, a thing of the past.

CONTRIBUTORS

David Alvarez is Associate Professor of English at Grand Valley State University in Allendale, Michigan, where he teaches courses on postcolonial Anglophone literatures as well as on various contemporary international literatures in translation. A comparatist by training, he has published articles on South African and West Indian poetry, on everyday life theory, and on colonialism in his native Gibraltar. Currently, he is working on a monograph that examines representations of clandestine crossings of the Strait of Gibraltar in Spanish and Moroccan fiction and film.

Blain H. Auer is Assistant Professor of Comparative Religion at Western Michigan University. He specializes on Islam in the context of South Asia. He is a contributor to the *The Encyclopedia of Islam in the United States* (2007). Publications include "Concepts of Justice and the Catalogue of Punishments from the Delhi Sultanate (7th–8th/13th–14th centuries)," in *Public Violence in Islamic Societies* (Edinburgh University Press, 2009). He is currently working on a book-length project that explores religion, politics, and history writing in the Delhi Sultanate. The work is titled *Symbols of Authority in Medieval Islam: History, Religion and Muslim Legitimacy in the Delhi Sultanate*. (I. B. Tauris) and is due for publication in 2011.

Monica Mona Eraqi was born and raised in Michigan by immigrant parents of European and Arab decent. She began teaching and coaching in Hamtramck Public Schools, Hamtramck, Michigan before moving in 2006 to Dakota High School in Chippewa Valley Schools, Macomb, Michigan. She graduated with a Masters Degree in Teaching in 2007 from Oakland University and an Education Specialist in 2010 from Wayne State University. A devout Muslim, Ms. Eraqi received many questions from students regarding Islam and the Middle East. Compelled by her students' questions she created the curriculum for a new course, Modern Middle East, which she teaches at Dakota High School. She is currently working on her doctorate in curriculum and instruction at the University of Michigan, Dearborn.

Jeffrey A. Patterson is a language arts teacher at the Volinia Outcomes School, an alternative high school, in Marcellus, MI, were he has taught for ten years. In 2009, Jeff, working with a group of seniors, developed a semester-long unit that explored ideas about their post-9/11 world. Students explored misconceptions and developed a clearer understanding of the events and issues surrounding the events of September 11, 2001 and the ensuing "War on Terror." Jeff has presented at the National Council of the Teachers of English, and its Michigan state affiliate. He is currently working towards a Masters Degree in the teaching of English at Western Michigan University, in Kalamazoo, MI.

Vivan Steemers is an Assistant Professor of French at Western Michigan University. Her areas of specialization are postcolonial theory, francophone Sub-Saharan literature and translation theory. A native of the Netherlands, she has studied and worked most of her life in a multilingual as well as a multicultural environment and taught at both Dutch and American institutions of higher education.

Allen Webb is a Professor of English Education and Postcolonial Studies at Western Michigan University. He has written or edited seven books, published over thirty articles and given more than 100 conference presentations primarily on the subject of teaching literature. He taught English at West Linn High School for six years, at the University of Oregon for five years, and at Western Michigan University for eighteen years. His master degrees and PhD are in English education and comparative literature.

BIBLIOGRAPHY

"11 U.S. Soldiers Court-Martialed for Crimes in Iraq." *Al Jazeera Magazine*. 16 Oct. 2006. Web. 15 Nov. 2010. www.aljazeera.com.

Abdel-Fattah, Randa. *Does My Head Look Big In This?* New York: Scholastic, 2008.

——. *Ten Hate Me*. New York: Orchard Books, 2010.

——. *Where the Streets Had a Name*. New York: Scholastic, 2010.

Abdul-Ghafar, Saleemah. *Living Islam Out Loud: American Muslim Women Speak*. Boston MA: Beacon Press, 2005.

Abouzeid, Leila. *Year of the Elephant: A Moroccan Woman's Journey Toward Independence*. Trans. Barbara Parmenter. Austin TX: University of Texas Press, 1989.

——. *The Last Chapter*. Cairo: American University in Cairo Press, 2004.

AbuKhalil, As'ad. "Women in the Middle East" *Foreign Policy In Focus*. 11 Oct. 2005. Web. 15 May 10.

Abulhawa, Susan. *Mornings in Jenin*. New York: Bloomsbury, 2010.

Ahmed, Akbar. *Journey Into America: The Challenge of Islam*. Washington DC: Brookings Institution, 2010.

Ahmed, Leila. *Women and Gender in Islam: Historical Roots of a Modern Debate*. New Haven CT: Yale UP, 1992.

Al Aswany, Alaa. *The Yacoubian Building*. Trans. Humphry Davies. Cairo: The American University in Cairo Press, 2004.

Alcott, Louisa May. "Lost in a Pyramid: The Mummy's Curse." Sioux Falls SD: NuVision Publications, 2010.

Al-Ghitani, Gamal. *Zayni Barakat*. New York: Viking, 1988.

Algosaibi, Ghazi. *An Apartment Called Freedom*. London: Paul Kegan Press, 1996.

Al-Hakim, Tawfiq. *Fate of a Cockroach*. Washington DC: Three Continents Press, 1980.

Al-Koni, Ibrahim. *The Bleeding of the Stone*. Northampton MA: Interlink Book, 2001.

——. *Gold Dust*. Cairo: The American University in Cairo Press, 2008.

Allah Made Me Funny: Live in Concert. Dir. Andrea Kalin. 2008. DVD.

Al-Nowaihi, Magda M. "The 'Middle East'? Or . . ./Arabic Literature and the Postcolonial Predicament." *A Companion to Postcolonial Studies*. Eds. Henry Schwarz and Sangeeta Ray. Wiley On-Line Library, 2007.

Al-Qaid, Yusuf. *War in the Land of Egypt*. London: Al Saqi Books, 1986.

Alsamari, Lewis. *Escape from Saddam: The Incredible True Story of One Man's Journey to Freedom*. New York: Crown, 2008.

Alsanea, Rajaa. *Girls of Riyadh*. New York: Penguin, 2007.

Al-Shaykh, Hanan. *Only in London*. New York: Pantheon, 2001.

Al-Windawi, Thura. *Thura's Diary: My Life in Wartime Iraq*. New York: Penguin, 2004.

"The Arab Community in Canada." *Statistics Canada*. Web. 20 June 2010.

Armstrong, Karen. *Muhammad: A Biography of the Prophet*. New York: HarperOne, 1993.

——. *Islam: A Short History*. New York: Modern Library, 2002.

——. *Muhammad: A Prophet For Our Time*. New York: HarperOne, 2007.

Arranged. Dirs. Diane Crespo, Stefan. C. Shaefer. Cicala Filmworks, 2007.

Atkins, Sarah and Giovanni Belzoni. *The Fruits of Enterprise: The Travels of Belzoni in Egypt and Nubia*. Boston, MA: Monroe & Francis, 1824.

Atwell, Nancie. "Afterward." *Adolescent Literacy: Turning Promise into Practice*. Eds. Kylene Beers, Robert Probst, Linda Rief. Portsmouth NH: Heinemann, 2007. 311–14.

Auer, Blain. "Spelling Quran." Email to the author, 1 Sep. 2010.

——. *Symbols of Authority in Medieval Islam: History, Religion and Muslim Legitimacy in the Delhi Sultanate*. London: I.B. Taurus, forthcoming, 2012.

Bakhtin, M. M. *The Dialogic Imagination: Four Essays*. Austin: University of Texas Press, 1982.

Bakr, Salwa. *The Wiles of Men and Other Stories*. Austin TX: University of Texas Press, 1993.

"Battle of Algiers." Dir. Gillo Pontocorvo. Rialto Pictures, 1966.

"Battle over History." *60 Minutes*. CBS: 28 Feb. 2010.

Bayoumi, Moustafa. *How Does it Feel to be a Problem? Being Young and Arab in America*. New York: Penguin, 2008.

Beaufort. Dir. Joseph Cedar. United King Films, 2007.

Benjamin, Walter. "The Task of the Translator." *The Translation Studies Reader*. Ed. Lawrence Venuti. New York: Routledge, 2004 (2000). 75–85.

Bennis, Phyllis. *Ending the Iraq War: A Primer*. Northampton MA: Olive Branch Press, 2009.

Bergeron, David M. "'Are we turned Turks?': English Pageants and the Stuart Court." *Comparative Drama* 44.3. (2010).

Bermann, Sandra and Michael Wood. *Nation, Language, and the Ethics of Translation*. Princeton, NJ: Princeton UP, 2005.

Blood and Oil. Dir. Michael Klare. Media Education Foundation, 2007.

Boccaccio, Giovonni. *The Decameron*. New York: Penguin, 2003.

Bosquet, Alain. *Yasar Kemal on His Life and Art*. Syracuse, NY: Syracuse UP, 1998.

Bourdain, Anthony. *No reservations Istanbul*. Travel Channel. 2009. Television.

Bowden, Mark. *Black Hawk Down: A Story of Modern War*. New York: Penguin, 2000.

The Boys from Baghdad High. Dir. Ivan O'Mahoney and Laura Winter. Arte and BB, 2008.

Braiker, Brian. "Americans and Islam: The latest NEWSWEEK Poll paints a complicated portrait of attitudes toward America's Muslims." *Newsweek*. 20 Jul. 2007. Web. 15 Nov. 2010.

Burden, Matthew Currier. *The Blog of War: Front-Line Dispatches from Soldiers in Iraq and Afghanistan*. New York: Simon & Schuster, 2006.

Burnham, Gilbert, Riyadh Lafta, Shannon Doocy, and Les Roberts. "Mortality after the 2003 invasion of Iraq: a cross-sectional cluster sample survey." *The Lancet*, 21 October, 2006; 368(9545): 1421–1428. Web. 15 Nov. 2010. www.thelancet.com/journals/lancet/article/PIIS0140-6736%2806%2969491-9/fulltext.

Butler, Judith. "You Will Not Be Alone." *The Nation*, 14 Apr. 2010.

Call of Duty 4: AC-130 "Gunship." Created by Activision. Uploaded by syoun678.11-6-2007. Web. 15 Nov. 2010. www.youtube.com/watch?v=xAscuD4loh8.

Call of Duty 4 HD "War Pig." Created by Activision. Uploaded by Shadowzack. 12-10-2008. Web. 15 Nov. 2010. www.youtube.com/watch?v=lMkl6g7sCHE.

Carey-Webb, Allen. *Literature and Lives: A Response-based, Cultural Studies Approach to Teaching English*. Urbana IL: NCTE Press, 2001.

Carmi, Daniella. *Samir and Yonatan*. New York: Scholastic/Blue Sky Press, 2002.

Carter, Bucky. Ed. *Building Literacy Connections with Graphic Novels: Page by Page, Panel by Panel*. Urbana IL: NCTE Press, 2007.

Carter, Jimmy. *Palestine: Peace Not Apartheid*. New York: Simon & Schuster, 2006.

Cesari, Joceylyne. *The Encyclopedia of Islam in the United States*. Santa Barbara, CA: Greenwood Press, 2007.

Charara, Hayan, Ed. *Inclined to Speak: An Anthology of Contemporary Arab American Poetry*. Fayetteville AR: University of Arkansas Press, 2008.

Charlie Wilson's War. Dir. Mike Nichols. Perf. Tom Hanks, Julie Roberts. Universal, 2007.

Chaucer, Geoffrey. *The Canterbury Tales*. New York: Penguin, 2005.

Chill, A. *Teaching about the Middle East*. Culver City, CA: Social Studies School Service, 2002.

Collateral Murder – Wikileaks – Iraq. Footage from a U.S. Apache helicopter in 2007. Released by Wikileaks. Uploaded by sunshinepress on Apr 3, 2010. Web. 15 Nov. 2010. www.youtube.com/watch?v=5rXPrfnU3G0.

"Court Martial in Iraq Rape Case." 2006. BBC News. 19 Oct. 2006. Web. 15 Nov. 2010. http://news.bbc.co.uk/2/hi/americas/6064444.stm.

Cryan, Phillip. "Defining Terrorism." *Counterpunch Magazine*. 29 Nov. 2001. Web. 1 Sept 2010.

Curtis, Edward E. IV. *Muslims in America: A Short History*. New York: Oxford UP USA, 2009.

Daniels, Harvey. *Literature Circles: Voice and Choice in the Student-Centered Classroom*. Portland, ME: Stenhouse, 1994.

Dante, Alighieri. *The Inferno*. Trans. Henri Barbusse. Project Gutenberg Archive. Web. 15 Sep. 2010.

Dehqan, Ahmad. *Journey to Heading 270 Degrees: A Novel*. Trans. Paul Sprachman. Costa Mesa, CA: Mazda Publishers, 2006.

Denny, Frederick. *An Introduction to Islam: Third Edition*. New York: Prentice Hall, 2005.

Donovan, Jennifer. "Literary and Suspenseful" Review of *Rooftops Over Tehran*. Amazon.com. Web. 30 May 2010. www.amazon.com/Rooftops-Tehran-Novel-Mahbod-Seraji/dp/045122681X.

Dozier, Kimberley. "US Intelligence on Arab Unrest Draws Criticism." *Associated Press*, 4 Feb. 2011.

Dumas, Firoozeh. *Funny in Farsi: A Memoir of Growing up Iranian in America*. New York: Villard, 2003.

——. *Laughing Without an Accent: Adventures of an Iranian American, at Home and Abroad*. New York: Random House, 2009.

Duwayhi, Jabbur. *Autumn Equinox*. Fayetteville, AR: University of Arkansas Press, 2001.

Eisner, Will. *Fagin the Jew: A Graphic Novel*. New York: Doubleday, 2003.

Elalamy, Youssouf Amine. *Les Clandestins*. Paris: Au Diable Vauvert, 2001.

——. *Two Novellas by YAE: A Moroccan in New York and Sea Drinkers*. Lanham, MD: Lexington Books, 2008.

Ellis, Deborah. *The Breadwinner*. Berkeley, CA: Groundwood Books, 2001.

Elmessiri, Nur and Abdelwahab Elmessiri. *A Land of Stone and Thyme: An Anthology of Palestinian Short Stories*. London: Quartet Books, 1996.

El Saadawi, Nawal. *Woman at Point Zero*. New York: Zed Books, 1983.

Encounter Point. Dir. Ronit Avni. Just Vision, 2006.

Esposito, John. *Islam and Democracy*. Oxford UP: New York, 1996.

——. *What Everyone Needs to Know about Islam*. New York: Oxford UP, 2002.

Esposito, John and Dalia Mogahed. *Who Speaks For Islam? What a Billion Muslims Really Think*. New York: Gallop Press, 2008.

Fanon, Frantz. *Wretched of the Earth*. Trans. Constance Farrington. New York: Grove Press, 1961.

——. "The Pitfalls of National Consciousness." *Wretched of the Earth*. Trans. Constance Farrington. New York: Grove Press, 1961. Web. 17 June 2010. www.marxists.org/subject/africa/fanon/pitfalls-national.htm.

Finkle, Sheryl and Tamara Lilly. *Middle Ground: Exploring Selected Literature from and about the Middle East*. Urbana, IL: NCTE Press, 2008.

Fitzgerald, Edward and Omar Khayyam. *Rubaiyat of Omar Khayyam*. New York: FQ Classics, 2007.

Ford, Peter. "Why do they hate us?" *Christian Science Monitor*. Web. 27 Nov. 2001.

"Four Pairs of Interfaith Fellows." *Speaking of Faith*. Dir. Krista Tippett. American Public Media. National Public Radio. 15 Oct. 2009. http://being.publicradio.org/programs/2009/newground.

"Four U.S. Soldiers Charged with Rape and Murder." CNN. 18 Oct. 2006. Web. 15 Nov. 2010. www.cnn.com/2006/LAW/10/18/soldiers.court/index.html.

Friedl, Erica. *Women of Deh Koh: Lives in an Iranian Village*. New York: Penguin, 1991.

Glazebrook, Phillip. "The View from Behind the Veil." *New York Times Book Review*, 14 May 1989.

Gravett, Paul. *Graphic Novels: Everything You Need to Know*. New York: Harper, 2005.

Grossman, David. *Smile of the Lamb*. New York: Picador, 2003.

Haddad, Yvonne, Farid Senzai, and Jane Smith. *Educating the Muslims of America*. New York: Oxford UP USA, 2009.

Halaby, Laila. *West of the Jordan*. Boston MA: Beacon Press, 2003.

——. *Once in a Promised Land*. New York: Beacon Press, 2007.

Hammelman, Steven. "Orientalism and sympathy in Maria Susanna Cummins's *El Fureidis*." *Legacy: A Journal of American Women Writers* 25.1 (2008).

Hart, Alan. *Zionism: The Real Enemy of the Jews, Vol. 1: The False Messiah*. Atlanta, GA: Clarity Press, 2009.

——. *Zionism: The Real Enemy of the Jews, Vol. 2: David Becomes Goliath*. Atlanta, GA: Clarity Press, 2009.

——. *Zionism: The Real Enemy of the Jews, Vol. 3: Conflict Without End?* Atlanta, GA: Clarity Press, 2010.

Hatim, Basil. *Teaching and Researching Translation*. Harlow, UK: Longman, 2001.

Heavy Metal in Baghdad. Dir. Suroosh Alvi and Eddy Moretti. VBS TV and Vice Films, 2008.

Heide, Florence Parry and Judith Heide Gilliland. *Sami and the Time of the Troubles*. London: Sandpiper, 1995.

Heide, Florence Parry and Ted Lewin. *The Day of Ahmed's Secret*. New York: Harper Collins, 1995.

Higgins, M. "Great Film for Teaching About Islam." 1 Nov. 2002. Web. 17 Jun. 2010. www.amazon.com/Message-Anthony-Quinn/dp/6305020108.

Hosseini, Khaled. *The Kite Runner*. New York: Riverhead Books, 2003.

——. *A Thousand Splendid Suns*. New York: Riverhead Books, 2007.

Ibrahim, Son'allah. *Zaat*. Cairo: American University in Cairo Press, 2004.

Idris, Yusuf. "The Chair Carrier." *Arabic Short Stories*. Trans. Denys Johnson-Davies. Berkeley, CA: University of California Press, 1983.

"In His Own Words; Bush on Islam." Web. 17 Jun. 2010. http://muslimrepublicans.net/Article.asp?ID=164.

Inside Islam: What One Billion Muslims Really Think. Dir. Robert Gardner. Unity Productions, 2010.

Iran: Yesterday and Today. Dir. Rick Steves. PBS, 2009.

Iraq Body Count. Web. 17 Jun. 2011. www.iraqbodycount.org/.

Iraq Veterans Against War. *Winter Soldier: Iraq and Afghanistan: Eyewitness Accounts of the Occupations*. Chicago: Haymarket Books, 2008.

The Iron Wall. Dir. Mohammed Alatar, 2006.

Irving, Washington. *Tales of the Alhambra*. Powys: Lit, 2010.

Irwin, John T. *American Hieroglyphics: The Symbol of the Egyptian Hieroglyphics in the American Renaissance*. New Haven CT: Yale UP, 1980.

"Islam in the United States." Wikipedia. Web. 18 Jun. 2010. http://en.wikipedia.org/wiki/Islam_in_the_United_States.

Jacquemond, Richard. "Translation and Cultural Hegemony: The Case of French-Arabic Translation." *Rethinking Translation: discourse, subjectivity, ideology*. Ed. Lawrence Venuti. New York: Routledge, 1992. 139–158.

Jelloun, Tahar Ben. *Partir*. Paris: Gallimard, 2007.

Jerome. "Letter to Pammachius." *The Translation Studies Reader*. Ed. Lawrence Venuti. New York: Routledge, 2004 (2000). 21–30.

Johannessen, Larry. *Illumination Rounds: Teaching the Literature of the Vietnam War*. Urbana IL: NCTE Press, 1992.

Johnston, Sheila. "I Risked My Life to Make this Movie." *The Telegraph*, 7 Apr. 2006.

Kaladas, Pauline and Khaled Mattawa, Eds. *Dinarzad's Children: An Anthology of Arab American Fiction 2nd Edition*. Fayetteville, AR: University of Arkansas Press, 2009.

Kamguian, Azam. "The Liberation of Women in the Middle East." Web. 10 May 2010. www.ntpi.org/html/liberationofwomen.html.

Kanafani, Ghassan. *Men in the Sun and other Palestinian Stories*. London: Rienner Publications, 1999.

——. *Palestine's Children: Returning to Haifa and Other Stories*. Boulder CO: Lynne Rienner Publishers, 2000.

Kemal, Yashar. *Memed, My Hawk*. New York: NYRB Classics, 2005.

Keret, Etgar. *The Bus Driver Who Wanted to be God and other stories*. New York: Macmillian, 2001.

Keshavarz, Fatemeh. *Jasmine and Stars: Reading More than* Lolita *in Tehran*. Chapel Hill NC: University of North Carolina Press, 2007.

Khadra, Yasmina. *The Attack*. Trans. John Cullun. New York: Anchor, 2006.

Khalifeh, Sahar. *Wild Thorns*. New York: Interlink Books, 1999.

Kincheloe, Joe and Shirley Steinberg. *The Miseducation of the West: How Schools and Media Distort Our Understanding of the Islamic World*. Westport, CT: Praeger, 2004.

Kingdom of Heaven. Dir. Ridley Scott. Scott Free Productions, 2005.

Kinsley, Michael. "Defining Terrorism." *Slate Magazine*. 5 Oct. 2001. Web. 12 May 2010.

The Kite Runner. Dir. Marc Forster. Universal, 2007.

Klare, Michael. *Blood and Oil: The Dangers and Consequences of America's Growing Dependency on Imported Petroleum*. New York: Holt, 2004.

Koppes, Clayton R. "Captain Mahan, General Gordon, and the origins of the term 'Middle East'." *Middle Eastern Studies*. 12.1. (1976): 95–8.

Kurnaz, Murat. *Five Years of My Life: An Innocent Man in Guantanamo*. New York: Palgrave Macmillan, 2008.

Lalami, Leila. *Hope and Other Dangerous Pursuits*. New York: Mariner, 2006.

——. *Secret Son*. New York: Algonquin Books, 2009.

Lange, Christian. *Public Violence in Islamic Societies*. Edinburgh: Edinburgh UP, 2009.

Levine, Anna. *Running on Eggs*. Chicago IL: Front Street/Cricket Books, 2009.

Lima, Lazaro. "Washington Irving's Andalusia and the American Imagination." Web. 10 May 2010. www.nyu.edu/gsas/program/neareast/andalusia/pdf/7.pdf.

Lincoln, Bruce. *Holy Terrors: Thinking About Religion After September 11*. 2nd ed. Chicago IL: U Chicago P, 2006.

The Lion and the Hawk. Dir. Peter Ustinov. 1984.

The Lovers' Wind. Dir. Albert Lamorisse. Iranian Ministry of Culture and Art, 1969.

Luedtke, Luther S. *Nathaniel Hawthorne and the Romance of the Orient*. Bloomington, IN: Indiana UP, 1989.

Mackey, Robert. "Disobeying Israel's Law of Entry, for Fun." *New York Times*. The Lede. 21 Sep. 2010.

Mahfouz, Naguib. *The Time and the Place: And Other Stories*. New York: Anchor Books, 1992.

——. *The Day the Leader Was Killed*. New York: Anchor Books, 2000.

Mahi, Binebine. *Welcome to Paradise*. New York: Granta, 2003.

Mahmood, Saba. *The Politics of Piety: The Islamic Revival and the Feminist Subject*. Princeton, NJ: Princeton UP, 2005.

Mansour, Ahmed. *Inside Fallujah: The Unembedded Story*. New York: Olive Branch Press, 2009.

Matar, Nabil. *Turks, Moors, and Englishmen in the Age of Discovery*. New York: Columbia University Press, 1999.

McArthur, Shirl. "Conservative Estimate of Total Direct U.S. Aid to Israel: Almost $114 Billion." *Washington Report on Middle Eastern Affairs*. November 2008, 10–11.

McCloud, Scott. *Understanding Comics*. New York: Harper, 1993.

Meguid, Ibrahim Abdel. *The Other Place*. Cairo: American University in Cairo Press, 2005.

Mernissi, Fatima. *Dreams of Trespass*. New York: Basic Books, 1994.

——. *The Veil and the Male Elite: A Feminist Interpretation of Women's Rights in Islam*. Basic Books: New York, 1992.

The Message. Dir. Moustapha Akkad. Filmco International, 1976.

Michigan State Board of Education. *High School Content Expectations: English Language Arts*. Lansing, MI: Department of Education, April 2006.

Minah, Hanna. *Fragments of Memory: A Story of a Syrian Family*. Northampton MA: Interlink, 2004.

Mirzeler, Mustafa. "My Childhood Memories and the Legends of Kurdistan." *Remembering Childhood in the Middle East: Memoirs from a Century of Change*. Ed. Elizabeth Warnock Fernea. Austin, TX: U of Texas P, 2002.

"More than 1,000,000 Iraqis murdered. *Opinion Research Business*. PDF report." September 2007.

Mosteghanemi, Ahlam. *Memory in the Flesh*. Cairo: American University in Cairo Press, 2003.

"Most Recent U.S. Spousal Murder Statistics." Web. 15 May 2010. www.wildelife.com/worth/stats/stats2.html.

Munich. Dir. Steven Spielberg. Universal, 2005.

Munif, Abdelrahman. *Cities of Salt*. Trans. Peter Theroux. New York: Vintage, 1989.

"Muslims Widely Seen As Facing Discrimination." Pew Research Center. Pew Forum on Religion and Public Life. 9 Sep. 2009. Web. 15 May 2010. http://pewresearch.org/pubs/1336/perceptions-of-islam-religious-similarities-differences.

Mustafa, Shakir, Ed. *Contemporary Iraqi Fiction: An Anthology*. Syracuse NY: Syracuse UP, 2008.

Myers, Walter Dean. *Sunrise over Fallujah*. New York: Scholastic, 2008.

Myles, Anne. "Slaves in Algiers, Captives in Iraq: The Strange Career of the Barbary Captivity Narrative." *Commonplace* 5.1, October (2004).

"Nightmare At Guantanamo Bay." *60 Minutes*. CBS: 31 Mar. 2008. Web. 8 Feb. 2010. www.cbsnews.com/video/watch/?id=3980799n.

No End in Sight: Iraq's Descent into Chaos. Dir. Charles Ferguson. Magnolia Pictures, 2007.

"No Questions Asked: What Will Unconditional Aid Buy from Egypt's Hosni Mubarak." Editorial. *The Washington Post*. 7 May 2009.

Nye, Naomi Shihab. *Habibi*. New York: Aladdin Paperbacks, 1999.

Obenzinger, Hilton. *American Palestine: Meville, Twain, and the Holy Land Mania*. Princeton, NJ: Princeton UP, 1999.

Ochsenwald, William and Sydney Nettleton Fisher. *The Middle East: A History*. 6th ed. New York: McGraw Hill, 2003.

Ortega y Gasset, José. "The Misery and Splendor of Translation." *Theories of Translation: An Anthology of Essays from Dryden to Derrida*. Eds. Rainer Schulte and John Biguenet. Chicago IL: U of Chicago P, 1992. 93–112.

Osama. Dir. Siddiq Barmak. Barmak Film, 2003.

Oz, Amos. *The Panther in the Basement*. New York: Mariner Books, 1998.

Pamuk, Orhan. *The White Castle*. New York: Vintage, 1998.

——. *Istanbul: Memories and the City*. New York: Knopf, 2005.

Paradise Now. Dir. Abu-Assad. Augustus Film, 2005.

Pax, Salam. *Salam Pax: The Clandestine Diary of an Ordinary Iraqi*. New York: Grove, 2003.

Persepolis. Dirs. Vincent Paronnaud, Marjane Satrapi. 2.4.7 Films, 2007.

Poe, Edgar Allen. *Complete Stories and Poems*. New York: Doubleday, 1984.

Poonawalla, Aziz H. "The Burka and the Bikini." *AltMuslim Comment*. 20 Oct. 2002. Web. 20 Nov. 2010. www.altmuslim.com/a/a/a/the_burka_and_the_bikini.

Putz, Melinda. *A Teacher's Guide to the Multigenre Research Project*. Portsmouth NH: Heinemann, 2006.

The Quran. Center for Muslim–Jewish Engagement. University of Southern California. Web. 15 Nov. 2010. www.usc.edu/schools/college/crcc/engagement/resources/texts/muslim/quran.

Rahman, Fazlur. *Islam*. Chicago IL: University of Chicago Press, 1979.

Rastegar, Mitra. "Reading Nafisi in the West: Authenticity, Orientalism, and 'Liberating' Iranian Women." *WSQ: Women's Studies Quarterly* 34: 1/2. (2006): 108–128.

Reel Bad Arabs. Dirs. Jeremy Erp and Sut Jhally. Media Education Foundation, 2006. http://video.google.com/videoplay?docid=-223210418534585840.

Religion in the Public Schools: A Joint Statement of Current Law. Web. 8 Feb. 2010. http://candst.tripod.com/tnppage/jnt-sta.htm.

Ripples Cross. Dir. Mark Turner and David Schler. Arab Film, 2005.

Riverbend. *Baghdad Burning: Girl Blog from Iraq*. New York: CUNY Press, 2005.

Robinson, Douglas. *Becoming a Translator*. London: Routledge, 2003.

Rowson, Susanna Haswell. *Slaves in Algiers, or, A Struggle for Freedom*. Acton, MA: Copley Publishing Group, 2001.

Rozema, Robert and Allen Webb. *Literature and the Web: Reading and Responding with New Technologies*. Portsmouth, NH: Heinemann Press, 2008.

Sacco, Joe. *Palestine*. Seattle WA: Fantagraphics Books, 2002.

——. *Footnotes in Gaza*. New York: Metropolitan Books, 2009.

Sadat, Jehan. *Woman of Egypt*. New York: Simon & Schuster, 1987.

Said, Edward. *Orientalism*. New York: Vintage, 1978.

——. *The World, the Text, and the Critic*. Cambridge MA: Harvard UP, 1983.

——. "Impossible Histories" *Harper's Magazine*. Jul. 2002: 69–75.

Salih, Taleb. *Season of Migration to the North*. Trans. Denys Johnson-Davies. New York: NYRB Classics, 1989.

Samman, Ghadah. *The Square Moon: Supernatural Tales*. Fayetteville AR: University of Arkansas Press, 1999.

Sarroub, Loukia. *All American Yemeni Girls: Being Muslim in a Public School*. Philadelphia PA: University of Pennsylvania Press, 2005.

Sato, Hiroaki. *One Hundred Frogs: From Renga to Haiku in English*. New York: Weatherhill, 1983.

Satrapi, Marjane. *Persepolis I*. New York: Pantheon, 2004.

Satrapi, Marjane. *Persepolis II: The Story of a Return*. New York: Pantheon, 2004.

Satrapi, Marjane. *Embroderies*. New York: Pantheon, 2005.

Schleiermacher, Friedrich. "On the Different Methods of Translating." *The Translation Studies Reader*, Ed. Lawrence Venuti. New York: Routledge, 2004 (2000). 43–63.

Seraji, Mahbod. *Rooftops Over Tehran*. New York: New American Library, 2009.

Shafak, Elif. *The Bastard of Istanbul*. New York: Penguin, 2008.

Shahak, Bat-Chen. *The Bat-Chen Diaries*. Minneapolis MN: Kar-Ben, 2008.

Shaheen, Jack. *Reel Bad Arabs: How Hollywood Vilifies a People*. New York: Olive Branch Press, 2001.

Shakespeare, William. *Othello*. New York: Simon & Schuster, 2004.

Shakir, Evelyn. *Remember Me to Lebanon*. Syracuse NY: Syracuse UP, 2007.

Silver, Linda. "Israeli Encounters: Books for Teens about Israel." *English Journal*. 99.6. July (2010): 21–3.

Sirin, Selcuk and Michelle Fine. *Muslim American Youth: Understanding Hyphenated Identities Through Multiple Methods*. New York: NYU Press, 2008.

Skalli, Loubna. "Loving Muslim Women with a Vengence: The West, Women, and Fundamentalism." *The Miseducation of the West*. Eds. Joe L. Kincheoloe and Shirley Steinberg. Westport CT: Praeger, 2004.

Sperry, S. *Media Construction of the Middle East: A Digital Media Literacy Curriculum*. Unpublished manuscript. New York: Ithaca College, 2010. Web. 15 Dec. 2010. www.ithaca.edu/looksharp/?action=middleeast.

Spiegleman, Art. *The Complete Maus: A Survivor's Tale*. New York: Pantheon, 1996.

Staples, Suzanne Fisher. *Under the Persimmon Tree*. New York: Farrar, Straus, Giroux, 2005.

——. *Shabanu Daughter of the Wind*. New York: Laurel-Leaf Press, 2003.

Steiner, George. "The Hermeneutic Motion." *The Translation Studies Reader*. Ed. Lawrence Venuti. New York: Routledge, 2004 (2000). 193–198.

Stendahl, John. *The Charterhouse of Parma*. Trans. John Sturrock. New York: Penguin, 2006.

Steves, Rick. *Rick Steves' Greece, Turkey, Israel and Egypt*. PBS: 2000–07. Television.

Stevens, Michael S. "Spanish Orientalism: Washington Irving and the Romance of the Moors." Georgia State University: Dissertation, Department of History, 2007.

Taher, Bahaa'. *Aunt Safiyya and the Monastery*. Trans. Barbara Romaine. Berkeley, CA: University of California Press, 1996.

"Talk to an Iraqi." *This American Life*. Web. 6 Oct. 2011. www.youtube.com/watch?v=GPEX0PnV-LU.

Tergeman, Siham. *Daughter of Damascus*. Austin TX: UTP, 1994.

Time of Favor. Dir. Joseph Cedar. Kino International, 2000.

Todorov, Tzvetan. *The Conquest of America: The Question of the Other*. Norman OK: University of Oklahoma Press, 1999.

Tolan, Sandy. *The Lemon Tree: An Arab, A Jew, and the Heart of the Middle East*. New York: Bloomsbury, 2006.

Twain, Mark. *The Innocents Abroad: or The New Pilgrim's Progress*. Hartford: American Publishing Company, 1901.

——. *Tom Sawyer Abroad*. Charleston SC: BiblioBazaar, 2007.

Two Women. Dir. Tahmineh Milani. Facets, 2000.

Tyler, Royall. *The Algerine Captive or, The Life and Adventures of Doctor Updike Underhill*. New York: Modern Library, 2002.

Tymoczko, Maria. "Postcolonial Writing and Literary Translation." *Postcolonial Translation: Theory and Practice*. Eds. Susan Bassnett and Harish Triveda. London: Routledge, 1999. 19–40.

Under the Bombs. Dir. Philippe Aractingi. Fantascope Productions, 2008.

"US Intervention in the Middle East." Information Clearing House. Web. 1 Sep. 2010.

Vaughan, Brian K. *Pride of Baghdad*. New York: Vertigo, 2006.

Vengo. Dir. Tony Gatlif. Canal+, 2000.

Venuti, Lawrence. *The Translator's Invisibility: A History of Translation*. London: Routledge, 1995.

——. *The Scandals of Translation*. London: Routledge, 1998.

Visson, Lynn. "Simultaneous Interpretation: Language and Cultural Difference." *Nation, Language, and the Ethics of Translation*. Eds. Sandra Bermann and Michael Wood. Princeton, NJ: Princeton UP, 2005. 51–64.

Vitkus, Daniel J. "Turning Turk in *Othello*: The Conversion and Damnation of the Moor." *Shakespeare Quarterly* 48.2 (1997): 145–176.

——. *Turning Turk: English Theater and the Multicultural Mediterranean 1570–1630*. New York: Palgrave Macmillan, 2008.

Waltz with Bashir. Dir. Ari Folman. Sony Pictures. 2008.

Warren, John. "The Mummy's Curse." Web. 15 Nov. 2010. www.touregypt.net/featurestories/curse.htm.

Webb, Allen, and Brandon Guisgand. "A Multimodal Approach to Addressing Anti-Semitism: Charles Dickens' *Oliver Twist* and William Eizner's *Fagin the Jew*." *Page by Page, Panel by Panel: Building Literacy Connections with Graphic Novels*. Ed. James Carter. Urbana IL: NCTE Press, 2006.

"What is Terrorism?" *International Terrorism and Security Research, Terrorism-Research.com.* Web. 1 Sep. 2010.
"What is Zionism?" *Jews Against Zionism.com.* Web. 15 Jun. 2010.
White, Mathew. "Mid-Range Wars and Atrocities of the Twentieth Century." Web. 15 Nov 2010. http://users.erols.com/mwhite28/warstat4.htm#Israel.
"Why Do They Hate Us?" *SourceWatch: Your Guide to the Names Behind the News.* 7 July 2010.
Women of the Wall. Dir. Faye Lederman. New Day, 2008.
Wood, Trish. *What Was Asked of Us: An Oral History of the Iraq War by the Soldiers Who Fought It.* New York: Back Bay Books, 2007.
Wright, Evan. *Generation Kill.* New York: Penguin Berkley Trade, 2008.
Wristcutters: A Love Story. Dir. Goran Dukic. Lions Gate, 2006.
Yaklif, Yahya. *A Lake Beyond the Wind.* Northhampton MA: Interlink, 2003.
Yehoshua, A.B. *A Woman in Jerusalem.* New York: Mariner, 2007.
Zalman, Amy. "Definition of Terrorism Under U.S. Law." *About.com.* Web. 1 Sep. 2010.
Zangana, Haifa. *City of Widows: An Iraqi Woman's Account of War and Resistance.* New York: Seven Stories Press, 2007.
Zenatti, Valerie. *A Bottle in the Gaza Sea.* New York: Bloomsbury, 200.

INDEX

For Product Safety Concerns and Information please contact our EU
representative GPSR@taylorandfrancis.com
Taylor & Francis Verlag GmbH, Kaufingerstraße 24, 80331 München, Germany

www.ingramcontent.com/pod-product-compliance
Lightning Source LLC
Chambersburg PA
CBHW070527100726
47907CB00004B/1008
9780415874380